S0-CFV-246

John

DAILY BIBLE COMMENTARY

A Guide for Reflection and Prayer

John

Richard A. Burridge

HENDRICKSON PUBLISHERS

John
Daily Bible Commentary
Hendrickson Publishers, Inc.
P. O. Box 3473
Peabody, Massachusetts 01961-3473

ISBN 978-1-59856-188-3

Text © 1998 Richard A. Burridge. Original edition published in English under the title *The People's Bible Commentary: John* by the Bible Reading Fellowship, Oxford, England. © The Bible Reading Fellowship 1998.

Hendrickson Publishers' North American edition published by arrangement with the Bible Reading Fellowship.

All rights reserved. No part of this book may be reproduced or transmitted in any form or by any means, electronic or mechanical, including photocopying, recording, or by any information storage and retrieval system, without permission in writing from the publisher.

Scripture quotations from the New Revised Standard Version of the Bible, Anglicized Edition, are copyright © 1989, 1995 by the Division of Christian Education of the National Council of the Churches of Christ in the United States of America, and are used by permission. All rights reserved.

Scripture quotations from the Revised Standard Version of the Bible are copyright © 1946, 1952, 1971 by the Division of Christian Education of the National Council of the Churches of Christ in the United States of America, and are used by permission. All rights reserved.

Printed in the United States of America

First Printing — April 2007

Library of Congress Cataloging-in-Publication Data

Burridge, Richard A., 1955–
    John / Richard A. Burridge.
       p. cm. — (Daily Bible commentary ; 4)
    Includes bibliographical references (p.).
    ISBN 978-1-59856-188-3 (alk. paper)
    1. Bible. N.T. John—Commentaries. 2. Bible. N.T. John—Devotional literature. I. Title.
    BS2615.53.B87 2007
    226.5'07—dc22
                         2007003372

Introducing the
Daily Bible Commentary
Series
A Guide for Reflection and Prayer

Congratulations! You are embarking on a voyage of discovery—or rediscovery. You may feel you know the Bible very well; you may never have turned its pages before. You may be looking for a fresh way of approaching daily Bible study; you may be searching for useful insights to share in a study group or from a pulpit.

The Daily Bible Commentary series is designed for all those who want to study the Scriptures in a way that will warm the heart as well as instruct the mind.

- If you have never really studied the Bible before, the series offers a serious yet accessible way in.

- If you want to have both head and heart knowledge of the Bible, the series helps you first understand what the Bible is saying and then reflect on its meaning in your life and in the way you pray.

- If you help to lead a church study group, or are otherwise involved in regular preaching and teaching, you can find invaluable "snapshots" of a Bible passage through the Daily Bible Commentary approach.

- If you are a church worker or pastor, looking to recharge your faith, this series could help you recover the wonder of Scripture.

To help you, the series distills the best of scholarly insights into straightforward language and devotional emphasis. Explanation of background material and discussion of the original Greek and Hebrew will always aim to be brief.

Using a Daily Bible Commentary

The series is designed for use alongside any version of the Bible. You may have your own favorite translation, but you might like to consider trying a different one in order to gain fresh perspectives on familiar passages.

Many Bible translations come in a range of editions, including study and reference editions that have concordances, various kinds of special indexes, maps, and marginal notes. These can all prove helpful in studying the relevant passage.

The Daily Bible Commentaries are designed to be used on a daily basis, with you reading a short passage from the Bible and then learning more about it from the commentary entry. Alternatively, it can be read straight through, or it can be used as a resource book for insight into particular verses of the biblical book.

While it is important to deepen our understanding of a given passage, this series always aims to engage both heart and mind in the study of the Bible. The Scriptures point to our Lord himself and our task is to use them to build our relationship with him. When we read, let us do so prayerfully, slowly, reverently, expecting God to speak to our very being.

CONTENTS

ACKNOWLEDGMENTS

I have learned so much while I have been writing this book, despite my years of preaching and teaching it in Universities and churches. The list of books at the back contains the key works to which I have been indebted for so much of the material in this commentary.

I am also grateful to my undergraduate students at the University of Exeter (where I lectured a second-year course on John 1987–1994) and King's College London (first-year introductory courses on the Gospels from 1994 onward) for their encouragement and ideas, as well as to various postgraduates for their stimulation. Congregations in Exeter University Chapel, King's College Chapel and St Andrew's Church, Whitehall Park heard quite a lot of this preached over the years. While I was writing the commentary, I was asked to deliver the daily key note Bible Readings for the Diocese of Rochester's 'Forward in Mission' conference in October 1997; I was glad of the chance to study John's understanding of 'the God who sends' and for the feedback afterwards—my thanks to all who participated, especially the Bishop of Rochester and Canon Gordon Oliver, Director of Training.

The Revd Shelagh Brown of the Bible Reading Fellowship invited me to write this and was very encouraging as I started; her sudden death in June 1997 left us all the poorer. I am grateful to Naomi Starkey for her editorial assistance and the way she has taken over the project from Shelagh, as well as to my colleagues as Editors, David Winter and Henry Wansbrough. Many people have acted as 'trial readers' of the studies along the way, but I am particularly grateful to Jane Collins and Betty Jeffery for all their time, interest and helpful suggestions.

As always, it has been my wife, Sue, and our daughters, Rebecca and Sarah who have put up with author's stress and preoccupation at the computer. Without their love and understanding, it would not have been possible.

I am grateful to Professor Raymond Brown for the constant inspiration of his writings on John, and for his personal warmth and interest in this commentary; I gladly dedicate it to his memory.

JOHN: INTRODUCTION

'A book in which a child may paddle
but an elephant can swim deep.'

Welcome to all those who
cannot wait to get in the water

Whenever we go to the beach, my children rush to take off their shoes and socks and go paddling immediately—and I was the same at their age. So this is a quick word of encouragement and safety warning to those who want to jump straight into the text. John's gospel is a lovely story which can be enjoyed by those who know little of Jesus and nothing of the background, which is why it is often given out at churches and meetings to those who are enquiring about the Christian faith. So, go ahead and splash around in it! You can jump about and dip in here and there, because these little studies are all separate in themselves. On the other hand, you might want to use it for your early morning bathe and exercise, and take one or two sections each day for meditation and prayer. If you have the stamina, you can immerse yourself in reading it straight through, for each part flows into the next.

But, as that little saying above about John notes, it is also a book in which the real heavyweights, the mystics and the theologians, have been drowning for centuries! Beneath that placid surface run powerful undercurrents and eddies which will circle you around and bring you out some way forward or back from where you went in. I have tried to chart some of these as we go along, but if you get into difficulties, you might find it helpful to get out, sit on the beach and read these notes. And of course, if you want to do some serious wallowing in John, a little bit of preparation is always a good idea.

You will need a Bible, New Testament or gospel text open as you read. Each study is on a small section and we shall usually work through it verse by verse. Quotations tend to be from the Revised Standard Version or the New RSV, but often I will paraphrase the meaning of the original Greek. You should be able to follow it with any translation, and try several for variation.

What is this book?

It is called a 'gospel', or *eu-angelion* in Greek which means a 'good message' or 'good news', connected with the word 'angel' or messenger. In the Old Testament this means the 'good news' of God's peace and salvation, brought to poor and hurting people trapped in pain or oppression (Isaiah 52:7; 61:1). In the Graeco-Roman world, it was used for the latest proclamation from the local government or the emperor. But what it is called does not tell us what it is. In its form and content it describes a couple of years of the life and work of Jesus of Nazareth, a preacher, teacher and wonder-worker in the Roman province of Judaea, concentrating particularly on his trial and execution by the political and religious authorities and the rather strange things which happened afterwards. It is not what we would expect from a biography today.

On the other hand, it is very like many ancient accounts of teachers, philosophers, generals, and statesmen. They tended to be quite short; John is just over 15,000 words, or about a sixth of this book. It was the amount which could fit on a single scroll of papyrus and be read aloud in a couple of hours. Because they were relatively short, such works could not cover all of a person's life. So they would focus on some significant stories from someone's public life in society, including a concentration on their death, to show what they were really like. These books were not meant to be accurate historical reporting, nor were they fiction or legend; they would include stories about the person and the kind of things they said and did, to interpret their significance. So John makes it clear that he has made a similar selection from the 'many other things Jesus did' to show the reader who Jesus is, 'the Christ, the Son of God' (20:30–31; 21:25). Therefore we must expect to find both story and interpretative reflection, history and theology.

This explains why the book is structured in two main sections. The first describes Jesus' ministry, from his baptism and meeting his first followers through his teaching and miracles as some people come to believe and accept him while the opposition of others, particularly the authorities, grows over a couple of years (1:19—10:42). It is sometimes called the 'Book of Signs' because of the way Jesus' miracles are used to show who he is. The second half covers only his last few days, teaching his disciples and his trial, death and resurrection (13:1—20:31), often known as the 'Book of Glory' because John uses 'glory' to describe what happens to Jesus. From these two parts emerges a clear picture of who Jesus is and what happened to him. Around these sections, the writer has arranged a prologue, like an overture to set out the main themes (1:1–18), an interlude at half-time to help change gear (11:1—12:50) and an epilogue to tie up some loose ends (21).

How was it composed and produced?

This book is called 'the gospel according to John'. It does not say it was written *by* him, but is 'according to' his teaching and interpretation. In fact, even this description is not original, but dates from the second century when the four gospels were collected together and given these titles to distinguish them from one another. Furthermore, John is never mentioned in the text. There is an unnamed disciple described as 'the one Jesus loved' who is present at the last supper, the trial, the cross and the resurrection (see on 13:23; 18:15–17; 19:26–27; 20:2–8 below). In the epilogue, he is claimed as the 'witness' who caused it all to be written but who may have since died (see on 21:24). Since the only possibilities in that chapter are the 'sons of Zebedee and two others' (21:2), he has been traditionally identified as the apostle John, son of Zebedee.

It was quite common in the ancient world for the followers of a great man to write up his ideas and teachings, as Plato did for Socrates. If John had led this particular early church for many years, it might be better to think of him as the 'authority' rather than the 'author' of the gospel 'according to John'. Since we do not know who actually wrote the book, in this commentary we shall use 'John' to refer to the 'writer', 'author' or 'evangelist', and sometimes even to describe the text itself in the traditional manner.

Whoever wrote it seems to have worked independently of the other three gospels. Matthew, Mark and Luke are often called the 'Synoptics' because when you 'see' them 'together' (*syn-optic-* in Greek), it is clear that the texts are related, probably with Matthew and Luke using Mark as a source. While John has some of the same people and similar stories, he uses different words and writes in a completely different style with many individuals, events and teachings occurring only in this gospel.

Because of the interlude and the epilogue, and the way the story jumps around between Galilee and Jerusalem, some scholars think the gospel may have gone through several editions before reaching its final form. Certainly it seems to show the effect of years of theological reflection and teaching. However, the attempts to reconstruct earlier versions vary so much that it is probably impossible. Furthermore, with the one exception of the woman taken in adultery (see on 7:53—8:11 below), all the ancient manuscripts have the gospel in the form we have it today. So we shall take the gospel as we find it and work through it verse by verse.

How does it read?

This gospel is written in a very distinctive style, which seems to have emerged through years of teaching and prayer, meditation and theological reflection. Furthermore, the whole gospel uses this style and vocabulary. Punctuation marks were not put into manuscripts until a thousand years later and sometimes it is difficult to see where they go. Thus it is not clear whether the most famous verse, 'God so loved' (3:16) is spoken by Jesus, or is a comment from the writer; the same difficulty makes it unclear whether 3:31–36 is spoken by John the Baptist or another narrative comment (see on 3:9–36 below).

Style and vocabulary

In fact, we could all probably write in John's style after spending a while immersed in the gospel. It has a limited vocabulary with a number of key words repeated over and over again like look, see, witness, know, believe, have faith, world, glory, abide, remain, hour, send. Other words are in contrasting pairs, light and darkness, truth and falsehood, life and death, above and below, love and hate, father and son. The sentences tend to be short, but they build on each other in steps and stairs and spirals, connecting and reconnecting. Someone has said these words over and over and over again in prayer and teaching. It is ideally suited, therefore, for use now in contemplation and the little prayers and suggestions at the end of each section in this commentary are designed to help you reflect on the passages and let them soak into you.

Time

Time also seems to behave in a similar way for John. Unlike the other gospels which seem to relate only one season of ministry leading to a Passover, John has a logical sequence over several years with three Passovers (2:13; 6:4; 12:1). But time seems to go round and round, to speed up and slow down. The first half of the gospel occupies at least two years, while the second half is little more than a week. Little references like 'now', 'already', 'recently', 'day' abound. At first, Jesus' 'hour' has 'not yet come' (2:4; 7:30; 8:20), but when it arrives it is both the 'hour of glory' and the Passion (12:23, 27; 13:1; 17:1). There are 'flash backs' and 'flash forwards' which connect parts of the narrative: for example 7:50 and 19:39 refer back to Nicodemus' visit by night in 3:2, while 11:2 looks forward to Mary's anointing in 12:3. There are even references out beyond the story to the disciples' later reflections (2:22; 7:39; 21:23).

Levels of meaning

Like many in the ancient world, John tends to see the world in different levels, with earthly things reflecting or foreshadowing heavenly realities. This is also true of the way he writes. To go back to our opening analogy, the surface looks very placid, but underneath flow ever deeper currents of meaning. Most of Jesus' conversations begin with natural things like birth (3:3), water (4:7), bread (6:25), sight (9:1), but questions and misunderstandings soon follow. As Jesus takes his questioners deeper, John invites us to look beyond earthly things to spiritual realities, to the 'true' bread or 'true vine'. If we look closely at what is happening, some of the stories and images like the manna in the desert or the figure of the good shepherd and the sheep are being played out in Jesus' life, and eventual death. There is tremendous irony below the surface so that Jesus' talk of 'being lifted up' actually means a cross (3:14; 8:28; 12:32) or the soldiers' mocking someone who really is the 'King of the Jews' (19:1–3, 19–22).

Signs and discourses

While John narrates several of Jesus' miracles, he never calls them this. They are 'signs', which 'reveal his glory' (2:11). People believed in him because of the signs (2:23; 7:31; 10:41). The writer tells us that Jesus did many more of them of which these are only a selection to help us believe in him (20:30–31). Most analyses of the gospel suggest that there are seven signs:

- changing water into wine (2:1–11)

- healing the official's son (4:46–54)

- healing the paralysed man (5:1–15)

- feeding the five thousand (6:1–15)

- walking on the water (6:16–21)

- giving sight to the blind man (9:1–7)

- raising Lazarus from the dead (11:17–44)

In addition, there is the huge catch of fish in the epilogue (21:1–11). In order to include this one but still keep to the perfect number '7', some remove one of the others, like the walking on water because it does not seem particularly to 'sign' anything. Certainly, some of the signs lead naturally into Jesus' debates and discourses which draw out the meaning of the 'sign' and some are linked to the seven 'I am' sayings. Thus the feeding leads to the debate about the 'bread of life' (6:25–59) and the blind man is connected to 'the light of the world' (8:12; 9:5). However, other signs like the water into wine or the official's son do not lead to a discourse, and John never mentions the word 'seven', so perhaps we should be careful about trying to be too clever sometimes!

These notes on John's style and way of writing might help us in our studies ahead. The levels of meaning suggest that we should start by reading each passage as a whole at the surface level, but then be ready to go back over it looking more deeply. Use any connections John makes by word echoes or references to time to see how it all links together and to the rest of the gospel. Meditate upon the words he uses and let the simple style and vocabulary sink into you in prayer as you use each section as a 'sign' to reveal God's glory in Christ.

What was the situation?

Whoever was involved in writing and producing this gospel was very familiar with the multi-faith multi-cultural world of the eastern Mediterranean in the first century. It was a real melting pot because of the Romans' deliberate policy of bringing all the countries and peoples together in one empire of peace and easy communications.

Probably nothing was seen like it again until today's 'global village'. Just like today, lots of ideas and beliefs were circulating and being mixed together and their effect can be seen in the gospel.

The Greek background

The dominant Greek philosophical tradition from Socrates and Plato was essentially dualist, contrasting the real but invisible realm of the intellect, the soul and the gods with our material physical universe. In addition, Stoicism stressed the logical stability and rationality (called *logos* in Greek) behind the cosmic order which made ethical demands on people's lives. Meanwhile, religious cults and sects abounded with stories of divine figures who came from the realm of light above to save us from this dark world, and they often had initiation ceremonies into the 'mystery' or 'secret knowledge' which could set people free. The influence of all this can be clearly seen on this gospel, both in the prologue and in the way John portrays Jesus coming into the world to bring salvation. This need not imply that the writer had ever belonged to or studied any of these groups in particular detail. The ideas saturated the culture, and like any good evangelist, John is trying to present Jesus in a way that people will understand.

The Jewish background

At the same time, he is obviously steeped in the Hebrew scriptures and Jewish beliefs. Many of the stories are set against the background of the great Jewish festivals, such as the Sabbath (5), Passover (6), Tabernacles (7—8), Hanukkah (10), and Passover again (13—20), and draw their themes from the rituals and beliefs at each feast. Many of the events take place in and around the temple in Jerusalem. The debates between Jesus and his opponents are conducted according to Jewish customs about witnesses and evidence (see on 5:30–47 below) and great heroes like Moses and Abraham are brought in. The themes of the law, the prophets and the scriptures run constantly just below the surface, and particular quotations and prophecies are used through the Passion (see on 12:15; 19:24, 28, 36). Furthermore, modern study of other groups like the Essenes and the Qumran community near the Dead Sea and of the development of the rabbinic traditions has all shown many links with the ideas and beliefs described in this gospel.

This Jewish background is not surprising. After all, with the exception of a few Samaritans, Greeks and Romans like Pilate (4:7, 39; 12:20; 18:28) everyone in the gospel is Jewish—Jesus, the disciples, the crowds, the leaders, the priests. Jesus is explicitly called 'a Jew' and he says that salvation is 'from the Jews' (4:9, 22). John uses the phrase "the Jews" nearly 70 times, in contrast to only a few mentions in the other gospels. So it is quite a shock to discover that it often describes Jesus' opponents, particularly among the religious leaders (see on 1:19 below)—so we shall denote this with inverted commas. People are frightened of "the Jews" in case they are put 'out of the synagogue', *aposynagogos*, (9:22; 12:42; 16:2). While people could be punished by being barred from the synagogue for a week, or a month, or even totally excommunicated in the Old Testament (see Ezra 10:8), this does not seem to have happened to Jesus and his disciples who went to synagogue as good Jews regularly in the gospels and Acts. Of course, there was opposition and conflict (Luke 6:22), but this technical term, *aposynagogos*, seems to belong to a later period.

After the Jewish War and the destruction of Jerusalem and the temple by the Romans in AD70, the surviving rabbis regrouped Judaism around the synagogue and study of the Torah. A prayer called 'the blessing against the heretics' was put into the synagogue liturgy, probably at the Council of Yavneh in AD85, asking that the '*nosrim* and the heretics perish quickly'. If the *nosrim* mean 'Nazarenes' this would make it very difficult for Jewish Christians to attend synagogue and pray against themselves. Regrettably, the split between the early churches and the synagogues developed rapidly after this.

Thus it is possible that John's gospel is being written in the late first century after the War in the period leading to the Council of Yavneh, or even after it, and John's use of the phrases "the Jews" and *aposynagogos* reflects that unhappy time. Perhaps he is aware that some of his readers may have suffered the traumatic experience of excommunication. So he relates their current painful situation to the conflict and opposition from the leaders in Jesus' own day. This is important to remember as it shows John's careful attempt to make his story of Jesus relevant to the people he was writing for. It does not give any justification for the anti-Jewish way the gospel has sometimes been used in later centuries, particularly most recently by the Nazis (see on 8:44 below).

So John is probably writing for a mixed group of people, reflecting the multi-cultural situation of that period. They would know something of Greek philosophy and near eastern religious cults, as well as recognize the allusions to Jewish beliefs and practices. Some might be converts from Hellenistic religions or Jews who have found their faith fulfilled in Jesus as Messiah.

John the Baptist

Another possible group would be followers of John the Baptist. The Jewish historian, Josephus, refers to the Baptist's ministry of preaching and baptizing people. Some people may have been baptized while on pilgrimage or visiting Jerusalem and then taken their new faith back to the cities of Asia Minor or Greece. Thus Paul finds disciples of John the Baptist in Ephesus (Acts 19:5). John shows that some of Jesus' early followers had also been disciples of the Baptist (1:35–37). Whenever John the Baptist appears in this gospel, he directs people to Jesus. It is made clear that he is 'not the light' himself, but a witness 'to the light' (1:8). His 'witness' is then repeated and expanded (see on 1:24–34). He does not even mind when his followers complain that Jesus is baptizing more people, saying 'He must increase and I must decrease' (3:30). Some scholars have interpreted this material as an 'attack' on the Baptist, seeing it as an attempt to persuade his followers to join the new Christian church. Certainly, John is keen to encourage everyone to find life though faith in Jesus as Christ, but this need not imply a particular attack on any one, especially not the Baptist. Later Jesus pays him the compliment of 'bearing witness to the truth' as 'a burning and shining lamp' (5:33–35).

Peter and the beloved disciple

If the 'disciple Jesus loved' is the 'authority' behind the gospel, it is interesting to consider his relationship with Peter. They always seem to appear together and the beloved disciple usually goes one better than Peter. Thus he is next to Jesus at the supper and asks Peter's question for him; he gets Peter into the high priest's courtyard; he is at the foot of the cross when Peter is nowhere to be seen; he beats Peter to the empty tomb and is the first to believe; he tells Peter that the stranger on the lakeside is the risen Jesus, and he will live long when Peter is martyred (13:23–25; 18:15–17; 19:26–27; 20:2–8; 21:7, 22). Some scholars read this as a game of 'anything you can do, we can do better'; so they argue that John is promoting his church and attacking the churches linked with Peter.

On the other hand, there is a lot of positive material about Peter: Simon is one of the first to follow Jesus and is renamed 'Peter', the 'rock', by him; he is the one who makes the confession of faith when others are leaving; he wants to be washed all over by Jesus; he tries to defend Jesus; there is no cursing, swearing oaths or bitter weeping at his denial; the beloved disciple waits to give him the honour of being first into the tomb and the first to meet Jesus at the lakeside; finally he is restored by the Good Shepherd to the pastoral care of his flock (1:42; 6:68; 13:9; 18:10, 27; 20:6; 21:7, 15–17). This is all too much for an 'attack' on him. Peter is just another human being who tries to follow Jesus, who sometimes gets it wonderfully right and other times horribly wrong—but he is forgiven and restored by Jesus, so there is hope for us also. The anonymity of the beloved disciple makes him almost an 'ideal figure'—and we are all encouraged to fill in the blank with our own face and name and become a 'disciple Jesus loved'.

John and other early Christian groups

In recent decades, it has been fashionable to reconstruct the 'community of the beloved disciple', the church within which and for which the gospel was written. Some have even read the gospel as a kind of symbolic history of John's community, taking Jesus' encounters with people as allegories of the church being started from disciples of the Baptist and some Jerusalem Jews with missions to the Samaritans and the Greeks leading to its eventual expulsion from the synagogue. All of these people may well have been found in the communities which read John's gospel. However, if he had wanted to write recent church history for them, it would have been easier to do it like the Book of Acts. The variety of reconstructions and the lack of any external evidence has meant that such approaches are less common now. There is clearly a long process of prayer and reflection behind the gospel over many years, but all we have is the finished text.

Others have tried to relate the gospel to the epistles of John and the book of Revelation, calling them all 'Johannine' books. The epistles are certainly written in a similar style and share John's vocabulary. They are also involved in a situation of splits and conflicts, especially against early Docetic heretics, so called because they thought Jesus only seemed (*docein* in Greek) to be human (1 John 4:2–3; 2 John 1:7). This fits in with John's stress that the 'Word became flesh' (1:14). Revelation has many similarities to this gospel, but also differences of style, vocabulary and content.

Without any further evidence it is difficult to be sure about all of this and going much further into these complex issues would take us away from our task here of studying the gospel. What this brief survey has shown is how John does not write in a vacuum. Like all those who wrote ancient biographies, he is trying to tell people about his subject, Jesus, and to interpret him afresh for their situation. As we study his gospel today we can have no better aim.

What does it teach?

John is not just a beautiful writer who is clever enough to fit his message to the situation facing his initial readers, but he is also the sublime theologian of the early church. Debates raged about the meaning of his apparently simple words as ever deeper levels were explored. He was used by all sides in the various controversies over the formation of the creeds during the next few centuries and he was loved by groups in the mainstream, at the fringes and way outside what came to be seen as orthodox Christianity. Equally, over the last two millennia and all around the world he has provoked an extraordinary output of homilies, sermons, statements, books, lectures, courses, papers, essays, dissertations, and so forth. Here we can only sketch out briefly a few key aspects of his theology.

Christology

John is clear at the end of the gospel that his purpose is that we might believe that 'Jesus is the Christ, the Son of God' (20:31). He has perhaps the highest Christology, or understanding of Jesus, in the whole of the New Testament. At the same time, we must be careful about reading the arguments of later debates back into his text. John stresses that we see the 'glory of God' in the 'Word become flesh' against the philosophical and religious background of his own day; but the later arguments about the nature of Jesus and the Trinity were based on a much more complex philosophy. These debates were really about *ontology*, the nature of 'being' within the Godhead and *how* Jesus could 'be' both human and divine. John just asserts that

22

he *is*; he is more concerned for *function*—what Jesus said and *did* then, and still does now, for human beings. It is no accident that John's style is a lot more full of verbs and 'doing' things than 'static' nouns of 'being'.

As we shall see in the prologue, he draws upon the rich philosophical tradition of the 'Word', *logos*, behind the cosmos to explain who Jesus really is as that Word becomes flesh and dwells among us (1:14). He also uses the Jewish tradition about the Word of God, which he combines with the figure of God's Wisdom, who was with him at the creation and comes among men and women to teach them the way of God (Prov. 8:22–31).

He uses a number of *titles* to describe Jesus. The gospel opens with debate about who the Christ might be (1:20); John the Baptist says that it is not him. Soon Jesus is called 'Christ' by the first disciples, some Samaritans and other believers (1:41; 4:25, 29; 11:27). 'Christ' is the Greek form of the Hebrew 'Messiah' and both words mean God's 'anointed one'. In the Hebrew scriptures priests, kings and prophets were all anointed as a sign of God's special task for them. Later there emerged a longing for someone who would be *the* Messiah, God's anointed person to bring in his kingdom. When Jesus enters Jerusalem to be hailed as 'king' (12:13) the authorities are worried and he is executed as 'king of the Jews' which is also a messianic claim. John makes it clear that Jesus lived and died as the 'Christ'.

However, John's reason for writing connects 'Christ' with 'Son of God' (20:31). God is called Father over 100 times and Jesus is identified as the 'Son' about fifty, so John is making a clear statement about his relationship to God. The name of God was linked in the Old Testament with ultimate Being, 'I am who I am' (Exod. 3:14). In John's gospel, Jesus makes seven 'I am' statements, claiming to be the bread of life, the light of the world, the door to the sheepfold, the good shepherd, the resurrection and the life, the way, truth and life, and the true vine (6:35, 41, 51; 8:12, 9:5; 10:7, 9; 10:11, 14; 11:25; 14:6; 15:1, 5). Not only do these hint at the divine name, 'I am', but the descriptions are all central images of the Jewish faith and Law being now fulfilled in Jesus.

John also depicts Jesus being aware of his unique relationship with God, knowing that he was pre-existent with God and is going to return to him in glory. He is the source of all life and all judgment is committed to him (3:16–21; 5:19–29). The Father inspires and indwells all he says and does so much that to see him is to have seen the Father, for 'the Father and I are one' (14:9–10; 10:30). At the same time, 'the Word became flesh' (1:14), so John shows Jesus' humanity: he gets tired and thirsty in Samaria, he weeps at his friend's grave, he is tempted to shrink back from being crucified, and on the cross he is thirsty and really dies a human death (4:6–7; 11:33–38; 12:27; 19:28, 34).

This is indeed a highly developed Christology and shows how much John has thought and reflected on the meaning of Jesus over many years. And yet, it is only the logical outworking of the picture of Jesus in the other gospels who taught us to call God *Abba*, our Father, and who was bringing in the Kingdom of God through his parables and miracles. At the same time, John's understanding of Jesus was to set the tracks on a course which would lead to the later debates and creeds.

Eschatology

We have already noted John's interest in time. The Hebrew prophets looked forward to the 'last day', the 'day of the Lord' when God's justice would finally be revealed at the end of time. The Greek word for 'end' is *eschaton*, so the study of things to do with 'the End' is called 'eschatology'. In the other gospels, Jesus says that the End, the 'kingdom of God', when God's kingship will be recognized by everyone, was breaking into our time here and now through his teaching and miracles (Lk. 11:20). However, they also each contain long sections of Jesus' teaching about the End when he will come again on the clouds of glory to judge everyone (Mk. 13:3–37; Matt. 24—25; Lk. 21:5–36).

John does not have anything quite like these blocks of teaching about the coming of the End. Instead, Jesus talks as though his coming into the world has brought the End here already. So, although God did not send his Son to condemn the world, but to save it, the coming of light into darkness inevitably creates shadows; the arrival of Jesus has brought about the judgment, the 'critical moment' when some people reject the light and prefer to remain in the shadows (3:16–21). So we say that John sees eschatology as 'realized', made real in the present in our decision here and now. As people accept and believe in Jesus so they come into eternal life now, so much that

Lazarus can even be raised from the dead now without having to wait for the end of time (see on 11:17–44 below).

On the other hand, Jesus still talks of 'the last day' (e.g. 6:39–40; 12:48). While all the benefits of eternal life and knowing God can be received as we accept Jesus, there is still inevitably a future dimension to judgment. Perhaps the best section about John's understanding of eschatology is 5:19–29. Here Jesus says that all judgment and authority to give life has been granted to him by God the Father. In 5:19–24 this seems to be happening now in the present, while in 5:25–29 it is all repeated in the future tense. The two sections are linked by 'the hour is coming, and now is' (5:25). This is the heart of what John is trying to say: 'the hour is coming' when there will be judgment and eternal life, but it 'now is' available to us in Jesus, here, already.

Church and Sacraments

Perhaps no topic so divides scholars as John's understanding of the church and the sacraments. On the one hand, scholars of a more Protestant background point out that there is very little about this in the text of the gospel. In reply, those from a more Catholic tradition see images of the church and sacraments all over the gospel. In part, this situation arises from John's habit of writing on several levels at once; two commentators can look at the same passage and see different things depending on how deep they look.

On the surface level, the first group are quite right to point out that none of the key words about the church are ever used in John; there is little emphasis on the twelve apostles, but lots of stories about various people, most of whom are never heard of again—the Samaritan woman, the woman taken in adultery, the blind man and so on. It is all very individualistic, with individuals coming to Jesus, but not through the church or the community of faith.

In response, the other group look more deeply at Jesus' great images of the shepherd and the sheep, or the vine and the branches and notice how corporate these are. Part of the problem is that English does not distinguish between 'you-singular' (the old 'thee' and 'thou') and 'you-plural'; it is thus very easy to take all the wonderful promises of Jesus at the Last Supper in an individualistic way as addressed to each believer personally. However, closer inspection of the Greek reveals that these are all 'you-plurals'; we experience the promises of Jesus and the presence of the Spirit all together as the community of believers. We shall try to point out these 'you-plurals' in these studies. Furthermore, it is John's gospel where Jesus gives us the example of washing each other's feet and the 'new commandment' to 'love one another as I have loved you'. The mark of the church by which people will know we are his disciples is if we love one another (13:1–11, 34–35; 15:12–13). It is hard to have a higher understanding of the church than that!

Unfortunately, mention of the last supper causes the more Protestant scholars to jump up again. They note that it is very curious that there is no institution of the holy communion at the last supper, just the foot washing (13:1–11). What is more, there is no account of Jesus actually being baptized either, but it is just passed over briefly in a mention by John the Baptist (1:32–33). There is no command to baptize or to 'do this in remembrance of me' for the communion. Instead, there is a great stress on the Word, and on Jesus' teaching; we should get rid of our altars and fonts and build bigger pulpits!

The sacramentalists have to admit that the omission of the communion and baptism is rather embarrassing, on the face of it at least. But, if we look below the surface, suddenly we are awash with sacramental references. Water is in nearly every chapter at the start, from the Baptist, to water into wine, to being born of water and the Spirit, to living water, to healing by water, to streams of living water, and so on through to Jesus washing the disciples' feet (1:26–33; 2:1–11; 3:5; 4:10–15; 5:1–9; 7:38; 9:7; 13:1–11). Equally, water is turned into vast quantities of wine, Jesus calls himself the 'true vine' and there is lots of bread around, even at the last supper (2:1–11; 15:1; 6:1–14, 31–35; 13:26–30). The feeding of the five thousand looks like an open-air communion and it is difficult to interpret the debate about eating his flesh and drinking his blood as anything other than the eucharist (6:1–14, 50–58).

This is an excellent example of how the way we read John's style and manner of writing can affect our view of his theology, particularly with regard to the deeper levels of meaning. Are these things really there below the surface, or are they merely reflections of our own views? We will point out the main passages for the debate as we go through the gospel and you will have to think about it and ask the Holy Spirit to help you decide.

Truth, theology and history

Clement of Alexandria said towards the end of the second century that John was a 'spiritual gospel' written later to supplement the 'physical facts' described in the other three gospels (according to Eusebius, *Ecclesiastical History* VI:14:7). This came to represent how John was viewed up to this century—that John knew the Synoptics and wrote later to provide spiritual reflection upon their historical accounts.

The development of modern scholarship and literary criticism tended to confirm this approach to John. For most of this century, scholars thought that John was written at the end of the first century, or even into the early part of the second; his philosophical awareness seemed very Greek and to have lost touch with the Jewish background of Jesus and the early disciples; everything was seen to have a theological purpose or spiritual meaning and none of his events or conversations were thought to have any basis in history. The only possible historical material John had would have come from the Synoptic gospels. One example of such an approach is that the five porticoes at the pool of Bethesda were interpreted from St Augustine onwards as symbolizing the five books of the Law of Moses—identifying the sick but not able to heal them; then Jesus does what the old Law could not and makes the man whole (5:1–9). Obviously, in this view, the porches had no historical existence; Jerusalem was destroyed a generation or more before the gospel was thought to have been written so neither the writer nor the first readers would have known anything about what it had looked like.

Over recent decades, however, this approach has been seriously challenged. First, most scholars now consider that John was written independently of the other gospels, and they are therefore no longer the yardstick by which he is to be judged. Certainly he shares some old material with them which was passed on through the oral tradition which may or may not have had an historical basis; each must be assessed on its own merits. Furthermore, we have become more aware of the amount of theological interpretation in the other gospels which makes them more like John. Like other ancient biographies, all the gospels set out to explain and interpret their subject and his significance.

While the Synoptic gospels are now seen as more theological, conversely John has been shown to be more historical. Research on the

Dead Sea Scrolls and on the beliefs of the Essenes and other Jewish groups of the early first century has revealed lots of ideas and thoughts which are quite similar to John's approach. These groups were all destroyed in the Jewish War of 66–70 and their beliefs were lost. Without them, John's ideas used to look quite late and Greek. Now we know that they were not so different from other earlier, Jewish writings. Similarly, developments in archaeology in Israel and Palestine over recent decades have revealed a lot more about Jerusalem and Judaea before the Jewish War—and John's awareness of places and geography now seems quite good. Even the Pool of Bethesda has been excavated and we can now walk among its five porticoes! Of course, this cannot prove the historicity or otherwise of any miracle or conversation Jesus or anyone else may have held there—but it does caution us against assuming that everything is only symbolic and theological.

This all means that the process by which John's gospel came to be written is a lot more complex. Both the previous extreme views are too simplistic. John's awareness of Greek philosophy and the painful separation of the early churches from the synagogues in the latter part of the first century means that this gospel is not meant to be a straightforward eye-witness accurate record of what a Galilean fisherman heard and saw Jesus say and do. On the other hand, his knowledge of early Aramaic terms like 'Messiah' or 'Cephas' for Peter (1:41–42), his use of ideas common to Jewish groups wiped out—and awareness of places destroyed—in the Jewish War of 66–70 suggests that the gospel contains a good historical foundation dating back to the first half of the century. If the 'witness' behind the gospel, identified as 'the disciple Jesus loved', was John son of Zebedee some of it will have come from him. It is not just a later Greek symbolic invention.

As Pilate says in John, 'What is truth?' (18:38). To us today, truth is about tape-recordings of what an American President might or might not have said—and even then the truth is hard to discover! On the other hand, we consider 'myth' to be 'untrue', a fairy story. The people of Jesus' and John's day, however, had very different ideas and we must not impose our concepts of truth on to first-century texts like the gospels. To the ancients, 'myth' was the medium whereby profound truth, more truly true than mere tape-recorded facts could ever be, was communicated—hence John's use of the words 'true' and 'truly' nearly fifty times. John's gospel has an underlying basic level of historical information about the sorts of things Jesus said and did and the places where they happened, leading up to his trial and death. Over that are laid levels of awareness of the complex melting pot of the first century, including Jewish beliefs from before the destruction of Jerusalem and Graeco-Roman religious and philosophical systems. In writing his brief account of Jesus, he is trying to get from one level to the other. He has prayed and reflected on 'the many other things Jesus did' and makes a selection under the guidance of the Holy Spirit in order to 'bear true witness' in the situation of his first readers about the *truth* of who Jesus *truly* is and *really* means for them—'so that you may believe that Jesus is the Christ, the Son of God, and that through believing you may have life in his name' (20:30–31; 21:24–25).

The kids are splashing about and the elephants are enjoying wallowing; the children of God are enjoying new life in Christ and the theologians are plumbing ever greater depths. Breakfast on the beach is over and it is time for us to immerse ourselves in John's living waters. Enjoy it!

IN *the* BEGINNING

The opening of John's gospel is one of the most magnificent pieces of religious literature ever written. Not surprisingly, it has inspired vast amounts of analysis and interpretation. And yet, we are not even sure quite what it is: is it an introduction, a hymn or a poem? Arguments rage over whether it extends from verse 1 to verse 14 or to verse 18, whether or not the passages about John the Baptist belong here (1:6–8, 15), and how its structure might be analysed.

It is usually called 'the Prologue', although it is more like an overture, for it introduces some key themes and particular words which the writer will use over and over in the gospel. On the other hand, some of its ideas and phrases never appear again, including the central idea of 'the Word'. Therefore scholars have wondered whether it was written by the same author as the rest. Some suggest that it may have been an early hymn, which already existed and which the evangelist adapted for his purposes. Others think that it was composed later, and added to the already completed gospel. Indeed, I wrote the rest of this commentary first and came to the Prologue last!

So, read it now as the introduction to the gospel and these studies. It will give you a flavour of the great journey we are about to undertake and you will hear some of the major themes. Don't worry if some ideas are difficult or the motifs too grand at this stage. Come back and study it again after you have finished the whole gospel— and see how all the things you have learned and friends you have made are hinted at here.

Begin at the beginning

So we begin, as John does, at the beginning. Mark starts his gospel with Jesus being baptized by John the Baptist; Matthew begins with Jesus' birth, while Luke takes us back to the birth of John the Baptist as the one who prepared his way. John is traditionally symbolized by an eagle, and he certainly takes the high-flying perspective here! Jesus cannot be introduced in terms of time, place and human ancestry: he existed 'in the beginning' (1:1). This phrase would remind his readers immediately of the opening words of the Hebrew scriptures, 'in the beginning' (Gen. 1:1). Indeed, while *genesis* is the Greek word for 'beginning' or 'origin', the Jews called the first book of the Bible by its opening Hebrew words 'in the beginning'. Yet John goes even further, for Genesis starts with the creation of everything *at* the beginning; John takes us back *before* then, when only God existed.

The Word

John does not actually name Jesus until the end of the prologue (1:17). Instead, he calls him 'the Word'. The Jews thought that God's word was alive and active (Is. 55:11) from the creation, when God had only to say, 'Let there be…' for things to come into being (Gen. 1:3, 6, 9, etc.), to God's word coming through all the prophets. In Greek philosophy from early thinkers like Heraclitus to the Stoics, who were also popular among the Romans, the 'word', *logos*, was used for the logical rationality behind the universe. In later Jewish beliefs, this masculine principle was complemented by the feminine figure of Lady Wisdom, who was present with God at the creation (Prov. 8:22–31). This idea was developed in the writings between the times of the Testaments, as can be seen in the book of Wisdom in the Apocrypha (Wis. 7:22—10:21). There was further speculation in Jewish mysticism about the role of both wisdom and the Law with God.

But it is John who pulls all these threads together with the amazing idea that the Word was not only pre-existent with God but also personal. In 1:1–2 he states that 'the Word was with (the) God', including the definite article 'the' to stress how the Word existed with the creator Father God of Jewish monotheism—for there is no other god. Furthermore, 'the Word was God' without any article. He does not say 'the Word was *a* god', with the indefinite article, implying that Jesus was some sort of lesser divinity, as some groups believe who have split away from orthodox Christianity both in the past and today. Nor does he say 'the Word was *the* God', for that would imply that Jesus was all there is to God. No, he carefully writes 'the Word was God', divine, personal, existing in the unity of the Godhead and yet somehow distinct—for 'the Word became flesh and dwelt among us' (1:14). That is the wonderful story which John is setting out to tell us.

PRAYER

God our Father, inspire our study of these written words
that we may know your living Word, Jesus Christ.

2

LIGHT *in the* DARKNESS

Greek philosophy and many eastern religions had an essential 'dualism', a separation between the material world and the spiritual realm. God exists in brilliant light in the world above, while we live in the darkness of created matter. Therefore God can have nothing to do with the physical level. At best, this material universe is but a pale shadow of divine reality; however, many saw our world as positively evil, containing nothing good. Human beings were seen in a similar dualistic fashion: the physical body is sinful flesh or meaningless matter, inhabited by the soul which pre-existed in the divine light and strives to return there. Thus ancient philosophy from Socrates and Plato onwards sought 'enlightenment' or 'knowledge' to set the soul free into the bright intellectual realms, while many eastern religions offered 'salvation', often through 'initiation' into mysteries to enable the soul to leave the body after death and ascend back to the divine.

As a child of his time, John shares some of this. Thus he depicts the Word pre-existing with God in light, but descending into our dark world to bring salvation, before returning to the Father. John uses the separation of the divine 'above' and the world 'below' frequently, so the overture has introduced his first theme. However, he has also been nourished in the Jewish tradition that the world is the good creation of a loving God: 'the earth is the Lord's and all it contains' (Ps. 24). Thus he affirms the world's goodness and the Word's involvement in creation in a way abhorrent to a thoroughgoing dualist.

Life and light

First he asserts that 'all things came into being' through the Word and nothing exists without him (1:3). At a stroke, John inspires the great Christian involvement in the arts *and* the sciences. Scientific enquiry is possible if the world is not some malicious fantasy but the result of a creator's love—to study the laws of physics is to search out the mind of God, as many great scientists like Kepler and Newton believed. Equally, rather than trying to escape the material body, our humanity can be explored in sculpture and paint, poetry and prose, dance and drama, music and song—because 'in him was life' (1:4).

Suddenly two great fanfares burst out of John's overture to

announce the major themes of light and life, two words which he uses twice as often as the other gospels. Here all 'life' is found in the Word and he balances this neatly at the end with his purpose in writing that we 'might have life in his name' (20:31). Because 'God so loved the world', he gave his Son so we 'should not perish but have eternal life' (3:16). His life is also 'the light of all people' (1:4). The presence of the Word is the 'light come into the darkness' (3:19) and John uses light and darkness as a contrasting pair throughout, together with the images of night and day. Now, 'the light shines in the darkness and the darkness cannot master it' (1:5). The English 'master' reflects the double meaning of the Greek, both to 'understand' or 'comprehend' and to 'overcome' or 'extinguish'. The coming of light into darkness inevitably creates shadows, so there will be conflict and judgment.

A witness to the light

Next, John introduces two more themes—'sending' and 'witness'. John the Baptist was 'sent from God' (1:6). Unlike the dualist God who has no contact with the world, John stresses that the nature of God is to 'send'. He uses the verb 'send' about sixty times, nearly twice as frequently as the other gospels—and God does most of the sending. First he sends John the Baptist, and then Jesus. Finally, Jesus sends us into the world, 'as the Father sent me' (20:21).

John is sent as a 'witness to the light' (1:7). The Greek word for witness, *martur-*, gives us the English 'martyr' for a witness even to death. John uses the noun and its verb 'to bear witness' or 'to testify' more than the other three gospels put together, so it is another key idea. It recurs throughout as Jesus is constantly put on trial and asked for 'witnesses' for his claims, and with another careful balance the gospel ends with the witness of the writer himself (21:24). John the Baptist had many devoted followers, but the evangelist stresses that 'he himself was not the light', but came as a 'witness to the light' (1:8). The relationship of John the Baptist and Jesus will be explored in the first few chapters; for now, the writer states simply that John came to witness to the light 'so that all might believe through him', introducing another important theme—'believe'—into this overture.

PRAYER

Lord Jesus, shine your light into my life,
that I may be a witness for you.

3

ACCEPTANCE *or* REJECTION?

The overture is now in full swing, moving from its magnificent opening about the Word with God in the beginning to what happens when the Word enters into the world. This introduces many of the gospel's key themes. As God 'sends' the 'light' into the 'darkness' to bring 'life', some 'believe' and 'witness'. Unfortunately, this is not the only reaction possible and the gospel's main story is about the acceptance or rejection of the Word which the overture now introduces.

First, John distinguishes the Word as 'the true light' (1:9) from John the Baptist, whom many thought was the light, while actually he was only a reflection or witness to it (1:7–8). Another key motif, the words 'true' and 'truth' feature nearly fifty times in this gospel, three times the total in the others. Here too, John turns the dualists' ideas around; Greek philosophy stressed how true reality was only in the realm above, and everything in our world merely pale shadows and reflections. So for John, Jesus is 'the truth', foreshadowed by Jewish festivals, beliefs and ideas about the Law. But while dualists thought we had to leave this world to find truth, John announces that the 'true bread' and the 'true vine' has come to find us (14:6; 6:32; 15:1).

The Hebrew prophets looked forward to God's light coming in glory (Is. 9:2; 42:6; 60:1). That light, says John, is personal, as he breaks grammar from the neuter 'light' to the personal pronoun 'he', and available, 'coming into the world'. We do not leave the world to find enlightenment; he 'enlightens everyone'. The scale of John's insight is staggering: what is true and good in all philosophies and religions, thought and culture, arts and science—all of it comes from the enlightenment of the Word.

The world

John's stupendous claim, which no dualist would dare contemplate, is that the divine Word, the true light, has come 'into the world' (1:9). To them 'the world' was negative and evil. John is more subtle: he uses 'the world' nearly eighty times, over five times as often as in the Synoptics. Sometimes it is simply neutral, meaning 'the earth' or 'everyone', like the French *tout le monde* (e.g. 12:19). Essentially the world is positive, the good creation of the loving God, which he sent his Son to save (3:16). On the other hand, when the world rejects Jesus, it becomes negative, the source of opposition, especially later in the gospel (see on 15:18–19 below). All three usages are here: 'he was in the world (neutral), and the world was made through him (positive), yet the world did not know him (negative)' (1:10).

His own

The dualists thought that 'knowledge' was a way out of the world. Some who split away from Christianity were called 'Gnostics' from their stress on 'knowledge', *gnosis*, to get us back to the divine realms. 'Knowledge' and 'knowing' are used by John over 140 times—but it is often Jesus' knowledge of everything (e.g. 13:3; 18:4). Eternal life is 'to know God and Jesus Christ whom he sent' (17:3) and such knowledge comes through 'believing', which occurs nearly one hundred times, three times its usage in the Synoptics. The Word, the true light, came into the world 'to his own', a neuter phrase for his own possession, realm, or home. While 'the whole world' belongs to God, Israel was his 'special possession' (Exod. 19:5) and the Jews 'his people' (Deut. 7:6; 14:2). But John moves from the neuter to the personal pronoun to say that 'his own people did not accept him'. So 1:11 is a summary of the first half of this gospel, as Jesus comes to his own people but many, especially the religious leaders, reject him.

But alongside that theme of rejection, the overture plays the counterpoint of 'all who received him, who believed in his name'. Thus 1:12 is the summary of the second half of the gospel. Although 'his own people' do not accept him, Jesus calls together a group who 'know' that he was sent by God and who 'believe in him'. These become 'his own sheep' who 'know his voice'; at the last supper, he gathers together 'his own in the world' and loves them 'to the end' (10:4, 14; 13:1). To these he gives 'the authority to become children of God', who are born not by natural means, but a spiritual re-birth 'of God' (1:13). As the gospel unfolds, watch for people like Nicodemus, coming out of darkness to believe in Jesus, and to become 'his own', born of the Spirit (3:1–8).

PRAYER

Light of the world,
help me to know and believe in you
and make me a child of God.

4   JOHN 1:14–18

The WORD BECAME FLESH

Like an overture, the Prologue introduces the gospel's major themes. First, John arranged his composition against a cosmic backdrop of the realm of divine light above and our dark world below. Then John's middle section challenged this dualistic system as the Word from above enters into our world. In this final movement, he takes his themes more from the Old Testament, leading to a final climax which confronts Greek philosophy and Jewish beliefs alike.

The incarnation

'The word became flesh' (1:14) sounds four crashing chords to make any dualists listening jump out of their seats! The Word 'coming into the world' was bad enough, but for the divine to enter something as physical, messy and downright sinful as human flesh was outrageous. Even some early Christians (called Docetics) had problems with this, believing that Jesus only 'seemed' (*docein* in Greek) to be human. Of the four gospels, John has the clearest emphasis on the divinity of Jesus. As the story unfolds, Jesus knows all things, is aware of his pre-existence with the Father, and goes to his death serenely in control, confident of his return to the divine realm. Some scholars suggest that John stresses this so much that he risks going Docetic himself. Against this are all the places where John describes Jesus' humanity in the gospel itself, and this ringing declaration in his overture.

If the incarnation of the Word was difficult for Greeks, the next phrase would have startled Jews. 'He lived (*eskenosen*) among us' means literally 'dwelt in a tent', like the tent of the tabernacle (*skene*) where God resided during the Israelites' desert wanderings (Exod. 25:8–9). The prophets longed for God to 'pitch his tent' among his people again (Ezek. 37:27; Joel 3:17; Zech. 2:10). This, declares John, is what has happened in Jesus. The consonants of 'tent', *s-k-n*, are linked to the Hebrew *s-k-n*, to 'dwell', from which comes the *shekinah*, the glorious cloud of God's presence on Mount Sinai which then filled the tent and later the temple (Exod. 24:16; 40:34–35; 1 Kings 8:10–11). So John says, 'We have seen his glory'. The other gospels depict the glory of God coming upon Jesus at the transfiguration. John does not relate this event, for he sees the *shekinah* glory of God in Jesus in all he says and does; supremely the hour for Jesus to be glorified and 'lifted up' is the crucifixion (12:23; 13.32; 17:1).

Furthermore, Jesus shares God's glory as an only son resembles his father. This is John's favourite description for the relationship of Jesus and God. Jesus is frequently called 'the Son', and God is 'the Father' over 110 times, twice as often as in the other three gospels combined. As the proverb goes, 'like father, like son'. In the Old Testament God is always 'abounding in steadfast love and faithfulness' (Exod. 34:6). So here John translates this into Jesus being 'full of grace and truth'.

This is an astounding verse. In one sentence John breaches the dualistic divide of Greek philosophy, counters early Christian heresy about Jesus' humanity and divinity, and gathers together Jewish ideas of the presence, glory, mercy and love of God—all of this, he says, can now be seen among us in Jesus!

The revelation

So now we hear a reprise of the theme of John the Baptist, the last Jewish prophet, to 'bear witness' again to Jesus (1:15). Many thought the Baptist was fulfilling all the Jewish hopes, but he never appears in this gospel without 'witnessing' that it is Jesus who does this, not him. John uses two words frequent in Paul but occurring only here in the gospel—'fullness' and 'grace' (1:16). We saw that 'grace' represents the 'steadfast love of the Lord' so common in the Old Testament. As the Baptist witnessed to Jesus, so the evangelist shows throughout the gospel how all the Jewish beliefs and practices are fulfilled in Jesus—and even surpassed. Moses will be another important witness (see on 5:39–47; 6:25–50). Now John notes that 'the law was given through Moses, but grace and truth came through Jesus Christ' (1:17). No one has ever seen God (1:18). Even Moses was not allowed to see God's face (Exod. 33:18–23). But Jesus, the Word, who was with God in the beginning, the only Son who exists 'in the Father's heart'—he has revealed him and 'made him known'.

So the Prologue has come full circle, the overture has introduced all the themes, and it climaxes with a loud cry that Jesus is God come among us. That is why the story we are about to read is so important.

For REFLECTION & PRAYER

Read the whole Prologue slowly and meditate upon it phrase by phrase. What does Jesus show you?

QUESTIONS & ANSWERS

After the magnificent heights of the Prologue, the overture is over and a sense of hushed expectancy falls upon the audience as the curtain rises and the story begins. As so often in any great drama, John's opening scene introduces some key themes—but the star, the person at the centre of the story, is curiously off stage. However, the way is being prepared for his entry because the characters actually on stage are discussing the central question, 'Who is the Christ?' Messengers from the religious authorities have been sent to question the person at the centre of the action as the story begins, thinking, not unreasonably, that he might be the star: 'Who are you?' So let us consider this man and his questioners.

"The Jews"

The messengers are priests and Levites who have been sent by "the Jews" from Jerusalem (1:19). This is the first appearance in John's story of "the Jews". While this phrase occurs in the other three gospels only a few times, mostly in their accounts of Jesus' trial and death, it appears in John's gospel some seventy times: a few times in each chapter from 2 to 12, and then twenty times at the trial (chapters 18—19).

This statistic should make us pause for a moment and ask what John means by the phrase. "The Jews" appear here at the beginning as questioners, and the questions get sharper as they are directed away from John the Baptist to Jesus himself. The conflict builds until both Jesus and "the Jews" accuse each other of being demonic (8:44, 48). Here the phrase refers to priests and Levites from Jerusalem (1:19, 24) and it is used particularly of the Jewish leaders, especially when they bring about Jesus' trial and death (18—19). However, we cannot read this phrase today without thinking of the persecution of the Jews, particularly by the Nazis who used the accusation of 'being of the devil' as a justification for the Holocaust.

Yet Jesus is a Jew (4:9) and he tells a Samaritan that 'salvation is from the Jews' (4:22). In this gospel, all those who come to believe are Jews, just like those who do not believe. Jesus came into conflict with the Jewish religious authorities in his own day, which led to his death. This conflict continued 'within the family', between Jews who believed in Jesus as Messiah and Jews who did not—until, as the believers grew and included non-Jews among them, eventually they split away from the synagogue to the formation of the church. Such events do not happen without some bitterness and pain on both sides, and this is reflected in John's use of the phrase "the Jews" for Jesus' opponents.

So we must always bear in mind when reading this gospel that the phrase "the Jews" refers to the religious leaders who rejected what God was doing at that time in Jesus, rather than the Jewish people down through the ages. How often do *we* question what is happening and fail to recognize the activity of God?

John the Baptist

On the other hand, other Jews are portrayed throughout this gospel looking for the coming of the Christ, including the first disciples and others like Nicodemus, Martha and Mary. The first of these is John the Baptist. We know from the Jewish historian Josephus that John was seen by many as a prophet: he came out of the wilderness, preaching and baptizing people as a sign of their repentance. No wonder the religious authorities wanted to question him and find out who he was.

His answer at first is negative. In response to their questions, he states three times who he is not: he is not the Christ (1:20), nor Elijah, whom some expected to come before the Messiah, following the prophecy of Mal. 4:5, nor he is the prophet like Moses promised in Deut. 18:15–18 (1:21). Understandably, the questioners want a more positive answer to take back to Jerusalem, so John declares that he is 'the voice of one crying in the wilderness, "Make straight the way of the Lord"' as prophesied by Isaiah 40:3. Thus the evangelist depicts John the Baptist as a 'witness' (1:19) who prepares the way for the main star still to step on stage. He is not an opponent like "the Jews" but a proponent who will direct others to Jesus.

PRAYER

Lord, make me a voice crying in the wilderness,
not one who misses or opposes what you are doing,
but a true witness.

The WITNESS *of* JOHN *the* BAPTIST

John the Baptist's response to his questioners was to direct their attention away from himself to the 'star' of the show who has been off stage, waiting in the wings. Now, on 'the next day' after the questioners have departed, Jesus makes his arrival upon the scene (1:29), the first mention of him since the end of the Prologue (1:17). Modern biographies usually begin with their subject's birth, family, upbringing and education; ancient accounts of people's lives would often start straight in with their public debut, as John does here. Unlike the accounts in the other gospels, there is no narrative of the actual baptism itself. John the Baptist says he saw the Spirit descend upon Jesus as a dove (1:32), but in this gospel his role is less about being the one who baptized Jesus and more that of a witness to him: note how his 'witness' in 1:19 leads to what he says (1:32, 34). Here the Baptist declares four things about Jesus.

Jesus is greater than John

Before the questioners withdraw, John the Baptist tells them of the coming of one who is greater than himself. John is not worthy to untie his sandals, which is the work of a slave when his master enters the house (1:27). Perhaps this helps to explain why this gospel has no account of the actual moment of baptism, for this might imply that the baptizer is greater than the one baptized. Matthew also grapples with this problem by describing Jesus having to persuade John to baptize him (Matt. 3:14–15). This gospel consistently points out that the Baptist sees Jesus as greater (see on 3:22–30). In its own day, when the ancient Mediterranean was full of religious leaders and prophets, John's gospel stressed the pre-eminence of Jesus—and it proclaims the same message in our pluralistic society today.

Jesus is the Lamb of God

When Jesus appears, coming towards John, the Baptist points him out: 'Behold, the Lamb of God, who takes away the sin of the world!' (1:29). The 'lamb' immediately recalls the Passover story when the ancient Israelites wanted to leave slavery in Egypt: when all the first-born of Egypt were killed, the Israelites were saved because they had sacrificed a lamb and smeared its blood on their doorposts, causing God to pass over their houses (Exod. 12). John the Baptist has already quoted the prophet Isaiah to describe himself as the voice in the wilderness (1:23; cf. Is. 40:3). Now he uses Isaiah also to describe Jesus, the suffering servant of God who bears the sins of the people like a 'lamb to the slaughter' (Is. 53:4–7). In the literature written between the time of the Old and New Testaments, the image of a lamb is also used of the one who will destroy evil. Now the Baptist draws on all these images to describe not just who Jesus is, but what he will do—he will take away the sin of the world.

Jesus baptizes with the Holy Spirit

In John the Baptist's third description of Jesus, there is another contrast—between his own baptism in water and the baptism with the Holy Spirit which comes through Jesus. Even though John is forever identified as 'the Baptist', yet even here, Jesus' baptism is greater than his. As a prophet, John would have experienced the inspiration of the Holy Spirit on various occasions, particularly for his preaching. But the Spirit has descended from heaven and remains on Jesus. Because he possesses and is possessed by the Holy Spirit of God, Jesus is the one who can baptize others with that same Spirit (1:33).

Jesus is the Son of God

John the Baptist answered the religious leaders' questions by describing himself as the voice preparing the way (1:23). Now we see how great is the one who comes after him: he can take away the sin of the world and baptize with the Holy Spirit because he is nothing less than the very Son of God himself—another term with a rich Jewish background. The reason God wanted Pharaoh to let his people go was that 'Israel is my firstborn son' (Exod. 4:22). God's promise to David was that from his line there would come someone to rule Israel: 'I will be a father to him, and he shall be a son to me' (2 Sam. 7:14).

Thus the testimony of John the Baptist to Jesus is a rich tapestry, weaving together several strands from the Jewish scriptures to witness to the greatness of Jesus, the Son of God.

PRAYER

Lord Jesus Christ, Son of God, have mercy on me;
take away my sin and fill me with your Holy Spirit.

7

COME & SEE

Once again, this scene begins with John the Baptist declaring that Jesus is the Lamb of God (1:36). Two of John's disciples hear what he says, and, realizing that he is pointing away from himself to Jesus, leave John to find out about Jesus. It is very likely that Jesus' first disciples came from among followers of John the Baptist. John's preaching of repentance as preparation for the Kingdom would encourage his disciples to look for the next step. So here we have the origin of the community of faith, the church. A couple of people start following Jesus because someone else has pointed them that way. 1:36–37 use the key word 'follow' twice. Probably what they were doing, to begin with at least, was tagging along behind Jesus to see what he was up to and where he was going or staying (1:38) rather than the technical use of 'following' meaning like a disciple committed to a master. But, as so often, the one leads to the other. Why did we first start to follow Jesus? Was it because someone told us about him, or pointed us in his direction—a parent or grandparent, a teacher or minister—or because we tagged along just to see what was happening?

The invitation

The first words spoken by the main character are very important in a play. Now we hear Jesus' first words in this gospel, and they are a question: 'what are you looking for?' (1:38). This theme of seeking or looking for someone or something becomes quite important through this gospel. Many seek Jesus, some because they want to kill him, and others because they want to know about him and his teaching. On other occasions, Jesus asks, as here, 'what do you want? what are you seeking?' Even when he knows the answer, he graciously allows the other person to express their desire—even in the Garden asking the temple police who they are looking for (18:4). When Mary Magdalene is crying so much outside his tomb that she cannot recognize the risen Jesus, he will gently repeat this question: 'whom are you looking for?' (20:15).

The two new followers stammer a reply about finding out more about him, so Jesus follows up his open question with an invitation: 'come and see' (1:39). He does not force himself upon them—but asks what they are looking for and offers them the chance to find out the answer to their questions. As we read John's gospel, we are also asked the same question, what are we looking for—and we receive the same invitation from Jesus, 'come and see'.

Inviting others

When someone has pointed you to Jesus and you have responded and seen him for yourself, then you have to go and tell others and bring them also to 'come and see'. The news is too good to be kept to yourself. So it is here. Andrew and the other disciple stay with Jesus for the rest of the afternoon and evening—and then Andrew goes to find his brother, Simon, and tell him the good news, 'we have found the Messiah', using the Hebrew word which is translated into the Greek 'Christ', which means 'the anointed one' (1:40–41).

Andrew seems particularly good at bringing others to Jesus. At the feeding of the five thousand, it is Andrew who finds the little boy with the loaves and fishes and brings him to Jesus (6:8–9); later when some Greeks want to see Jesus, it is to Andrew that Philip brings them so Andrew can introduce them all to Jesus (12:22). In each case the consequences of these simple acts of bringing people to Jesus were significant: the hungry get fed, new races hear the gospel—and here, Simon becomes a disciple. Andrew could not have known the significance of what he had done in bringing his brother to the Lord—but Jesus looked at him and saw through the rough exterior to the enduring qualities of the man: so, he calls him *Kephas*, which means the same in Aramaic as the Greek, *Petros*—'Rocky', the foundation upon which so much will be built. We may not all be missionaries or famous evangelists, but perhaps there are people we could direct towards Jesus, or who need us to bring them to him— and who knows what the result may be?

PRAYER

Lord Jesus, thank you for your invitation to come and see;
help me to accept your call and to follow you.

8   JOHN 1:43–51

FOLLOW ME

The invitation, 'Come and see', leads to the command, 'Follow me'. In the other gospels, this is the first thing Jesus says to Andrew and to Simon Peter (Mk. 1:17), and in John's gospel, Jesus repeats it to Peter as his last word (21:22). Here, though, Jesus goes to Galilee to find Philip and give him this invitation (1:43). Philip comes from Bethsaida, where the Jordan flows into the Sea of Galilee in the north, in the territory of Philip the tetrarch (see Luke 3:1). The gospel writer tells us that it is also the city of Andrew and Peter (1:44), although Mark 1:21–29 suggests that they now live in Capernaum, a few miles to the west along the shore of Galilee. Like Andrew, Philip has a Greek name and he is often mentioned with Andrew (6:5–8; 12:20–22). Philip also shares Andrew's readiness to go immediately and tell someone else about Jesus—Nathanael, whose Hebrew name means 'God has given'. And so, in this cosmopolitan sea-side area the good news of what 'God has given' in Jesus begins to spread.

From disdain to faith

Unfortunately, like many others who think they are 'God's gift', Nathanael is not impressed. Philip tells his friend that they have found the one prophesied throughout the Hebrew scriptures, and identifies him as Jesus of Nazareth, son of Joseph (1:45). Nathanael comes from Cana (21:2) a village up the road from Nazareth—and he is quite clear about the likelihood of God giving anything of value to his local rivals: 'Can anything good come out of Nazareth?' (1:46). Nathanael's disdain reflects our natural human expectations. If God is going to give something special, it will come in a special way, not from a carpenter's shop up the road! While this gospel opened with Jesus' cosmic origins with God (1:1), it recognizes that Jesus' human origins are humble—and will prove a stumbling block to many (see 6:42; 8:40–43). Philip does not try to argue his friend out of his pre-judice, but rather he shares his own experience of Jesus and issues the same invitation as the others received—'Come and see'.

Jesus' knowledge of us

So Nathanael tags along with Philip, expecting his prejudices to be confirmed. Jesus, however, surprises him by taking the initiative and welcoming him as an Israelite in whom there is no guile (1:47). This is a compliment: all Israelites knew of the guile of the patriarch, Jacob, who stole his brother's blessing (Gen. 27:35); only one in whom there is no guile can serve the Lord (Ps. 32:2; Is. 53:9). Nathanael is taken aback: it is a shock when God lets us know that he believes in us more than we do in him! Jesus says that he saw Nathanael sitting under the fig tree. This may suggest he was studying the law: some rabbis used to teach under fig trees, while the prophets used sitting under a fig tree as an image of the peace of the Day of the Lord (e.g. Micah 4:4; Zech. 3:10). Later, St Augustine says that he was reading beneath a fig tree when he heard the call of Jesus to 'pick up and read' the New Testament (*Confessions* 8.28–29). Jesus sees us and brings his welcome and his invitation into the midst of our ordinary daily activities.

Greater things

It is not clear how Jesus knew him under the fig tree, but Nathanael is impressed and moves from provincial scepticism to a declaration of Messianic faith: 'Rabbi, you are the Son of God! You are the King of Israel!' (1:49). Jesus' somewhat amused response at this sudden turn around is in the best tradition of B-movie actors: 'You ain't seen nuthin' yet, kid!' Following Jesus is not about being impressed by his superior knowledge, or his ability to do supernatural things—but something much greater than these things (1:50). It is nothing less than the connection of God with all his creation. In the midst of his guile, Jacob received a vision of a ladder between heaven and earth upon which the angels ascended and descended (Gen. 28:12). So now to follow Jesus is to witness the bridge between the divine and the human, the means by which heaven is opened (1:51). From start to finish, this gospel is clear that Jesus is the way to God the Father, as Jesus explains to Philip later at the Last Supper (14:6–11).

For MEDITATION & PRAYER

Do I despise my local Nazareth, or can I find God there?

'Rabbi, you are the Son of God! You are the King of Israel!' (1:49).

9

The WEDDING *at* CANA

'There was a wedding at Cana in Galilee'. For a little town nestling in the hill-country above the Sea of Galilee a few miles from Nazareth, Cana has become remarkably well known down through the ages and across the world by being mentioned at the start of the wedding liturgies of many churches. Some couples save up for years to visit Cana to renew their marriage vows on significant anniversaries, and the little church there today is full of images of love and marriage. It is little wonder, then, that some people, particularly from Catholic traditions, interpret this story as being about the sacrament of marriage. Yet we are told nothing of the marriage itself, or the happy couple—just about the disaster of the wine running out at the party! The wedding serves merely as the backdrop for the occasion of Jesus' first miracle in this gospel. For the evangelist, the important thing is not the event—but the fact that Jesus was there (2:2). The Word made flesh, the God who dwells among us, goes to wedding parties, joins in our everyday activities and gets involved with human affairs.

When resources run out

It is so embarrassing: the guests are here, the party is going well and then you realize that the special item for the dinner menu must have been left behind at the supermarket check-out, or a miscalculation of amounts per person has left you short. Given the tendency of ancient near-eastern weddings and parties to go on for days, supplies must have run out occasionally—but it would still have been a disgrace for the family. And so Mary turns to Jesus for help. It is futile to speculate why she does so, or to surmise that they are related to the wedding couple, or that Jesus has caused the shortage by bringing his friends along. None the less, Mary clearly expects that simply explaining the situation to her son will lead him to do something about it. When we come to the end of our human resources, and we simply have nothing left to say, or do, or give in a situation, so too we can turn to God in prayer and tell him what has happened.

Jesus' initial response is not encouraging. The address, 'Woman' is not as brusque in Greek or Aramaic as in English, and indeed he uses it to his mother again while on the cross (19:26). However, 'what is that to you and me?' does not suggest that he is going to do anything, because his 'hour has not yet come' (2:4). John uses the word 'hour' about twenty-five times. Twice more we are told that Jesus' 'hour had not yet come' (7:30, 8:20). When it does arrive, it refers to Jesus' death and glorification (12:23; 13:1; 17:1)—the very hour when Mary again stands at her son's side and is addressed as 'woman'. Thus we have a link in John's account between the beginning of Jesus' ministry when Mary turns to him when resources run out, and the end when Mary watches his human life ending.

Do whatever he tells you

Mary, however, is not put off by Jesus' response. She tells the servants to do whatever he tells them. This motif of someone persisting despite an apparent initial rebuff from Jesus recurs later with the official who wants his son to be healed (4:47–50). Sure enough, Jesus now acts, and turns to the large stone jars holding the water used for purification, for washing people's feet when they came into the party, or for their hands before eating, and even between courses (see Mk. 7:3–4). Jesus tells the servants to fill the jars, and not only do they obey, but they fill them 'to the brim' (2:7); then he tells them to take what is apparently water to the person in charge of the feast—and they take it, without protest. So the miracle happens through the persistence of Mary and the obedience of the servants. It is as though the evangelist is saying that simply expecting Jesus to take over when human supplies fail is not enough: persistence in faith is needed, together with the willingness to do whatever he says. God in Jesus dwells among us in times of joy, like that of bridegroom and bride, and of need at the end of our resources—but in both he desires our co-operation to grant us his grace.

PRAYER

Lord, when resources run out and things seem hopeless,
grant me the faith to trust in you
and the willingness to do whatever you say,
that your abundance may be shed on this world.

10

WATER *into* WINE

John describes the events at Cana as the first of Jesus' 'signs' and thus it stands at the start of his ministry as a foretaste of what is to come and an introduction to the rest. So what is the meaning of this miracle, apart from merely saving the blushes of the wedding family whose supplies had run out? After all, the sheer quantity of the water turned into wine is remarkable. The evangelist notes that each jar held 'two or three measures'; a measure—a *bath* or firkin—was between twenty and thirty gallons, so six jars works out around 150 gallons, or 800 bottles of the best-quality wine! It was clearly going to be quite a party…

This prodigious amount has invited comparisons between Jesus and the Greek god of wine, Dionysus. Various stories are told of bowls being miraculously filled with wine in his temple at Elis, or of a fountain flowing with wine in his temple at Andros. In fact, we do not need to go so far afield for inspiration. The prophet Amos uses the image of 'the mountains dripping with sweet wine and the hills flowing with it' for the great Day of the Lord to come, and similar examples of wine as a sign of so-called 'messianic abundance' can be found in other Hebrew prophets (Amos 9:13; Hos. 14:7; Jer. 31:12). Isaiah looks forward to the Lord giving a huge party, 'a feast of rich food, a feast of well-aged wines' (Is. 25:6) and likens God's rejoicing over his people to a wedding (Is. 62:4–5). Jesus uses this image of a wedding banquet for the kingdom of heaven in his parable of a marriage feast and those who refused the invitation (Matt. 22:1–10; Lk. 14:15–24), and he likens himself to the bridegroom in Mark 2:19. All of this, says the fourth evangelist, is being inaugurated in the here and now as Jesus begins his ministry at this wedding feast in Cana.

New for old

Christians, of course, look forward to the heavenly wedding feast of God with his people every time we celebrate the Holy Communion, and so it is not surprising that some have seen an allusion to the sacrament of the Eucharist as well as marriage here. But in the absence of any mention of bread, or of blessing, this seems unlikely, except in the sense that John sees everything as sacramental: he fills his gospel with symbols of the grace of God being found in bread and wine, water and light. The great richness of this gospel is that so many levels of understanding can be found, but at the surface level of the story, the climax is the proclamation of the master of ceremonies that the best has been saved until last (2:10). Here at the start of his story of Jesus' activity, the evangelist says that we 'have seen nothing yet', that all which has gone before in the writings and prophecies, the hopes and beliefs of God's people, is now being made new in Jesus. The old order is passing away, as the new is inaugurated among us— and we should celebrate.

A sign to reveal his glory

This is the whole point of the miracle—it is not so much about what was done as who did it. As we saw in the Introduction (see p. 16 above), John uses the word 'sign', *semeion*, for Jesus' miracles, rather than 'mighty act', *dynamis*, more common in the other gospels. This, 'the first of his signs', points to Jesus; it 'revealed his glory, and his disciples believed in him' (2:11). The purpose of the sign is not for public display; apart from the servants, no one knew what had happened and so the person in charge compliments the bridegroom (2:9–10). For the disciples, however, the miracle of changing water into wine is the sign which moves them on from their call in Chapter 1 to putting their faith in Jesus. At the end of the gospel, the evangelist tells us that he has selected these signs from the many done by Jesus 'in the presence of his disciples' that we might believe that 'Jesus is the Christ, the Son of God' and so have life in him (20:31). So, as Jesus brings life to the wedding party when things ran out, so he comes to us with the superabundance of his grace to make all things new.

For REFLECTION & PRAYER

What are the 'signs' around you where God is changing the ordinary things of life into the new wine of his kingdom?

Lord, thank you that you have kept the best until now; grant me insight to see your signs and courage to believe in you.

HOUSE CLEANING

Many signs in this gospel are followed by a debate to explain the sign's purpose—as the story of the feeding of the five thousand leads into the discourse about Jesus as the Bread of Life (see on chapter 6 below). However, the first of Jesus' signs, the changing of the water into wine, has no such dialogue. Instead the scene shifts a hundred miles south to Jerusalem for the incident in the temple, which the other gospels use to introduce the final week of Jesus' life and the crucifixion. In these next studies, therefore, we will consider why the temple incident comes here in John, and how it is connected to the water into wine story.

The Passover in Jerusalem

'The Passover of the Jews was near, and Jesus went up to Jerusalem' (2:13). In the other gospels, only one Passover is mentioned, that during the final week of Jesus' life. However, John mentions three Passovers, introducing them each time with this phrase, 'the Passover of the Jews was near'—this Passover in 2:13, another a year later at the time of the feeding of the five thousand (6:4), and the final Passover introduced in 11:55 and 13:1, upon which Jesus dies (19:14). John's dating gives us the traditional chronology of Jesus' ministry lasting three years. We have already noted John's interest in time with the mention of Jesus' 'hour' in the previous story (2:4). In fact, this gospel abounds in references to time, with words like hour, day, time, moment, now and already occurring frequently.

We also note that it is the Passover of "the Jews". Festivals of "the Jews" punctuate this gospel: in addition to three Passovers, we have the feast of Tabernacles in chapter 7 and the Dedication in chapter 10, with an unspecified festival in chapter 5. In each case, Jesus goes up to Jerusalem for the feast, like any pious Jew. This portrayal of Jesus the Jew is important in the light of John's use of the phrase "the Jews" to denote his opponents. The other gospels concentrate on Jesus' ministry in Galilee and show him going to Jerusalem only once to die at Passover time—indeed Luke structures the whole of his account around Jesus' journey to Jerusalem (Lk. 9:51—19:27). In contrast, John shows Jesus visiting Jerusalem regularly over several years.

This incident in the temple must come at the end of Jesus' ministry in the other gospels since it is the only time he is in Jerusalem, but historically that makes good sense also, since it precipitates the events of Holy Week leading to his arrest and death. Even today, the temple site in Jerusalem is heavily policed and any demonstration quickly attracts the authorities' interests! Since it is unlikely that Jesus could have done this twice, we must assume that John places it here at the start for theological rather than chronological reasons. So what are they?

A good clean-out

The common description of Jesus' removal of the traders and animals as the 'cleansing of the temple' suggests that it is some form of protest about its system. The other gospels' use of Jeremiah's phrase 'you have made it a robbers' den' (Jer. 7:11) implies a protest at the financial trading and exploitation of people through money changing and the sale of sacrificial animals (Mk. 11:17, Matt. 21:12, Lk. 19:46). Others have inferred from the reference about a 'house of prayer for all nations' (Is. 56:7, also in Mk. 11:17, etc.) that Jesus' action in the Court of the Gentiles was a protest about the exclusion of women and Gentiles from worship in the inner courts reserved for Jewish men, especially the priests. But there is none of this here. Jesus does drive out the traders and money changers, even using a whip, but the saying is simply a pun about making 'my Father's house' into a 'trading house' (2:16). There is no reference to robbers or financial exploitation. It is almost as though the temple itself and its whole use is the focus of Jesus' action as he begins his ministry.

John would have known the prophecy at the end of our Old Testament canon that the messenger of the Lord would suddenly come to his temple, like a refiner's fire (Mal. 3:1–4). This may be why John places the temple incident here, almost as programmatic for Jesus' ministry. Now it makes the same point as the story of water into wine—the replacement of the old order by the new, for the Lord has come. Everything is changed as Jesus fulfils the festivals and the very temple itself—if only they would recognize him.

PRAYER

Lord may I recognize when your time comes
and may the 'inner courts' of my life be ready for you.

DESTROY THIS TEMPLE

It is not only in his placing of the temple incident at the start of Jesus' ministry that John differs from the other gospels. He also has this story concerning a saying of Jesus about the destruction of the temple. We have already noted that sometimes a sign or action in John's gospel is explained by a dialogue afterwards, so this next incident, acting as a counterbalance to the water-into-wine story, can further illuminate the meaning of the temple event placed between them.

Zeal for the temple

It is introduced by the disciples remembering a quotation from Psalm 69:9, 'Zeal for your house will consume me' (2:17). The early Christians often saw Messianic prophecies in this Psalm, and John will refer to it again for Jesus' thirst at the crucifixion (19:28, quoting Ps. 69:21). This gives a different atmosphere to the story, moving the attention away from a protest *by* Jesus about the temple to a concentration *on* Jesus himself, telling us of his zeal for God's house and warning us that it will lead to his death. Thus the temple event becomes a foreshadowing of the crucifixion.

The response by the religious authorities, identified again simply as "the Jews", is to question Jesus' authority. The old prophets, like Jeremiah, prophesied in and against the temple, and were questioned by the authorities (see Jer. 7:1; 19:14; 36:5) and Mark records a similar challenge to Jesus' authority after his account of the temple incident (Mk. 11:28). So here, "the Jews" ask Jesus, 'What sign can you show us for doing this?' (2:18). The prophetic word could be accompanied by an action, such as Ezekiel's dramatic acting out of the siege of Jerusalem as a sign (see Ezek. 4:3). However, we have already noted that 'sign' in John's gospel (*semeion*) is used for a miraculous action which reveals something about Jesus—and this happens here too.

Destruction and the temple

However, instead of giving them a confirming miracle, Jesus replies with a *mashal*, a riddle, about destroying the temple and raising it up in three days (2:19). The second part alludes to Hosea 6:2, 'after two days he will revive us, on the third day he will raise us up', which should warn the hearers that something prophetic is being suggested. However, in this gospel, John often makes use of ironic misunderstandings between Jesus and his hearers, where he tries to explain something on a more spiritual level to someone who can only (mis-) understand it on a literal level. So here "the Jews" interpret the comment literally as a rebuilding of the temple in three days and curtly dismiss such a preposterous idea! After all, Herod had begun to rebuild the temple during 20BC and after forty-six years it was still under construction. It would be finished finally in AD63, only to be destroyed by the Romans a few years later in the Jewish War in 70.

Forty-six years from the start of construction would bring us to AD26, when Jesus was about thirty years old. This is probably a little too early for the actual temple demonstration leading to Jesus' death. However, if Jesus' ministry lasted three years, AD26 could have been around its start, so John may be right to place the *saying* here. It is also interesting that various versions of this saying about destroying the temple are quoted against Jesus by the false witnesses at his trial (Mk. 14:58, Matt. 26:61; see also Acts 6:14) and at the cross (Mk. 15:29, Matt. 27:40). If John is correct in placing the debate about the temple right at the start of Jesus' ministry, it would explain why the witnesses disagree about the saying several years later.

Thus this saying reinforces the point from the previous section by directing our attention away from interpreting this incident in the temple as a protest about particular abuses and back to Jesus himself. In the new order, when water is turned into wine, a prophecy about the destruction of the temple actually refers forward to Jesus' own death. The temple sacrifices will be replaced by his sacrifice on the cross.

For REFLECTION & PRAYER

What are the practices in my life and my ways of worshipping God which need to be replaced by the new order in Jesus?

Father, give me a proper 'zeal for your house,'
renewed in the death of your Son, Jesus Christ.

13 JOHN 2:21–25

REALIZING & BELIEVING

We have seen that the evangelist is carefully linking the incident in the temple with the changing of water into wine, so that both stories reveal the arrival of the new age with Jesus. Of course, this is only realized with the benefit of hindsight, as the early Christians prayed and reflected upon the events of Jesus' life and death. As John makes clear in 2:22, it was only after the resurrection that the disciples remembered and finally understood what had been said and done—and in the light of the resurrection, they began to see how God's new life in Jesus transformed everything, even prophecies about the temple.

Resurrection and the temple

If 'zeal for your house' would lead to Jesus' death, and the saying about the temple be quoted at his trial, the evangelist is keen to point out that the rest of the saying refers to his resurrection. After the three Passovers and the three years, the phrase 'three days', with its roots in Hos. 6:2, would instantly remind any early Christian reader of Jesus being raised from the dead. We have noted John's interest in time, and he will often refer ahead to what is still in the future in the story-time, but which is now in the past from the point of view of the time of the writer and the reader. Thus Jesus' death and resurrection, which are still three years in the future in the story, dominate everything for the evangelist. So everything is all brought together in this story about the temple, which is placed at the start of Jesus' ministry but which looks ahead to the consummation of it all in his death and resurrection.

Now we really see the meaning of the whole chapter and how John likes to order events more for their theological significance. This whole incident is not about a prophetic cleansing of the temple, nor an anti-racial or financial protest; rather it reveals John's understanding of Jesus. The link with the water into wine is now clear—the new and better for the old. Just as the water became the abundant new wine, so this incident looks ahead to the replacement of the temple and its sacrifices by Jesus' sacrifice and his new life. The temple may have been destroyed only a few years after its final completion, and never rebuilt, but Jesus rose again after his death. Something beyond the physical level is happening and to argue about the timing of this event or that saying is to make the same mistake as the Jewish leaders who were so concerned about construction timetables that they could not understand who was standing before them, challenging them with his actions and his words.

Believing and trusting

John tells us that Jesus did many other signs, but that he has selected certain ones to describe so we may believe that Jesus is the Christ (20:31). This is clear here since, in between the 'first of his signs' of water into wine (2:11) and the 'second sign' (4:54), we are told about people believing in Jesus' name because of the signs he was doing (2:23). But belief which is based upon miraculous signs is not enough—hence Jesus' refusal to give one to "the Jews" to prove his authority (2:18). While the disciples can 'believe' or 'trust' (*pisteuein* in Greek) his word after the resurrection (2:22), and others similarly 'believe' because of the signs (2:23), Jesus will not 'entrust' himself to them, as John uses the same word *pisteuein* here in 2:24 as in the preceding verses. He knows what people are like (2:25). His supreme knowledge of all is stressed throughout this gospel, from knowing Nathanael under the fig tree in 1:48 to knowing 'all things' at the end (13:3; 21:17).

This is the one who has come from being with God in the beginning to call disciples in Chapter 1. So in Chapter 2, this is the one who makes all things new, who can change water into wine and temple worship into resurrection faith. Both stories point clearly to Jesus and challenge us to respond, either with the questioning of the authorities, the following of the crowd or the dawning belief of the disciples. This challenge will become clearer and sharper in the next few chapters as more and more people come face to face with Jesus.

PRAYER

Lord Jesus, teach me to see all things in the light of your resurrection and to believe the word you have spoken.

14 JOHN 3:1–8

NICODEMUS *by* NIGHT

In the last chapter, Jesus did not 'trust' himself to people who 'trusted' in him because of his signs (2:23–24). Over the coming chapters, many people come to Jesus because of his signs—the Samaritan woman (4:29), the official whose son is healed (4:47), the paralytic (5:9), the crowd who were fed (6:14), the blind man (9:25)—who all need to move on from trusting in the signs to faith in Jesus himself. The first is Nicodemus, a Pharisee and 'a ruler of the Jews', a member of the Sanhedrin, the Jewish council (3:1). He is a man of influence and wealth (he buys spices in 19:39), whom Jesus calls 'a teacher of Israel', a theologian perhaps!

He comes 'by night', which may be caution arising from his fear as one of the authorities of being seen talking to Jesus (3:2). However, the rabbis also saw the night as a quiet time for study of the scriptures. Whether it is out of fear, or that he wants to talk to Jesus undisturbed, the evangelist depicts Nicodemus as someone still in the dark—but who comes to the light. In due course he will come out into the open to speak for Jesus (7:50) and to bury him (19:39); at this point he simply wants to ask questions.

You must be born again

We have noted John's habit of using the way people misunderstand Jesus to get at deeper levels of meaning. This happens in Jesus' conversation here. Jesus responds to Nicodemus' trust in the signs (3:2), by telling him that he must be born over again, *anothen* (3:3). Just as "the Jews" misunderstand Jesus to mean literally rebuilding the temple , so Nicodemus interprets this as a man trying to climb back into his mother's womb (3:4). So, what does *anothen* mean? Some Bible translations will have 'born again', and others 'born from above'. In fact, *anothen* can have both meanings, in the way our phrases 'start over' or 'from the top' use language from 'above' to mean 'again'. The evangelist probably intends both meanings. Jesus has come from above, with God (1:1ff) and wants his followers to be with him there (17:24). However, both Jews and Greeks used the idea of rebirth to mean starting again in a new life, for Gentiles wanting to follow Judaism and for initiates in the Greek mystery cults. So Nicodemus' misunderstanding allows Jesus further explanation.

Water and the Spirit

Jesus replies to this misunderstanding by explaining that we have to be 'born of water and the Spirit' to enter the kingdom of God (3:5). There is a lot of water in this gospel: John baptizes in it (1:26); Jesus turns it into wine (2:9), offers it to the woman at the well (4:14), heals by a pool (5:7), walks on it (6:19), offers it again to the thirsty (7:37), and uses it to heal (9:7) and to wash the disciples' feet (13:5). There is something cleansing, healing, and satisfying about it all. Little wonder, then, that many have interpreted 'born of water' as referring to Christian baptism, seeing 'of the Spirit' as meaning Confirmation, or a Pentecostal second blessing or baptism in the Spirit. The paradox of this gospel is that although John's theology is supremely sacramental in the way ordinary things like water, bread and wine are used to convey great spiritual truths and meanings, he never actually describes the sacraments of baptism and communion, or indeed any others. It is thus unlikely that he has any reference to any 'two stages' of Christian initiation here.

Instead, he is contrasting Nicodemus' literal understanding of getting back into the womb with the spiritual rebirth from above offered by Jesus. When my wife's waters broke at the birth of our daughters, I was amazed by how much water had protected them in the womb—but now they had to take their first breaths of air. So too we must move from our physical natural birth through a new spiritual birth to enter the kingdom of God. 'That which is born of the flesh is flesh' but to be born of the Spirit is to be like the wind, which comes and goes at will, invisibly (3:6–8). The Greek word, *pneuma*, which gives us words like pneumatic tyres, means wind, breath and spirit, from the air in our lungs to the Holy Spirit of God. Nicodemus has to come out of the darkness, be born again, take a big breath and let himself be carried on the winds of God.

For REFLECTION & PRAYER

What are the darknesses and misunderstandings out of which we
need to be born again?
Do we have the courage to launch out in the Spirit?
Lord Jesus, grant me God's Holy Spirit
that I may be born again to your new life.

The TEACHER IS
TAUGHT HEAVENLY THINGS

After Jesus' comparison of the Spirit with the wind, poor old Nicodemus has to ask for yet further explanation (3:9). As 'a teacher of Israel' (3:10), he should have known the old prophecies about God giving his people 'a new heart and a new spirit' (Ezek. 18:31; 36:26) and writing his covenant on their hearts (Jer. 31:33). In response to his question, Jesus embarks on a section of teaching introduced by the phrase 'Amen, amen I tell you' (3:11), variously translated as 'truly, truly' or 'very truly'. While the other gospels use only one 'Amen' to introduce Jesus' teaching, John stresses it by using this doubling effect some twenty-five times.

Furthermore, something strange happens in verse 11, for Nicodemus disappears from view: the first 'you' in the verse is singular, still addressing Nicodemus, but after that the speech moves into plural pronouns, 'we' and 'you-plural'. Also, it is not clear when Jesus' speech ends. Since ancient manuscripts had no punctuation marks, which were only put into the text centuries later, modern editors have to work out where to put inverted commas around someone's speech. Usually it is clear where someone stops speaking and the narrator restarts—but not in John. Some Bible translations end the quotation in 3:15, while others run it right through to 3:21, since both the narrative and Jesus' speech use the same style and words. It is as though the quiet night-time conversation between Jesus and Nicodemus has been replaced by Jesus speaking through the evangelist and the early Christians to the rest of the Jews and, indeed, to the whole human race, asking them to 'receive our testimony' (3:11).

Earthly and heavenly things

The misunderstanding of "the Jews" about the temple saying and by Nicodemus about the new birth arose because they interpreted Jesus just on a literal or earthly level, when he wanted to direct them to a higher, heavenly one (3:12). This happens regularly throughout this gospel. So here Jesus has been speaking of earthly things like a birth or the wind, but uses them to refer to the heavenly things of a new beginning with God and his Spirit.

In fact, John often distinguishes a heavenly divine realm from the earthly world we inhabit. The problem is that we cannot ascend from our level to God's. Jesus, however, is the Son of Man who has descended from heaven to our lowly depths (3:13). We saw this in Chapter 1, in the great Prologue describing Jesus as the Word with God in the heavenly realm (1:1–14), and also in Jesus likening himself to Jacob's ladder connecting the two levels in his conversation with Nathanael (1:51). We should not assume that John held a primitive two- or three-tier view of the physical universe; rather, this distinction between a 'superior' level of the world of ideas and the divine over an 'inferior' realm of the physical universe of material bodies runs right through ancient writings from the Greek philosophy of Plato to Jewish prophecy. Thus we must expect to find it often in this gospel.

Moses' serpent and the Son of Man

Next, the Old Testament allusions move away from the prophets and Jacob's ladder to Moses and the Israelites in the wilderness. In Numbers 21:4–9, we find the story of the Israelites grumbling against Moses and God, and being punished by a plague of poisonous snakes. As a remedy God told Moses to make a bronze snake and lift it up on a pole—and anyone who looked at it was healed (Num. 21:9). The bronze snake itself was eventually smashed as an idol by Hezekiah (2 Kings 18:4). However, the later Book of Wisdom, which was written in intertestamental times and can now be found in the Apocrypha (see Glossary), described it as a 'symbol of salvation' (Wis. 16:6). This is exactly how John uses it here. He seizes on another word capable of several levels of meaning—the verb *hypsoun*, to 'lift up'. Of course, it has the positive meaning of to raise or exalt, but when Jesus talks here and in 8:28 and 12:32–4 of the Son of Man being 'lifted up', we know that it will be on a cross. Once again, we are asked to look beyond the earthly level to spiritual things. Like the dying Israelites looking to the snake 'lifted up' for healing, we are to see in Jesus' broken body 'lifted up' on an instrument of torture our means of healing and the source of eternal life (3:14).

PRAYER

*Lord Jesus, give me grace to see beyond earthly things
and to receive your salvation as you are lifted up.*

16   JOHN 3:16–21

GOD SO LOVED *the* WORLD

As we saw before, this passage can be read either as the end of Jesus' conversation with Nicodemus, or as a separate comment by the evangelist. Who says it, is less important than what it says, for it is one of this gospel's supreme passages, full of John's favourite vocabulary and themes, including, of course, probably the most famous verse in the Bible, 3:16. But this verse, rich in the love of God, is set within a whole series of contrasts. John is fond of balancing sets of opposites such as above and below, life and death, truth and falsehood. Such pairings are also found in Greek philosophy, and within Judaism, notably in the Dead Sea Scrolls found at Qumran. Again we see how John explains the gospel in words and ideas accessible to his own day, but which also have had a profound influence upon human history ever since.

Eternal life or perishing

John's use of contrasting pairs and seeing the heavenly realm as opposed to the earthly could lead to accusations of dualism, seeing everything as either positive or negative. Certainly, the dualism of Greek philosophy valued the heavenly above the earthly, seeing the physical, material world as something from which to escape. While John does sometimes use 'the world' in a negative sense for those opposed to God, especially in the Last Supper discourses, this section shows us that the world can never be seen totally negatively. 'For God so loved the world' tells us that it is the *world*, for all its sin and shortcomings, which is the object of God's love, which has a universal scope. Sometimes Christians act as if Jn. 3:16 read, 'For God so loved the *church* that he gave...' in their neglect of the world! Yet this gospel makes it abundantly clear that God acts for the whole world in sending his 'only Son'. This phrase recalls another Old Testament story, where Abraham is told to take 'your son, your only son, Isaac whom you love' up the mountain for sacrifice (Gen. 22:2, 12). While Abraham was spared this ultimate sacrifice, God did not spare his Son, Jesus, but gave him so that the world should not perish. For this is the ultimate choice John puts before his readers: to perish apart from God, or to receive his gift of eternal life in his Son. There is no other option—and for this reason 'God sent his Son into the world'.

Belief or condemnation

This idea of God 'sending' Jesus is one of John's most frequent, occurring over fifty times in this gospel. But he is also clear why God sent the Son—not to condemn the world but to save it (3:17). The Greek verb *krinein* means to judge or to condemn, and it gives us the English words 'crisis' and 'critic'. The coming of Jesus provokes a crisis both for the world and for all who dwell upon it, a 'critical moment' of judgment and decision. It is not that he comes as Judge, to condemn the world, for those who do not believe are already lost in their darkness and evil deeds (3:18–19). Instead, he comes to save, that they might turn to him and receive eternal life. It is often thought that judgment is something which happens at the End of all time and space on Judgment Day. But John makes it clear that this deciding, this judgment is already happening in every 'critical moment' in the here and now. As we saw in the Introduction (see p. 24), for John, 'eschatology' (things to do with the End, *eschaton* in Greek), is made real in the present, as Jesus comes into the world to save us.

Light or darkness

Of course, the coming of light into darkness creates shadows, and this, says John, is the crisis, the judgment, because some prefer to remain in the shadows (3:19). Thus we have another contrast, between those who practise what is true, who come to the light, and those who do evil, who hide (3:20–21). But since Jesus comes not to condemn the world but to save it, it is not the case that only those who do truth may come forward. Those who do not know how to live truly, or who stumble in the darkness, may come to the light as Nicodemus does by night and find love and acceptance. Later in the gospel, as Nicodemus comes more out into the open, we will also read of Judas, who leaves Jesus to go out into the darkness of the night (13:30). The options, the opposing contrasts are always before us at each critical moment, which is why God sent his Son into the world, that we should not perish but have eternal life.

PRAYER

Lord Jesus Christ, may I recognize the 'critical moment';
let me come to you out of my darkness to receive your eternal life.

JESUS & JOHN *the* BAPTIST

The next scene gives us a glimpse of the ministry of Jesus and his disciples baptizing, in much the same way as John the Baptist and his followers. It was a good job there was 'much water there'! (3:23). This reminds us of how similar their ministries were at first, before John was put in prison (3:24). In fact, this is the last appearance the Baptist makes in this gospel, although he is mentioned in comparison with Jesus later (e.g. 4:1; 5:33–36; 10:41). Such comparisons were bound to raise the possibility of rivalry between the two men and their respective groups. Disciples of John the Baptist were known around the Mediterranean for some time later, as is shown by St Paul's baptizing some at Ephesus in the name of Jesus (Acts 19:5). Thus it would not be surprising if there was debate among the Jews about these rites of purification, and whether Jesus' or John's was better (3:25). Even more understandable is the complaint of John's disciples that Jesus is doing better business, 'all are going to him' (3:26). What is not perhaps expected is John's reaction.

Bearing witness

Even John the Baptist's disciples who are complaining know perfectly well that Jesus had been with John 'across the Jordan' and that John had borne witness to him (3:26). This gospel shows John the Baptist as satisfied to accept the success or otherwise of the ministry given to him by God (3:27). He reminds his followers that he had denied any claims to be the Christ, but was only the one sent before him (3:28, referring back to 1:20–23). He has given his fourfold witness to Jesus being greater than himself as the Lamb of God and Son of God who baptizes in the Holy Spirit (see on 1:24–34). While this understanding of Jesus is more theologically developed than John's questioning of Jesus in the Synoptics (see e.g. Matt. 11:3; Lk. 7:19), it need not be interpreted solely as a later 'attack' by the early Christians against the followers of the Baptist. John the Baptist's ministry is clearly attested in all the gospels and in the writings of the Jewish historian Josephus as preaching and baptizing for forgiveness in preparation for the coming of the kingdom of God. Thus he was looking forward to something greater to come.

He must increase, but I must decrease

Matthew makes this point by showing John as reluctant to baptize Jesus at first, recognizing him as greater than himself (Matt. 3:14). In this gospel, John uses the analogy of the bridegroom and his friend (3:29). It is a bit like our custom of having a 'best man' at a marriage—and the old joke about the bride not marrying the best man at her wedding! In Jewish weddings of the time, the bridegroom would be assisted by one or two friends who would make the arrangements and escort the bride to the groom, and eventually to the bridal chamber. The reference to rejoicing at 'the bridegroom's voice' may refer to the friend standing guard at the chamber and only admitting the groom, whose voice he recognizes, or to hearing his voice calling out joyfully when the marriage had been consummated—the sign for the friend to slip away quietly, his duty done. Of course both the Baptist and the evangelist, as well as their readers, would have been very familiar with all the bridal imagery used to refer to the people of God in the Hebrew prophets: 'as the bridegroom rejoices over the bride, so shall your God rejoice over you' (Is. 62:5; see also Is. 49:18; 54:6; Ezek. 16:8–14; Hos. 2:16–20). The same idea recurs later in the Revelation of St John, 19:7 and 21:2, 9–10.

Thus with this imagery, the Baptist is saying that his task is done and it is time for him to disappear: 'he must increase, but I must decrease' (3:30). I remember as a best man enjoying all the festivities and basking in the reflected joy of the happy couple—and there is sometimes the same temptation in the Christian life and ministry, especially when God is blessing our work. But while it is perfectly right to rejoice at such times, we must always remember that we are not meant to be centre stage, only the Groom and his bride—and like John the Baptist, slip away quietly, happy as God is magnified.

PRAYER

Lord Jesus, teach me to follow the example of John the Baptist
that I may bear witness to you
and decrease while you increase.

18

JESUS—THE ONE *from* ABOVE

This last section is 'free floating' like 3:16–21; again it is unclear who is the speaker. John the Baptist started talking in 3:27 and some translations continue his speech through to 3:36, while others make this a comment by the evangelist. Some scholars even see this as a separate speech by Jesus. Since both the Baptist and Jesus speak in the same style of the evangelist and quotation marks had not yet been invented, it is not vital. Far more important is how it sums up this chapter's themes by redirecting our attention, as John the Baptist does, back once again to Jesus.

The origins of Jesus

The section begins by using the phrase 'the one from above' to refer to Jesus (3:31) and this picks up the earlier conversation with Nicodemus where Jesus described himself as the one who has descended from heaven (3:13). We saw how this dualism of the heavenly realm above and the world of earthly things below dominates John's thought (see on 3:12), so this recapitulation is not surprising. From the heights of the Prologue through to when Jesus ascends to return to his Father, John makes it clear that he is the one who has come down from heaven into our world. It is so central to John's view of Jesus that he does not even name him in this passage at all—the phrase 'the one from above' is quite sufficient to refer to Jesus. Here, 'from above' is *anothen* once again, the word Jesus used when he told Nicodemus that he needed new birth 'over again, from above' (3:3, 7). This is why we need to be born over again, so that we can participate with Jesus in the realm where he belongs with God.

The mission of Jesus

If Jesus has come down from above, then we next need to ask the question why? and what for? As John the Baptist constantly bears witness to Jesus, so too Jesus testifies to what he has seen and heard in the presence of God (3:32). Again, this picks up his conversation with Nicodemus, where the transition to the more general statement happened with 'we bear witness to what we have seen' (3:11). Throughout this gospel, Jesus is identified as 'the one whom God has sent' (3:34), which reminds us that the expression of how much God loves the world is that he sent his Son into the world (3:17). Jesus is well aware of this, and his favourite description of God in this gospel is 'the one who sent me' (e.g. 7:28, 8:26–9). His mission is to speak 'the words of God' as the one who 'gives the Spirit without measure', abundantly (3:34). This also reminds us of how Jesus taught Nicodemus about being born of water and the Spirit, the Spirit which blows where God wills like the wind (3:5–8). Jesus warned Nicodemus that some will not accept his testimony (3:11) and this is reinforced here in 3:32. But, thanks be to God, there are those who do accept it, who are prepared to put their names to it, to sign up and 'certify that God is true' (3:33).

The Father of Jesus

If Jesus is the one who bears witness to God, the Father is the one who loves the Son and gives all into his hands (3:35). This stress on God's love for Jesus and his entrusting of everything to him is common in this gospel. If, however, God has made Jesus the centre of everything, then the consequences of any response to him are great. As well as John's typical dualism of above and below here, we also find another one of belief and disbelief or disobedience, which brings either life or death (3:36). This recalls the themes of the previous teaching section about the coming of Jesus as a crisis, a critical moment of decision and judgment (3:15–21). In both sections it is clear that whoever believes in Jesus has eternal life (3:36, cf. 3:15–18). However, the alternative must also be true, that rejection of Jesus leaves us under God's wrath (3:36). This is not some 'temper tantrum' of a malicious deity, for God so loved the world that he sent his Son to bring us into his light. But if men and women choose to remain in the darkness (3:19), the God of love cannot force them out. The late Bishop Lesslie Newbigin has expressed this sober truth well in his commentary on John, aptly entitled *The Light Has Come*, thus: 'if we turn our backs upon light, where shall we go but into darkness?' (p.48).

PRAYER

Lord Jesus, help me to accept your testimony
that God has sent you,
and give me your eternal life.

19 JOHN 4:1-9

A SAMARITAN WOMAN *at a* WELL

This gospel's geographical setting moves between north and south, from Jesus calling disciples in Galilee (1:43) and the wedding in Cana (2:1) to the temple in Jerusalem (2:13) and Nicodemus' night visit (3:1). Now, after the debate about Jesus' baptism compared with John's (4:1), Jesus leaves Judaea and heads back to Galilee. The hundred-mile journey takes about three days in a straight line north, which goes through Samaria, an area Jews would prefer to avoid. However, the alternative route going up the Jordan valley to the east needs twice the time, so Jesus sets off through Samaria (4:4), and this becomes the scene for yet more contrasts and meetings of opposites.

Jews and Samaritans

Jesus arrives at the city of Sychar, or Shechem, a place with a history stretching back to the patriarch, Jacob (4:5). This immediately recalls 1:51, where Jesus described himself as the connection between the heavenly realm and the earth just like Jacob's vision of a ladder with angels ascending and descending. It was the same Jacob who bought this land on his return (Gen. 33:18–9), and then gave it to Joseph before he died in Egypt (Gen. 48:22); the Israelites later buried Joseph's bones there after the occupation of Canaan (Josh. 24:32).

Centuries later, after the great kingdom of David split apart on Solomon's death, King Omri made it the capital of the Northern Kingdom around 870BC (1 Kings 16:24). It was captured by the Assyrians in 721, who settled non-Jews there; their intermarriage with the locals offended later ideas of Jewish purity (2 Kings 17:6, 24). The Southern Kingdom also fell and the people were deported to Babylon in 586BC; those who returned from Exile fifty years later prided themselves on their purity. Those in Samaria offered to help the exiles rebuild the temple in 520BC since they shared the same sacrificial worship of God, but this was spurned (Ezra 4:1–3). So the Samaritans built their own temple. From these roots came the bitterness still so strong in Jesus' day. The irony is that ancient Samaria is now the 'West Bank', occupied by modern Israeli soldiers locked in continuing conflict with its inhabitants—and so the ancient troubles persist, despite their shared history going back to a patriarch who dreamed that even the gulf between heaven and earth could be bridged.

Men and women

So Jesus, the bridge between heaven and earth, arrives in this place and immediately confronts yet another division. He is tired with the journey and sits down by the well in the noonday heat (4:6). A woman comes to draw water, which reminds us of how the patriarchs met their wives by wells. Jacob himself met his future wife Rachel by a well (Gen. 29:1–20), which was also where his mother Rebecca met the servant searching for a wife for his father Isaac (Gen. 24). Moses met Jethro's daughters at a well (Exod. 2:15–21). After a wedding with no mention of the happy couple in 2:1–11, and Jesus likened to a bridegroom in 3:29, we might expect this woman coming to a well to be the bride. The problem is that she is a Samaritan. Furthermore, the barriers of race and creed were complicated by gender divisions in Jesus' day. The rabbis taught that a man should not talk to a woman in the street. Some even refused to acknowledge their wives in public, while certain Pharisees sported bruises from bumping into things when their eyes were shut to avoid looking at a woman! What is more, this woman has come in the hottest part of the day, which can only be to avoid others, implying that she is immoral as well.

If Nicodemus was the representative Jew with whom Jesus debated (3:1–11), this woman is the representative Samaritan. But now we have a real meeting of opposites—of a Jew with a Samaritan, a man with a woman, a rabbi with a sinner, the one 'from above' confronting the lowest of the low. It sums up all the bitterness of human separation by race, creed, class, sex, profession, status—yet Jesus, alone, without even his disciples to protect him, asks her for a drink (4:7–8). No wonder there follows her disbelieving, even sarcastic reply—'are *you* talking to *me*?!' (4:9). Yet this is what it means for him to be the ladder at Jacob's well, bridging not only the gulf between God and the world, but also all the barriers human beings put between themselves. It was for this reason that God sent his Son into the world, and for this reason there is hope for us all, from modern Samaria on the West Bank to our daily petty differences.

PRAYER

Lord Jesus, great bridge-builder and ladder into heaven,
forgive us our divisions and reconcile us to God and one another.

LIVING WATER

The woman is surprised that Jesus, a Jewish man, should talk to someone of her gender, race and status—but talk he continues to do. As the conversation unfolds, a dynamic develops similar to that with Nicodemus, as Jesus gently leads her through levels of misunderstanding from the earthly and the literal to the heavenly and spiritual. As this happens, she gradually becomes more aware of who Jesus is. At the moment she thinks he is simply a Jewish man who ought to know better than to talk to her, or can only be doing so for some ulterior motive (4:9). So he teases her by hinting at 'a gift' and suggesting that she does not know who he is; if she did, she would have asked him and would receive 'living water' (4:10). The English translation hides the pun and the beginning of the shift of level, for *zon*, living, with water means 'running, moving' as opposed to the still, or even stagnant water found in a well. Jesus has aroused her interest, and she addresses him with respect, 'Sir'. But he does not even have a traveller's skin bucket—so how is he going to get 'running/living' water? (4:11). Who does he think he is? Even the great patriarch, Jacob, had to dig the well very deep to provide for his family (4:12). How is this man going to get to its actual source?

Wells and springs

Jesus' reply suggests that despite Jacob's greatness, the water in the well cannot satisfy, but people will be thirsty again—which is why the woman has to come to draw water (4:13). However, if people drink the water he is offering, they will never be thirsty again; the still water of the well will be replaced by a 'spring welling up for eternal life' (4:14). This contrast between ordinary water and a leaping fountain reminds us that water is a key theme in this gospel (see on 3:5). The use of water as a spiritual metaphor is very common in the Old Testament scriptures, where the Psalmist's soul is as thirsty for God as a deer for flowing streams (Ps. 42:1–2) and God calls all who are thirsty to come and drink freely (Is. 55:1). A century or so before Jesus, the phrase 'the well of living waters' is used in the Dead Sea Scrolls to describe the Jewish law, while the wisdom writers used water as a symbol of wisdom itself: 'those who drink of me will thirst for more' (Ecclesiasticus 24:21). Jesus' offer goes even beyond that, with the promise of never thirsting (4:14). In the new order where water turns into abundant wine and the temple is replaced by Jesus, even wisdom and the law itself must give way to the superior gift of God in Jesus.

Not surprisingly, however, the woman again misunderstands it literally; if what Jesus says is true, he is to be respected as someone to save her work and the trouble of carrying water: 'Sir, give me this water, so that I may never be thirsty or have to keep coming here to draw water' (4:15).

Husbands and gods

If the woman has to keep drawing water, she must have a family to care for, so Jesus tells her to call her husband (4:16). After the betrothal hints in the story so far of Jesus, the bridegroom, asking for water from a woman at a well, her reply that she has no husband (4:17) is only to be expected; does this mean she is available? Now the conversation moves into another level, as the gentle teasing is replaced by the blunt truth, that she has had five husbands as well as her current man (4:18). The Jews permitted three marriages at most, and so this is why she is slinking around the well in the quietest, but hottest part of the day. As with Nathanael under the fig tree (1:48), so now Jesus demonstrates his knowledge of all things and everyone. He confronts her with herself so that her impurities can be cleaned out and the living water run freely.

Some interpreters see in the five husbands a reference to the five non-Jewish groups brought in to intermarry with the remaining members of the Northern Kingdom after the fall of Samaria in 721BC, as listed in 2 Kings 17:24, each with their own gods and worship. Thus the woman becomes an allegory of the racial impurity of the whole Samaritan people. However, since seven gods are mentioned in 2 Kings 17:30–31, this is unlikely. What is more, the woman now reacts in a very human way. Her estimation of Jesus goes up another notch; for him to know the truth about her, he must be more than 'Sir'—he must be a prophet, and what better way to move him off her private life than to throw a theological conundrum at him? (4:19–20).

PRAYER

Lord, give me this water, that I may never be thirsty.

21 JOHN 4:19–30

PROPHET *or* MESSIAH?

As the story unfolds, Jesus has gently led the woman to a greater understanding of who he is, from her initial ignorance (4:9) to calling him 'sir' (4:11, 15); as he confronted her with the facts of her life, she began to wonder if he might be greater than Jacob. Now Jesus must take her further.

The place of worship

When Jesus reveals that he knows all about her sex life, the woman thinks he must be a prophet. If he knows all these things, perhaps he knows the answer to the theological question which divided Jews and Samaritans—where should we worship? (4:20). We suggested that she throws this 'hot potato' at him to deflect him away from her personal difficulties. We too sometimes avoid the embarrassing truth about ourselves by debating knotty problems or church politics! Alternatively, since the place of worship is where sacrifice for sin was made, the woman's question might not be a diversionary tactic but a response to the truth Jesus has revealed: yes, you are right about my life, so where can I go to find forgiveness?

The woman is correct that the patriarchs worshipped on this mountain in Samaria, not only Jacob (Gen. 33:20) but Abraham also (Gen. 12:6–7). Of course, Mount Gerizim, as it was called, was later eclipsed by the great temple built by Solomon on Mount Zion in Jerusalem. However, after the Samaritans' offer to help rebuild the temple was rejected (Ezra 4:1–3), they built their own temple here around 400BC. Relationships deteriorated further when some Jews led by John Hyrcanus destroyed it in 138BC. No wonder this Samaritan wants to ask this Jew where she should go with her sinful life to find God (4:20).

Jesus says that the place is not important, as the time is coming when neither mountain will have a temple (4:21). As we saw in 2:13–22, the earthly temple will be destroyed and replaced by Jesus himself. Furthermore, as in the conversation with Nicodemus, suddenly the verbs move into 'we' and 'you-plurals' (4:22, cf. 3:11). Although John uses the phrase "the Jews" to describe Jesus' opponents among the religious authorities, he is clear that Jesus himself is a Jew ('we') and 'salvation is from the Jews' (4:22). However, while salvation may come *from* the Jews, who have worshipped God faithfully in the temple for centuries, and *through* the Jew Jesus, it is not solely *for* them. 'The hour is coming and now is' for worship to be not tied to a place but open for all. John uses this phrase to show how God's heavenly future is breaking into our earthly realm now (see also 5:25). As was made clear to Nicodemus, only through the Spirit can we enter into God's kingdom, for 'God is spirit, and those who worship him must worship in spirit and truth' (4:23–4, cf. 3:5–9 above).

Who is this?

Now it has become too much for the woman and she wistfully repeats her trust that One will come to explain all this (4:25). The Samaritans revered the first five books of the Hebrew scriptures, and so were waiting for the 'prophet like Moses' foretold in Deut. 18:15, which they called the *Taheb,* the restorer. The term 'Messiah' used here means 'the anointed one' in Hebrew, as does 'Christ' in Greek. Jesus realizes that the woman has now progressed as far as she can, so the moment has come to reveal himself (4:26). Again, however, John's language works on two levels: on the surface Jesus says, 'That's who I am', but the verb *ego eimi*, 'I am', on its own in the sentence, recalls the name of God revealed to Moses, 'I am who I am' (Exod. 3:14; see also Is. 41:4; 43:10). This is the first time this phrase appears in the gospel, but it will become a very important way of understanding who Jesus is.

Meanwhile, the disciples have returned from their shopping expedition and are amazed to discover their rabbi talking with a Samaritan woman (4:27). The woman realizes that it is time to go and return into the city, extraordinarily forgetting to take her water jar with her—an indication of how flustered and excited she is by what has happened perhaps, or even a sign that she intends to return (4:28). But she has changed; she came to the well in the hottest, quietest part of the day to avoid people—but now she goes to find them and tell them what has happened to her. Now the fact that Jesus knows all she has done is not something to be avoided with a theological hot potato—but the hottest news to be shared: 'can this really be the Christ?' (4:29).

PRAYER

Lord Jesus, help me to worship you in spirit and truth
and to know you as Messiah.

FOOD & HARVESTS

The woman has gone, but her abandoned water pot is a silent reminder to the disciples that their rabbi was talking with a woman, a Samaritan and a sinner, openly in the middle of the day. But too embarrassed to mention it directly, they can only stammer two words, 'Rabbi, eat' (4:31). In their confusion, they concentrate on simple necessities. But Jesus will not allow them to deflect him like this, any more than he let the woman divert him with questions about the place of worship. So he teases them that he has food which they do not know about (4:32). Just as the woman misunderstood the living water for a labour-saving spring, so the disciples, tired from their shopping, wondered why they bothered: 'who has given him something to eat?' (4:33). You can almost hear the scandalized whisper— it cannot have been that woman, can it?! Like both 'that woman' and Nicodemus, the disciples are stuck on the earthly, literal level of meaning, while Jesus is talking about heavenly nourishment, simply to do the work of the One who sent him, his heavenly father (4:34). Now it is the disciples' turn to progress to a deeper understanding .

Lift up your eyes

In the other gospels, Jesus uses images from farming frequently in his parables, about a Sower, or seeds growing secretly, or about the harvest (see Mk. 4). Remarkably, John has no parables in his gospel, but this little section uses the same imagery, like a parable. Jesus begins with a common saying, that there are four months between the sowing, in January or February, and the harvesting, in May and June. He then invites them to look around at the fields, 'white for harvesting' (4:35). If the story is set around harvest time, reapers may have been working in the fields; certainly this plain of Samaria on the West Bank of the Jordan is one of the few open expanses of arable land. At harvest time, the sowers and the reapers, those who began and those who ended the process, can rejoice together in their success (4:36–37). The disciples, still clutching the bread they have brought from market, look at the fields and wonder what the point of this agricultural lesson is.

By now we have learned to expect that they will interpret Jesus' words on the literal, earthly level. But perhaps, as they look at the white-flowering fields surrounding the well, they begin to notice instead the white robes of the Samaritan villagers who have been listening to the woman's testimony and are now on their way to see Jesus (4:30). Here again, the level shifts, from shopping for food to sowing and harvest, and then on to the spiritual meaning. The conversation between Jesus and the woman is where the sowing took place (4:37), 'others' have laboured (4:38)—but the seeds sown by Jesus the Sower and disseminated by the woman have not needed four months to come to harvest. If only the disciples could 'lift up their eyes' beyond the ordinary level of worrying about food and prejudice against women and Samaritans, they would see that the work of God, the One who sent Jesus, is being done. Now they are invited to the joyful climax, reaping the fruits of that little talk by the well in the noonday heat. So this section comes full circle: the disciples were embarrassed about Jesus talking to a woman—but he not only explains what he was doing, but also corrects their prejudice and invites them into God's work.

The Samaritan harvest

In fact, the woman has been doing the work of a disciple—giving her testimony, her witness, through which others are coming to faith for themselves (4:39). The short cut through Samaria ends up taking as many days as the long way round, since the Samaritans invite Jesus and his disciples to stay with them (4:40). First, the woman wondered who this person able to tell her all she ever did might be, then others came to faith through her, but now many believe because of Jesus' words (4:41). The testimony of others may enable us to see how God acts in each of our lives individually, but in the end we all have to hear and believe for ourselves that Jesus is indeed 'the Saviour of the world' (4:42). And so, Jesus' real identity is finally revealed: he is not just a Jewish man talking to a woman, or a rabbi, nor even the Prophet or the Christ—but the Saviour, a term reserved in the Hebrew scriptures for God alone: 'For I am the Lord your God, the Holy One of Israel, your Saviour' (Is. 43:3; see also, Is. 45:15; 49:26).

PRAYER

Lord of the harvest and Saviour of the world,
feed me with your Father's will, that I may sow your seed.

HEALING *an* OFFICIAL'S SON

After all the excitement in Samaria, Jesus finally returns to Galilee (4:43). Although the Galileans welcomed him, it was only because they had seen what he had done at the festival in Jerusalem (4:45). Once more the evangelist notes that Jesus was aware of how fickle such a welcome could be, especially in his home locality (4:44). This reminds us of his previous comments about Jesus' knowledge of human hearts in 2:23–4. The move to Cana also takes us back to chapter 2 with the reminder about the changing of water into wine (4:46). Thus chapters 2 to 4 form a little section from Cana to Cana with this passage balancing 2:23–5 like a pair of bookends.

Unless you see signs

The story concerns a 'royal official' who asks Jesus to heal his son. Such an official would have worked for Herod, perhaps as a soldier or as an administrator, and could be Jewish, Greek or Roman. In a similar story in Matthew and Luke he is a centurion (Matt. 8:5–13; Lk. 7:1–10). If this man is a Gentile, he balances Nicodemus the Jew and the Samaritan woman. However, John does not tell us his nationality, just that his son is ill in Capernaum. Jesus' response is rather brusque, turning to address the crowd, 'Unless you (plural) see signs and wonders, you will not believe' (4:48). The official does not have time for all this debate and presses Jesus harder, 'Sir, come down before my little boy dies' (4:49). This reminds us of the other miracle in Cana, where Mary's request to Jesus for help at the wedding also seemed to receive a rebuff at first. Her persistence then was rewarded by Jesus telling the servants to fill the water jars and take it to the top table; through their obedience it became wine (2:1–11). So too here, as the official believes Jesus and obeys him when told to go, so he meets his servants who bring him the good news that the fever had left his son (4:50–52). This same basic structure in both of the signs at Cana of request–rebuff–persistence–obedience–miracle cannot be coincidental. This is John's answer to human fickleness and sensation seeking: Jesus responds to those who persist in their prayerful request.

Your son lives

Throughout the fourth gospel, the evangelist stresses Jesus' authority and power. Capernaum, where the little boy is sick, is 20 or 30 miles from Cana—but when Jesus tells the official 'your son lives', the fever leaves him straight away (4:50–53). Jesus has only to speak and it happens, regardless of the distance, which will take the official most of a day to cover. To stress this, John repeats the phrase, 'your son lives', no less than three times—when Jesus tells the official, when the slaves meet him with the good news, and when he reflects on when Jesus said it (4:50, 51, 53). No wonder not only the man himself but also his whole household came to believe, not just in the sign but in Jesus (4:53).

Signs in John's gospel

John ends this section by pointing out that this was the second sign Jesus did (4:54), in the same way that he began it by noting that the water into wine was his first (2:11). This careful numbering, which does not take into account the other signs Jesus did in Jerusalem which impressed the Galileans (2:23, 4:45), has fascinated biblical scholars. John's statement at the end of his gospel that he has selected these signs to convince his readers that Jesus is the Christ (20:31) has stimulated much discussion. It is usually noted that there are seven main signs in this gospel: water into wine, 2:1–11; this boy's healing 4:46–54; the lame man 5:1–15; feeding the five thousand 6:1–15; Jesus walking on water 6:16–21; the blind man 9:1–11; and the raising of Lazarus 11:1–44. Some signs are linked to discourses, such as that about the bread of life in 6:25–58 and the light of the world in 8:12–59. There is no obvious discourse for these two signs in chapters 2 and 4, but we have seen how Jesus' actions in the temple pick up the idea of 'new for old' in the water into wine. Similarly, Jesus' discussions with Nicodemus about being born again to eternal life and with the Samaritan woman about 'living water' are brought to a climax here as Jesus gives this little boy new life, even at a distance. It is easy enough to promise life, says John—but Jesus actually brings his promises into the reality of our pain and suffering.

PRAYER

Lord Jesus, help me to persist in my praying
and bring your new life to us all.

24

Do You Want *to be* Healed?

This new chapter begins with the mention of 'a feast of the Jews' (5:1). Various Jewish feasts provide the backdrop for the next chapters: we have already seen one Passover in 2:13, and the next Passover happens in 6:4. Then the feast of Tabernacles is the background for chapters 7—8, with Hanukkah or the Dedication for 10, before we come back to Passover again in 11:55. It is thus curious that John does not identify this feast. This may be because he wants to draw attention not to an annual feast but to the weekly festival of the Sabbath which dominates this chapter. Whatever the feast is, Jesus once again goes to Jerusalem. Some scholars suggest that chapters 5 (in Jerusalem) and 6 (back in Galilee) should be swapped around to give a more coherent flow to the story. However, all ancient manuscripts have them in this order. It gives us a sequence of each sign being followed by a visit to Jerusalem: so the changing of water into wine is followed by the temple incident in 2 and the Feeding of the Five Thousand in 6 is followed by the Tabernacles visit in 7. This visit to Jerusalem in chapter 5 not only follows the sign of the official's son (4:43–54) but includes the healing of this lame man. Both signs then lead into discussion with the Jews and a discourse from Jesus about his authority and identity.

The healing pool

The healing takes place at a pool, variously called in the manuscripts Bethesda or Bethzatha, which had five porticoes (5:2). Since so many things in this gospel have symbolic meanings, these five porticoes have often been interpreted as representing the five books of Moses—Genesis, Exodus, Leviticus, Numbers, Deuteronomy—known together as the Pentateuch. There are other references to Moses and the Exodus in this chapter, but more recently a double pool near the Sheep Gate in Jerusalem has been excavated which does have four porticoes around the sides with a fifth down the central divide between the two baths. The site also contains the old church of St Anne, a cool, peaceful building with a marvellous acoustic, quite suited to a place of healing!

Once again we notice the presence of water. After baptism in chapter 1, water into wine in 2, being born of water and spirit in 3, being thirsty at a well in 4, now we find that water is also a source of healing. The best manuscripts do not contain the story of the waters being troubled by an angel (5:3b–4), but it is assumed in the lame man's later comment (5:7). Spas have been very important throughout history where waters stirred up by a bubbling spring have often contained curative minerals. The Roman baths at Bath are a very good example, where patients at the Hospital for Rheumatic Diseases are still helped into the waters. No wonder so many invalids lay in the porticoes around these pools (5:3).

Wanting to be healed

However, the image of 'troubled waters' is often more one of mental distress than physical, of getting agitated as something disturbs us, even at an unconscious level. When Jesus realizes how long the man has been there, he confronts him with the key question, 'do you really want to be made well?' (5:5–6). After all, 38 years is a very long time, as long as the main wanderings of the Israelites in the wilderness (Deut. 2:14), which makes another link back to Moses. There are lots of other people here, but this man is alone—and he has his answer ready. 'I am all abandoned and helpless. Even when the water bubbles, I cannot get there. Someone else always enters first' (5:7). The word used here for paralysed (5:3) is *xeron*, which means all dried up, 'withered' in the AV. The man has withered into his loneliness and isolation and hope has all dried up: it is not fair, he complains.

But Jesus cuts straight through the man's prepared speech with a direct command. He does not need the troubled waters, just to stand up, pick up his simple mattress and walk away—healed. It is an extraordinary idea which leaves us all wide-eyed with gaping mouths, astonished and asking why this one was healed and not the others. Yet something of the waters of Jesus' new life which we have seen in the previous chapters pour into this man's heart and wash through his body—and off he goes, healed and carrying his mat!

For PRAYER & REFLECTION

What causes the 'troubled waters' around me?
Which parts of my life have dried up and withered?
Do I really want to be healed?
Can I trust Jesus' word of life?

The SABBATH & JESUS' CLAIMS

This day is not only 'a festival of "the Jews"', but also a Sabbath (5:1, 9b). So "the Jews" notice the man carrying his bed on the Sabbath and accuse him of doing something unlawful (5:10). Since the man who was healed and Jesus who healed him were both Jews, as were all those attending the festival, it is curious to find the phrase denoting a separate group—especially since we have just been told that 'salvation is from the Jews' (4:22). Once again, this phrase seems to denote the Jewish authorities, who questioned both John the Baptist and Jesus himself (1:19–22; 2:18–20). Now they move on beyond mere questioning, as their opposition to Jesus starts to gather momentum.

The first complaint is that it is not lawful for this man to carry his mat on the Sabbath. Observance of the Sabbath is central to the Jewish way of life. It was a day which God had made holy after he finished his work of creation (Gen. 2:2–3), setting it aside for worship and a rest from work. The problem is how to define what constituted 'work'. In the collection of rabbinic teaching about the Sabbath, compiled just after New Testament times, thirty-nine types of activity were prohibited (*Mishnah Sabbath* 7:2). Even today in some cities with a large Jewish population, some of the Orthodox would like to link the houses and streets together into one residential area within which they are allowed to carry objects on the Sabbath without breaking the law. Certainly, for this man to carry his bed, even if it were only a simple mat, would have been seen by some as 'work'. Once again, however, he has his answer ready: it is not my fault, I am only doing what I was told by the man who healed me (5:11).

Jesus found him

However, this attempt to 'pass the buck' runs into problems because the man does not know who Jesus was. Jesus' ability, especially in Jerusalem, to appear in public to do or say something and then to merge back into the crowd happens frequently in this gospel (5:13). On the other hand, it is also typical that he seeks out and finds those in need and those whom he has helped. So now, while "the Jews" are looking for him, Jesus takes the initiative and finds the man in the temple. First, he points out that he is now well, and then warns him to 'sin no more, so that nothing worse happens' (5:14). This need not imply that Jesus shared the common belief that sickness and suffering were results of, or even punishments for, someone's sin. Actually he denies that view later (see 9:2–3). But if such a simplistic cause and effect is rejected, the biblical idea is still that we are a unity of body mind and spirit, that what we say or believe, think or feel affects who and how we are—and this is borne out by the 'psycho-somatic' approach of much modern medicine. Perhaps Jesus is warning the man about lapsing back into his old self-centred attitude developed in so many years by the pool side; if so, he does not seem to heed the warning, for he promptly goes off to tell the authorities that it was Jesus who had healed him on the Sabbath! (5:15).

At this point, "the Jews" move from questioning Jesus to actively opposing him—not just because of this one incident, but because he made a habit of it, as is shown by John's use of the continuous imperfect tenses in 'doing such things on the Sabbath' and 'breaking the Sabbath' (5:16, 18).

My Father is working

Jesus' response was to draw attention to the fact that God was still working on the Sabbath (5:17). The rabbis and theologians soon realized that God could not be completely idle on the Sabbath, since it still rained and crops grew, still people were born and died. Thus God did not cease from giving life and declaring judgment, for that is his very nature as ruler of the universe. But Jesus' offence was now something worse than merely breaking the Sabbath. To call God his Father and to connect his healing activity with the giving of life and judgment by the Father was a claim they could not ignore. In fact, this is not actually 'making himself equal to God', as the next verse makes clear Jesus' total dependency upon God and his inability to do anything without him (5:18–19). None the less, the whole of Jesus' ministry and teaching could be seen as acting in the place of God, as his representative or agent, in giving life and proclaiming judgment. No wonder they sought 'all the more to kill him' (5:18).

PRAYER

Lord Jesus, thank you that you have made me well;
grant that I may sin no more,
but rather work with you and your Father.

26

The SON GIVES LIFE & JUDGES

We now come to the first of the 'discourses' common in this gospel, sections of teaching delivered by Jesus. Speeches were used not just in ancient biography, but also in history writing to help readers understand the true meaning of what was happening, rather than as an exact account of what was actually said. As we have seen punctuation marks were not added until a thousand years later. So too, John, drawing on his years of meditation under the guidance of the Spirit on what Jesus said and did, connects these discourses to the signs to explain their significance. In these two signs Jesus gave life to the official's son and to the paralysed man; to the latter, he also spoke a word of warning and judgment. In the Old Testament, both of these activities belong supremely to God (see e.g. Deut. 32:35–41 and 1 Sam. 2:6). The giving of life and death in judgment is also ultimately connected with the End of all things (see Introduction, p. 24, on 'eschatology'). We have already noted John's interest in time with words like 'hour' and 'day' (see on 2:4 and 2:13 above). Now he shows how the End is breaking into time in Jesus' deeds and words.

The Father and the Son

If Jesus is giving life and acting in judgment, then this is a claim to be acting for God here on earth. Thus we begin with the relationship of Jesus with his Father. Far from 'making himself equal with God', in fact he can do nothing on his own. Although John has no parables, this saying is like a parable when read without the capital letters: a son can only do what he sees his father doing, and whatever the father does, so does the son, because the father, out of love for his son, shows him everything he is doing (5:19–20). It reminds us of a child watching his father, in a carpenter's workshop perhaps. Yet in this gospel no other description says more about Jesus. John uses 'the Father' to describe God over 100 times, with the corresponding 'Son' for Jesus about 50 times—much more often than in the other gospels. This elucidates perfectly Jesus' relationship with God in which he has equality and identity with God as he speaks and acts for God here on earth, but yet he is totally dependent on his Father who loves him to show him all things.

Judgment now

In the light of that relationship between Father and Son, the next few verses explore how Jesus gives life and acts in judgment in the present, as the events of the End, the *eschaton*, are made real among us. God raises the dead and gives them life, as in Ezekiel's vision of the valley of dry bones (Ezek. 37:1–14). Now he shares this with Jesus who 'gives life' to whomever he wishes (5:21). Judgment has also been given to Jesus, since people's reaction to the Son now is a reaction to the Father who sent him (5:22–23). Thus anyone who hears Jesus and believes him has already passed from death into eternal life; there is no judgment to come (5:24). Eschatology is not about 'pie in the sky when you die'; it is realized—made real—in the here and now. In the last two signs, the official's son received new life as soon as his father believed Jesus and the paralytic got up and walked immediately upon Jesus' command. Unfortunately, the opposite is also true, that those who refuse Jesus are rejecting God the Father who sent him (5:23).

Future judgment

And yet, the End can never be totally realized in this life, so now we get the same themes repeated with a future dimension. Thus the time is coming when the dead and those 'in their tombs' *will* hear Jesus' voice (5:25, 28). This is because God has given him the authority to execute judgment, now and in the future. Those who have done good will rise from death to life, while evil doers will come to judgment (5: 27, 29). Jesus can do all this because of the relationship of the Father and the Son: only God is totally self-sufficient, with 'life in himself', but he shares this with his Son (5:26). Thus those who have received the Son's life, like the official and the paralytic, will come into eternal life, while those who go on opposing him risk judgment at the End.

In other words, we can never escape the inevitable tension between the present and the future, the 'now' and the 'not yet'. In Jesus the Son, the End is breaking into our present, so the two passages are linked with the phrase, 'the hour is coming and now is' (5:25; see also 4:23). This is what his signs point towards.

PRAYER

Lord Jesus, grant that I may hear your voice
and receive your life now, and for ever.

BEARING WITNESS

So far Jesus has made some claims through his signs, which have then been challenged by "the Jews". He has repeated the claims directly through this discourse, arguing that he shares in God's activity of giving life and judgment both in the present now and in the future at the End. The obvious question must then be, where is the evidence for this claim? When people claim today that God has told them to do something, it needs careful examination; some seem quite right, but others end up being looked after in prison or hospital. Similarly, the next few chapters examine the evidence for Jesus' claims. It is as though Jesus is on trial before "the Jews", long before the formal proceedings which lead to his crucifixion. This is why the word 'witness' or 'testify/testimony' is so important in this gospel. It occurs about 35 times, especially with John the Baptist and in debate between Jesus and "the Jews" (as here and in 8:13–18).

Witnesses were very important in any ancient trial. Without our modern techniques of forensic science and evidence gathering, the testimony of witnesses was the main way to discover the truth. Thus the Jewish law did not allow anyone to be convicted on the statement of a single witness, but only if their evidence was corroborated by one or two others (Deut. 19:15). In order to deter malicious or false accusations, judges had to subject witnesses to a thorough investigation. If the witness was found to be false, he would suffer the fate intended for the person he accused. In this way, others would be deterred from making such false claims (Deut. 19:16–20). Paul also requires two or three witnesses for any charge (2 Cor. 13:1). So, in these chapters where Jesus is on trial for what he claims, the issue of his witnesses is crucial.

Jesus' own witness

First, Jesus states once again that his claim to exercise judgment is not based on his own authority. He is only doing the will of God, who sent him (5:30). Therefore, the discourse moves away from Jesus' claim to the evidence for it. As a good Jew, Jesus accepts immediately the point of law that his witness to himself is not enough (5:31). However, he argues that there is another witness on his behalf whose testimony is true (5:32). So, let us call this next witness.

The witness of John the Baptist

So the discussion moves to John the Baptist. Jesus reminds "the Jews" that they had already questioned John and heard his testimony to the truth (5:33; see 1:19–28). Even in the prologue to his gospel, the evangelist described the Baptist's role as to 'bear witness to the light' in Jesus (1:6–8) and John the Baptist made this clear to his disciples (3:28–33). Now Jesus returns the compliment by bearing witness to him. If John was not the light, he was at least like an oil lamp with its wick burning and shining bright. What is more, even "the Jews" were grateful for his light (3:35). But Jesus' claim will need more than the human testimony of John to be upheld, however much the questioners may need to be reminded of it to avoid becoming false accusers (3:34).

The witness of the Father

So Jesus now calls something greater than John's testimony to the witness stand. He appeals to the works he is doing, such as the healing of the paralysed man which started this debate, as well as his other miracles. Thus this gospel calls such works 'signs' since they bear witness on Jesus' behalf that God has sent him (5:36). Even one of "the Jews", Nicodemus, accepted that such miraculous signs indicated that God was with Jesus (3:2). But in appealing to the evidence of his works, Jesus is actually calling God as his final witness. The problem is that the opponents have 'never heard his voice nor seen his form' as God used to appear in the Old Testament (5:37). Nor indeed, do they have his word, the prophecy which was the other way God communicated with their forebears. Ultimately, this is because they have not believed in Jesus, whom God has sent as his supreme word (5:38). So, who is on trial here? Is it Jesus, who must call these witnesses to prove his claims—or his questioners, who refuse to recognize and accept the evidence God gives them? We need to find a judge to decide this, which takes us into the final section.

PRAYER

Lord Jesus, give me grace to accept your testimony
and to believe in the one who sent you.

The SCRIPTURES & MOSES

Chapter 5 has given us a good example of how John weaves together signs, dialogues and discourse to develop his story of Jesus. The sign of healing the paralysed man on the Sabbath led to accusations about Jesus' work and his claims, which have then been tested through the dialogue and the discourse. In his defence, Jesus has called to the witness stand himself, John the Baptist, his miraculous signs, and God his Father. So who will judge the witnesses and decide whether the accusation is correct? The ultimate arbiter for Jews is always Moses and the Law. After all, it all began with Jesus being charged of violating the law of Moses by breaking the Sabbath with his work of healing.

The witness of the scriptures

The accusers have appealed to the scriptures for their witness, namely the commandments about the Sabbath and keeping it holy, as evidence that Jesus is wrong. What Jesus does is to claim that their witness actually testifies to him, to bring the 'hostile witness' onto his side. He compliments them on the way they search the scriptures; the word used for 'search', *ereunan*, implies proper rigorous study and analysis (5:39). Unfortunately, this detailed search has missed the main point which is to find life in God and Jesus whom he has sent (5:40). It can often be like that for us in our Bible reading. Rigorous detailed study is vital, but not so that we cannot see the wood for the trees and end up missing the main point, which is to bring us to life in Christ. This is particularly important when studying the gospels, whose primary focus is the life and work, death and resurrection of Jesus of Nazareth. They were written to testify to Jesus, that we might come to him and have life (5:39–40).

Receiving glory

Jesus makes it clear that he is not interested in being judged by human beings' opinion of his work (5:41). Their inability to understand the scriptures and to believe the witnesses he has called, in addition to their failure to recognize God at work in his healing signs, all show that the accusers do not have the love of God in them (5:42). To make matters worse, he suggests that they will accept others who come in their own name (5:43). There were many Messianic claimants in the first century, each with their various supporters. In any group or society, those who work within the system are likely to be praised by the others. This is as true of any 'mutual admiration society' today as it was then. Does our searching of the scriptures, our preaching, teaching or writing, merely lead to human praise, to receiving 'glory from one another'? (5:44). To go beyond 'you scratch my back, and I'll scratch yours' to seek the glory from God alone is difficult. Jesus implicitly denies the charge of claiming 'equality with God', since there is 'one who alone is God' (5:44). He has simply come in his name, dependent upon God for everything, and to accept or reject him is to accept or reject 'the one who sent me'.

Judgment by Moses

So we come to the end of this first round of trial by witnesses. Jesus has been accused of breaking the law of Moses by violating the Sabbath, but he is more than happy to appear before Moses. For Moses is the judge who will turn the tables and accuse the accusers (5:45). If we search the scriptures, we will find that the commandments and the law point towards Jesus, in whom God's people are to find their Sabbath rest and their healing (5:46).

So here all this chapter's themes come together. The story of the paralysed man spending thirty-eight years in the five porticoes was full of allusions to Moses, the five books of the Law and the years of the Exodus. Those hints continue through the discourse about judgment and witness, asking us some questions as we search the scriptures. Who is actually on trial here—Jesus, his accusers, or those of us who read this chapter today? Will what we trust in actually come back to accuse us? Do we seek glory from the only true God, or merely each other's approval? These are vital questions, since the final judgment breaks into our present here and now in Christ, according to this whole chapter. If we respond to what God has done in Jesus whom he has sent, then we pass from death to life (5:24).

PRAYER

O God our Father, grant that we may
so search the scriptures and seek your glory,
that we may find life in the one you have sent,
Jesus Christ our Lord.

29

JOHN 6:1–13

FEEDING *the* FIVE THOUSAND

Jesus' miraculous feeding of a vast crowd is such a well-known story. This is the only miracle narrated in all four gospels—indeed, it is the only incident from Jesus' ministry before his last week which they all include. The Synoptic gospels each describe the feeding of five thousand people (Mk. 6:31–44; Matt. 14:13–21; Lk. 9:10–17), and a feeding of four thousand occurs in Mark 8:1–9 and Matthew 15:29–38. Here, we shall concentrate on the details unique to John, especially its link with the 'bread of life' discourse with its eucharistic overtones.

The story begins back in Galilee, as Jesus goes to the other side of the lake (6:1). John alone tells us that the crowd followed Jesus because 'they saw the signs he was doing' (6:2). This recalls the last few chapters, especially the signs done in Cana. More importantly, only John tells us that Jesus went up a mountain at the time of the Passover (6:3–4). Chapter 5 hinted at the Israelites in the wilderness and appealed to Moses; now we are reminded of Moses who began the Passover and who went up the mountain to meet God. So what will Jesus do on this mountain?

How to feed so many?

In all the accounts, Jesus sees the crowd coming to him, but as so often in John, here Jesus is the one in control, and he takes the initiative. He begins by questioning Philip (6:5), of whom we have heard nothing since his call in chapter 1. Since then, Philip has seen Jesus at work in the miraculous signs—but he does not seem to have learned much from them. After all, where did the 'good wine', the 'living water' and Jesus' food come from (2:10, 4:10, 33)? It is also typical of this gospel that Jesus knows what he is going to do and is only testing Philip. Philip fails the test by suggesting that 200 denarii would not buy enough for everyone to have even a little (6:6–7). A denarius is a day's wage (according to Matt. 20:2) so this sum is about six or seven months' wages.

Every little helps

Next the evangelist brings Andrew into the story. Andrew and Philip came from the same town and often feature together in John (see

1:40–44). In his last appearance, Andrew brought his brother Simon Peter to Jesus (1:42). Now, keen as always to help, Andrew goes beyond Philip's despair by bringing a 'little boy' to Jesus. Only John's gospel mentions this lad and, in addition, tells us that the loaves are 'barley loaves' and the fish are dried. Barley loaves were the food of the poor, a third of the price of wheat (see Rev. 6:6), while the word *opsarion* means a small dried or pickled fish. In the other gospels, the word is *ichthys*, used for fresh fish as we might expect so near the lake. John stresses how meagre is this offering of a poor little boy's packed lunch. No wonder Andrew is tempted to follow Philip's despairing attitude, 'but what is this among so many people?' (6:8–9). But Jesus accepts it, however small it was and told everyone to sit down to eat (6:10).

When he had given thanks

In the other gospels' accounts, Jesus says grace, that is, he blesses (*eulogein*) both the bread and God for it. But John says he 'gave thanks' over the bread—*eucharistesas*. This is the very word which gives us 'eucharist', which is rather curious, considering that there is no account of the institution of holy communion in this gospel (see on 13:1–20). Equally, while the people pick up the fragments in the other gospels, here Jesus specifically instructs the disciples to do this 'so that nothing may be lost' (6:12). This may anticipate Jesus' concern that no one should be lost, in 6:39, but it could also reflect the tradition of consuming all the consecrated bread at communion.

So if we pull all these hints together, we can see how John has carefully told this story so that it goes beyond just an account of a miraculous feeding, amazing though that might be. The references to the mountain and Passover remind us of how Moses fed people in the wilderness, just as Jesus does now. But to do so, he wants our co-operation. What we have may be meagre, but like Andrew or the boy, we are to offer it to Jesus. When he has given thanks for it (eucharist) and shared it around in communion, then everyone is satisfied and all can be gathered together. These hints about Moses and the communion are developed further in the events and discourse which follows.

PRAYER

*Lord Jesus, give us courage to offer the little we have to you
that you may use it to satisfy all your people.*

WHO IS THIS?

After this amazing sign, it is hardly surprising that people wonder who such a person can be, which gives us the theme of this next section. People seek, Jesus hides; Jesus finds, people seek. The miraculous feeding of a multitude in the mountains would make people think of Moses and remind them of Moses' promise: 'the Lord your God will raise up for you a prophet like me from among your own people' (Deut. 18:15). After all, John the Baptist was asked if he was this prophet right at the start (1:21) and the Samaritan woman wondered if Jesus was the prophet (4:19, 25). No wonder the crowd concluded that Jesus was the prophet they were expecting and would have sought to acclaim him (6:14). But Jesus does another of his disappearing acts and withdraws up into the mountains, perhaps to be alone and pray. The writer explains that this was because the crowd would not stop at prophet but would make him king as well, whether or not he wished it (6:15).

Walking on water

The disciples seem to have taken the hint as well, and keep out of the crowd's way by going back down to the shore (6:16). The Sea of Galilee is about four miles across at its northern end, and they set out back to Capernaum by boat. The lake is surrounded by the mountains, and as evening draws on and the hills cool, so the wind springs up and it can get rather strong, making rough seas (6:17–18). As the disciples are struggling to row back, they see Jesus coming towards them (6:19). It has been noted that the phrase translated 'on the sea' can also mean 'by the sea' on the shore, as is the case when it is used of Jesus on the beach in 21:1. On this reading, the disciples have almost rowed back across the lake, and then they see Jesus walking around it alongside them. However, their reaction of fear suggests that here John intends us to understand that Jesus is walking on the water to find them. After the allusions to Moses in the wilderness, now we are reminded of crossing the Red Sea. After the suggestions that Jesus might be the prophet and king, now we have hints about him acting like God: as the Psalmist referred to the Exodus crossing, 'your way was through the sea, your path through the mighty waters' (Ps. 77:19). So who is this person coming across the waves now?

I am

Jesus' reply is simple, 'It is I; do not be afraid' (6:20), except that nothing in John is as simple as it seems. Even on the lake, we find deeper waters underneath the surface! While it is true that the Greek phrase, *ego eimi*, can be used to identify the speaker in this way (see e.g. 9:9), its literal translation is 'I am'. As we saw when Jesus used it to introduce himself to the Samaritan woman (see on 4:26 above), it reminds us of the divine name revealed to Moses and used in the prophets (see, e.g. Exod. 3:14; Is. 41:4; 43:10). Jesus uses it about thirty-five times to refer to himself in this gospel, often with a description like bread or light; on other occasions, his use of it on its own as the divine name will invite stoning (8:58–59). Here too it stands alone; whether the disciples take it as his simple self-identification, or hear the resonance of the name of God is unclear—but it is enough to calm their fears and bring the boat to land immediately (6:21). Like those who 'went down to the sea in ships', who called to the Lord in the midst of a storm, they have been brought to the safety of the harbour (Ps. 107:23–30). The one who can feed them in the mountains can also bring them home afterwards.

Seeking Jesus

While the disciples have been safely found by Jesus, the crowd of would-be king-makers are having less success. When day dawns, they find that the disciples, the boat and Jesus himself have all gone (6:22). They are still at the place where 'the Lord had given thanks', again using the *eucharist* word to identify the Feeding (6:23). Therefore they have no option but to get into boats and go 'seeking Jesus' (6:24). Only when he lets them find him, will they be able to discover what this has been all about and who he really is.

PRAYER

Lord Jesus, my prophet, my king, my God,
come and find me when I struggle through the storm
and bring me safely to your rest.

More Questions & Answers

We have seen how John likes to move from signs into a dialogue between Jesus and others which ends with a discourse. So here, we start with three questions from the crowd, each answered by Jesus, which pick up the signs and begin to explore the themes they raise. Like Jesus' dialogue with Nicodemus and with the Samaritan woman, we progress through different levels from the obviously physical to the deeper spiritual meaning.

Perishable or eternal?

After the games of hide and seek earlier in the chapter, the crowd are surprised finally to find Jesus on the other side of the lake. Their question, 'When did you come here?' probably includes the questions 'how?' and 'why?' as well. In other words, they are still at the stage they were after the Feeding; they call him 'Rabbi' (as did Nicodemus) and still want to follow him on their terms, to hail him as prophet and make him king (6:25).

Jesus ignores their question, preferring to go straight to the heart of why they are seeking him. He suggests that it is nothing to do with his teaching as rabbi or his signs, but because they were getting free food (6:26). In other words, like Nicodemus or the Samaritan woman, they are stuck at the physical level. Jesus has to lead them on to the spiritual level, just as he did with the others. Like Isaiah calling people to stop working for bread which does not satisfy (Is. 55:1–2), so Jesus reminds them that the multiplied bread, like manna, is merely perishable—which is why they want some more. Instead, they need to work for food which leads to eternal life. The word, 'food', *brosis*, is the same as the food which nourished Jesus at the well when he had no bread (4:32). As Jesus told the woman to ask for the water of life instead of a physical well (4:10), so now he tells this crowd to work for the living food he offers (6:27).

The works of God

Like the woman, they are interested enough to ask what they must do 'to work the works of God' (6:28). Jesus' reply is brief: the work of God is not something we have to do, but someone we are to believe in. Throughout this gospel, Jesus is the one who does the works: they are his 'food' (4:34) and they are a witness that God has sent him (5:36), because in the end his works are those of his Father (5:17; 10:37–38). All we have to do is to believe in Jesus as the one God has sent (6:29). It is so simple, and yet so demanding. We can do no work to earn it, yet it will cost us everything. The crowd found it hard then, as we do today. Such is the life of faith.

Bread from heaven

If the work of God is that we should believe in Jesus, then again we need some evidence. So the crowd's immediate response is to ask what sign or work Jesus will do as proof for them (6:30). We have had several signs already and the last chapter introduced various witnesses, including Jesus' works and Moses as the judge. Now the crowd again remind us of Moses by referring to his work of providing manna in the wilderness. The text which they quote, 'he gave them bread from heaven to eat' (6:31) is from Ps. 78:24 mixed with allusions to the manna story in Exod. 16:4, 15.

Jesus could have replied by saying that this is exactly the sign which he has worked by feeding them in the mountains. Instead, he interprets the text as a rabbi would correct someone's understanding, by saying 'it's not this, but that', in three points. First, it was not Moses but God, identified as 'my Father', who fed them; second, it is not about the perishable manna, but the true heavenly bread; thirdly, it refers not to a single event in the past, 'gave', but God *gives* life to the world' now in the present (6:32–33).

After this succinct exposition, the crowd are even more eager for this bread. If God is giving out bread from heaven, this is much easier than going to the baker's all the time! It is hardly surprising that they want 'this bread always' (6:34). But like the woman who thought that 'living water' was better than coming to the well (4:15), they have not realized yet that Jesus is offering something beyond physical bread, or even magical provisions: it is nothing less than the very life of God.

For REFLECTION & PRAYER

Do I work for that which is perishable or eternal?
Father God, help me to believe in Jesus
as the one you have sent.

32 JOHN 6:35–40

I Am *the* Bread *of* Life

After the miraculous feeding and Jesus walking on the water and the discussion about bread, attention is now focused on Jesus by his direct claim, 'I am the bread of life' (6:35). Since the gospels are a form of ancient biography, the focus will be constantly redirected at the person of Jesus. The evangelists are trying to tell us about him, who he is and what he is doing, what it means and how it can change our lives. So what does it mean to identify Jesus with the Bread of Life? This phrase, 'I am the bread of life', is so well known from our liturgies, hymns and songs that we take it for granted—but what is it telling us about Jesus?

We saw in the walking on water story that the phrase 'I am' on its own recalls the name of God (see 6:20 above). However, in this gospel, 'I am' is also linked to seven well-known predicates, or descriptions of who Jesus is: the bread of life (6:35, 51); the light of the world (8:12; 9:5); the door (10:7, 9); the good shepherd (10:11, 14); the resurrection and life (11:25); the way, truth and life (14:6); the true vine (15:1, 5). Some of them are linked to signs, as with bread here and the feeding, or light with the healing of a blind man (9:7), and resurrection with the raising of Lazarus (11:43). Some of them also include the word 'life' or 'living' which we know is a key theme of this gospel. But what all these images share in common is a very strong Jewish background. We have seen that this section of the gospel is structured around the Jewish feasts, in which Jesus takes the key aspect of the Feast and goes beyond it (see on 5:1 above). In these 'I am' sayings, something similar is happening, as these key Jewish ideas—of bread and so forth—are taken and reapplied to Jesus and identified with him. In each case, we will need to explore their background and meaning and see what this tells us about Jesus.

The bread of life

According to Deuteronomy, Moses told the Israelites that God fed them with manna to make them realize that 'one does not live by bread alone, but by every word that comes from the mouth of the Lord' (Deut. 8:3). Over the years, the Jews often used manna and bread as images of the word of God, for the Law and for divine wisdom. Thus Wisdom invites people, 'Come, eat of my bread and drink of the wine I have mixed' (Prov. 9:5). The Wisdom of Jesus son of Sirach (written around 190BC) says that Wisdom feeds those who fear the Lord and hold to the Law 'with the bread of understanding'; therefore those who eat of her 'will hunger for more' and those who drink of her 'will thirst for more' (Ecclesiasticus 15:3; 24:21). But this Jesus, the son of his Father who sent him (6:37–38), is even better than that. Just as he promised the Samaritan woman that those who drink his living water would never thirst again (see on 4:14 above), now, as the Bread of Life, he is superior to the bread of the Law and wisdom. Whoever comes to him 'will never be hungry', and whoever believes in him 'will never be thirsty' (6:35). As Jesus offers more than the Jewish feasts, so 'I am the Bread of Life' is saying that he is better than the very centre of Jewish devotion, the Law itself. It may only be a simple phrase, but it is a staggering claim!

The Father's will

Thus it is not surprising that people could see Jesus, but not believe (6:36). It is one thing to be miraculously fed by him and even to want to make him prophet and king—but quite another to accept that he is superior to all you have ever believed. We may claim to want to do the work of God and to want the bread (6:28, 34)—but to come to Jesus on these terms demands everything we are and have ever been. He, however, is clear that he is not interested in exalting himself; his only purpose is to do the will of God who sent him, which reminds us of John's theme of Jesus' dependency upon his Father (6:38). All that the Father gives him will come to him so that nothing may be lost (6:37, 39), any more than any of the 'eucharisticized' bread was to be lost after the feeding (6:12). Because Jesus is the Bread of Life, to see him and believe in him is to receive eternal life, to become a fragment which he will gather up on the last day (6:40). This phrase means nothing more, and nothing less, than that.

PRAYER

Lord Jesus, thank you that you reject none who come to you;
feed me now and raise me up on the last day.

BREAD *from* HEAVEN

Jesus and the crowd have been debating the meaning of the feeding and the last section concentrated on the issue of Jesus' identity. Suddenly it is no longer a matter of whether he is 'the prophet like Moses' who can feed people in the mountains as Moses did. His claim to be 'the bread come down from heaven' has taken the debate to a much higher level where Jesus is portrayed as superior to the whole of Jewish faith and practice; acceptance of this and faith in him are necessary for eternal life.

It is no wonder that such a claim leads to 'murmuring' or 'grumbling' introducing the wonderfully sounding word, *gongusm-*, which will feature regularly over the next chapters (6:41, 43, 61; 7:12, 32). Until now Jesus' hearers have been simply called 'the crowd'; but now they are identified as "the Jews". We have noted before that, although Jesus and his disciples are all Jews, this term is used here to denote Jesus' opponents. The murmuring of the crowd has now brought them into conflict with Jesus. Their dissent has been growing through the chapter, from their desire to make Jesus their kind of king, through chasing him around the lake, to asking for a sign (6:15, 24–25, 30). Grumbling is also what the Israelites did in the wilderness; in fact, it was as a result of their complaining, that God sent them the manna (Exod. 16:2–15). Thus we have another link between Jesus' feeding of the crowd and the experiences of Moses and the Israelites in the wilderness.

Who is Jesus' Father?

The complaint centres around how Jesus can make such grand claims for himself in the light of his origins. Once again John gives us one of his typical contrasts between two levels, the earthly and the heavenly. The crowd know Jesus' earthly origins; he is the son of Joseph—and they know not only his father, but his mother also. Who does he think he is to start making claims about coming down from heaven? (6:42). As at the start of this dialogue (see 6:25–26), Jesus chooses not to answer the question asked, but goes to the heart of the matter. He warns them not to grumble and complain (6:43). If he has only an earthly origin, then no one will pay him any attention, in the way that we are cautious about claims to divine revelations from people who are mentally ill. No one will come to him unless 'drawn' by his real Father, the one who sent him (6:44). The prophets knew all about the attractive power of God's love. Hosea says that God has 'drawn' us with cords of love (Hos. 11:4), while the Greek version of Jer. 31:3, 'I have drawn you with an everlasting love', uses the same word for 'drawn' as here in John. These prophets looked forward to a time when everyone would learn about God and this, says Jesus, is what is happening now (6:45). His claim is not blasphemy or self-seeking megalomania; the initiative always remains God's, whom no one has ever seen. Even Moses could not see God and live, but had to be hidden in a cleft of rock as he passed by (Exod. 33:18–23). But if Jesus is the bread come down from heaven, then he has seen the Father (6:46).

Death or life

This is no debate merely about different interpretations of the story of the Exodus. Just as the claim that Jesus is 'the bread come down from heaven' is staggering, so the consequences of acceptance or rejection of him are vital. Thus it is restated with the solemn introduction, 'truly, truly I tell you' (6:47). To call Jesus the bread of life means that belief in him brings life, the eternal life of the age to come (6:47–48). Because the Israelites in the wilderness grumbled, God fed them with manna; but their grumbling also led to their death, as they wandered around for years and none came into the Promised Land (6:49; see Num. 14:26–35).

Thus we reach the final contrast in this section. All the comparing of Moses with Jesus, of manna in the wilderness with the feeding of the crowd, of earthly and heavenly origins, of complaining or believing—all come down eventually to the simple choice of death or life (6:50). As he offered 'living water' to the Samaritan woman, now Jesus offers the crowd 'living bread'; whoever eats this bread will live forever, for this bread is none other than his own flesh, his body given in sacrifice for us. Because he feeds us with living bread, we need not die; because he died for us, we can live forever with him (6:51).

PRAYER

Lord Jesus, draw me with the cords of your Father's love,
and give me the living bread from heaven,
that I may eat of it, and not die.

34　　JOHN 6:51–58

EAT MY FLESH & DRINK MY BLOOD

The debate between Jesus and the crowd since the miraculous feeding and walking on water has been exploring the text, 'he gave them bread from heaven to eat' (6:31). Like a rabbi preaching on the text, Jesus has taken each word or phrase in turn. First he stressed that it was God who 'gave' and still gives the bread (6:32–37) and then that the 'bread from heaven' is nothing other than himself (6:38–51). This only leaves the last part of the text, 'to eat', as the subject of this final section. It was introduced at the end of 6:51, where the bread was identified as 'my flesh'. Having begun with the overtones of the eucharist in the feeding through Jesus 'giving thanks' (6:11, 23), now we come back to communion themes again.

This explains why there has been little mention of such sacramental allusions in the earlier section, which focused on Jesus, using the material about Wisdom in the Old Testament and later Jewish writings. Because of this, some scholars think the two sections are separate, with 6:35–50 describing Jesus as the word and wisdom of God in an almost anti-sacramental way, and then 6:51–58 put in later to make everything more sacramental. Once we realize that the dialogue is working its way through this text, we would expect the central section to concentrate on Jesus coming 'from heaven' like God's word and wisdom, while 'to eat' would bring in more sacramental material at the end. Furthermore, the last section picks up the themes of the rest of the chapter beautifully and helps to round it all off.

The bread is my flesh

The middle section concludes with 'the bread that I will give for the life of the world is my flesh' (6:51). Two things immediately remind us of the words of Jesus at the Institution of Holy Communion: first, the Greek word for 'flesh' is a literal translation of the Hebrew word *basar* which is used with bread in Exodus 16:8, 12 and at the Passover *seder* meal. To say 'this (bread) is my flesh' is the same as 'this is my body'. Secondly, it is 'for the life of the world'; the word 'for' or 'on behalf of', *hyper*, also comes in the eucharistic words 'this is my body, which is given *for* you' (see Lk. 22:19; 1 Cor. 11:24). No wonder this direct statement produces a strong reaction from Jesus' hearers. Once again they are called "the Jews" and now they 'dispute among themselves'—the Greek word is actually 'fought'! (6:52). This was, and still is, a frequent reaction about Holy Communion—how can Jesus give us his flesh to eat? Quite apart from the general abhorrence of cannibalism, Jewish food laws specifically forbade eating flesh with the blood still in it, because the blood was considered to contain the animal's life (see Lev. 3:17; Deut. 12:23).

Yet the discourse continues with exactly this point, that if we want to have Jesus' life in us and be raised on the last day, we must eat his flesh and drink his blood (6:53–54). This picks up Wisdom's metaphorical invitation to eat and drink from the earlier section (Prov. 9:5, see on 6:35) and goes beyond it. The words are very vivid: 'flesh and blood' are given up in a sacrifice and the word for 'eat', *trogo*, literally means to chew or munch—stressing that Jesus' flesh and blood are 'really', 'truly' food and drink (6:55). This is strong stuff! Some early Christians could not accept that Jesus really came in the flesh, in human form (see 1 Jn. 4:2), while others saw Jesus as the word and wisdom of God in a non-sacramental way. Against both of these positions, this passage stresses that God sent Jesus to us in the flesh, and that he gives himself to us in his body and blood at the eucharist.

Live in me

It is through eating his flesh and drinking his blood that we abide in Jesus and he in us—in other words, Holy Communion is a way to union with him (6:56). After Jesus' words earlier about coming to him and not being rejected (6:37), now we see that we come to him and he feeds us so that we may live and abide in him. God the Father who sent Jesus is the source of all life, and even Jesus himself only lives because of the Father; thus any who receive his flesh and blood take the life of God into themselves (6:57). And so this whole discourse after the feeding of the multitude climaxes with one final contrast. The manna in the wilderness could not prevent the Israelites from dying ultimately; even those who are devoted to the Law and who eat of wisdom will hunger and thirst again. But those who eat the true bread from heaven, the bread of life in Jesus, will live forever (6:58).

PRAYER

Bread of heaven, feed me now and ever more.
W. Williams (1717–91)

35   JOHN 6:59-71

The PARTING of the WAYS

This chapter's setting has moved from up in the mountains for the feeding, across the storm-tossed lake to a crowd in Capernaum. The last part of this discourse at least has been Jesus' teaching in the synagogue at Capernaum (6:59). The impressive remains of the synagogue still visible there today date from a bit later than the time of Jesus, but there was an earlier building for study of the scriptures. This background of synagogue teaching explains why the debate has taken each part of the chosen text in turn for discussion, in the light of its context of Moses and the Exodus. We saw in 6:52 that 'the Jews disputed among themselves' and the subject of this chapter was hotly debated in synagogues across the Mediterranean during the second half of the first century, between Jews who accepted Jesus as Messiah and other Jews who did not. Central to the debate were the kind of claims made here about whether Jesus really had been sent by God from heaven, and whether he replaced the Jewish feasts, customs and laws. The 'parting of the ways' between the synagogue and the early church was happening gradually over these years (see Introduction, p. 19; also on 9:22; 16:2 below). However, Jesus' teaching and miracles led to argument and conflict even in his own day.

The hard saying

Thus it is not surprising that 'many of his disciples' said that this teaching was 'a hard saying' (6:60). These disciples are a larger group than the Twelve, who are mentioned separately later (6:67). They may have witnessed Jesus' healings and miraculous signs, like the Feeding, or heard him teach and joined in the debates. After all the dialogue and discourse in this chapter, the teaching is not difficult to understand, for it has been rigorously clarified section by section. On the contrary, its stark clarity makes it all the harder to believe and accept. As Mark Twain is reputed to have said, 'It is not the parts of the gospel which I do not understand which cause me difficulty—it's the demand of that which I do understand.'

Jesus is aware that the grumbling and murmuring is taking place even among disciples who follow him and asks them why they are 'scandalized' or offended (6:61). If they find difficult all this talk about him having descended from heaven to bring us life (6:38, 41, 51) what will happen when he goes back? (6:62). The word 'ascend' here has John's typical levels of meaning. At the simple level it refers to Jesus 'going up' to Jerusalem, where he will be 'lifted up'; but that lifting up on a cross will also be how he is exalted and ascends back to his Father. This will force a final decision on his grumbling disciples; for some, it may demonstrate that his claims are true, while for others it will be the final straw. Again he contrasts the natural life of the flesh with the supernatural life of the Spirit (6:63; see on 3:6 above). Jesus can give his flesh for people and speak the words of life, but unless they are drawn by the Father to believe, it is of no avail. Once more, John stresses Jesus' knowledge of all things and all people, including those who would not believe and even his betrayer (6:64–65).

Will you also go away?

The result is a parting of the ways even within Jesus' followers as 'many of his disciples turned back and no longer went around with him' (6:66). In a wistful verse, Jesus tests the resolve of the twelve, asking them if they (the 'you' is plural) also wish to leave him (6:67). Peter answers with a rhetorical question: there is nowhere else to go— this whole chapter has demonstrated that Jesus is superior to everything else with the 'words of eternal life' (6:68, see 6:63). Then Peter speaks for them all with his confession of faith that Jesus is the 'Holy One of God' (6:69). This is another way of declaring that Jesus is the Messiah and may be compared with the story of Peter's confession in the other gospels (Matt. 16:16; Mk. 8:29; Lk. 9:20). Whether this is a version of that story or a separate occasion, it makes a good conclusion to the debate among the Jews and the disciples about the significance of the feeding and Jesus' claims. It ends with another reminder of Jesus' knowledge in calling all of them, including Judas Iscariot, who will 'hand him over' (6:70–71). Among the crowds who seek Jesus, there will always be those who want to make him king on their own terms, those who murmur and complain, those who question or oppose him, followers who turn back or betray him, and those who realize that he is their only hope of life and receive his body and blood.

FOR REFLECTION AND PRAYER

Where do we stand in the crowd who seek Jesus?
Lord where else can we go? You have the words of eternal life.

36   JOHN 7:1–10

TIMES & PLACES

This chapter begins with Jesus 'walking about' in Galilee (7:1). The verb, *periepatei*, describes the 'peripatetic' life Jesus lived as a wandering teacher and preacher. In John, Jesus moves between Galilee and Jerusalem frequently, especially in the sequence of chapters which we are following, rather than swapping chapters 5 and 6 around to bring the Jerusalem episodes together. In John's sequence, Jesus' times and places go like this. His first year of ministry begins with gathering disciples in Galilee and his first sign at Cana (1:35—2:12); at Passover time in the spring, he goes to Jerusalem for the temple incident and the conversation with Nicodemus (2:13—3:36). He then leaves Judaea and travels through Samaria back to Galilee for his second sign at Cana (4:1–54). At the end of this year, or early in the second, Jesus goes up to Jerusalem for an unnamed feast where he heals the lame man on the Sabbath (5:1–47). Because of this, "the Jews" wanted to kill Jesus (5:18), which is why he is now back home in Galilee (7:1). The second year was marked by the springtime feeding of the crowd at Passover and the subsequent dialogue (6:1–71). Now it is autumn and the Feast of Tabernacles is coming, so Jesus' brothers assume he will be going up to Jerusalem again (7:2–3).

There is no opening sign here, like the water into wine, the healing or feeding, to get things underway—just the reference to the Feast of 'Succoth'. This is celebrated at the harvest in September or early October. In a week-long celebration, people lived in temporary dwellings, called huts, tents, booths or tabernacles, as a reminder of their wanderings in the wilderness and coming into the Promised Land to settle down and harvest crops (Lev. 23:33–43). John may be suggesting that the 'peripatetic' wanderings of Jesus are also coming to an end; it is time for him to go to the heart of the Promised Land, to Jerusalem, to settle there until the final harvest of his ministry at the crucifixion. This is confirmed perhaps by the way the central drama of this Festival uses water and light, two of John's key themes which will dominate the next chapters (see 7:37–39 and 8:12).

Telling Jesus what to do

The water into wine, the healing of the official's son, the feeding and the walking on water have all been done in Galilee, with only the healing of the lame man described in Jerusalem, which led to the death threats (7:1). Now Jesus' brothers encourage him to go to Judaea so that his followers can see his signs and he can have more success (7:3–4). John mentions Jesus' brothers, while Mark even names them (Mk. 6:3). Because of the later tradition of Mary's perpetual virginity, some commentators suggest that these are half-brothers or cousins. Whichever interpretation is adopted, clearly Jesus' family did not believe in him and are challenging him to make a public demonstration of his power (7:4–5).

When Mary encouraged him to use his power to help the wedding couple, she was told, 'My hour has not yet come' (2:4). Similarly, Jesus tells his brothers now that his *kairos*, which means a special time, has not yet come (7:6, 8). He knows that this moment will come, because it is not only "the Jews" who seek to kill him, but the world itself which hates him (7:7). We have noted how Jesus is somewhat elusive in this gospel, playing games of hide and seek. He is not yet ready for an open demonstration to provoke the final crisis, and so he avoids the caravans of pilgrims, remaining for a while in Galilee (7:9).

And yet the odd thing is that he does eventually go up by himself, not in public with the others (7:10). For this will be his final journey to Jerusalem, from which he will not return. After Tabernacles, he will stay through the winter for the Feast of the Dedication (10:22–23), and on to the spring for the third Passover (11:55; 13:1) at which he will die. The paradox is that what the brothers asked for will happen: Jesus does go up to Jerusalem and, when the time is right, he will reveal himself. But the times and the places, the festivals and the results will be different, beyond their imagining. In John, Jesus is always serenely in control; others may think they are, or make suggestions to him—but he knows the right time and place for what he has come to do. This should be a warning when we seek to tell God the best thing to do, or the right time and place for everyone to see his power.

PRAYER

Lord, help me to trust that times and places are in your hands.

TEACHING *in* JERUSALEM

Jesus' brothers were not the only ones who were expecting him to make a public showing at the festival. "The Jews" were looking for him and speculating about him, which picks up the theme of seeking which we saw in the previous two chapters (7:11; see 5:13–14; 6:24–25). Also the 'muttering' or 'complaining', *gongusmos*, about him in the crowd here in Jerusalem reminds us of the reaction of those in Galilee in the previous dialogue with all the echoes of the Israelites grumbling in the wilderness (6:41). As there was in Galilee, so here again there is division about Jesus: some think he is a good man, but others believe that he is deceiving them, leading people astray (7:12). This is a serious charge. According to the Law, anyone who leads others astray, away from the worship of God, must be killed (Deut. 13:1–11). In fact, during the debate between Jews and Christians in the next couple of centuries, this became a common Jewish allegation. The writings of the Talmud state that Jesus had 'led Israel astray' and this is why he was crucified (*On the Sanhedrin*, 43a).

This explains the odd comment that people would not discuss Jesus openly 'for fear of the Jews' (7:13). Once again, we must remember that both Jesus himself and all those discussing him are all Jews. Here again, then, the phrase "the Jews" of whom people are afraid must mean the authorities. This is the first mention that others are afraid of them, but this will become more prominent as the gospel progresses.

Learning and authority

During the middle of the festival, Jesus decides to come out of his self-imposed privacy and goes into the temple to teach (7:14). After his previous reluctance, we might ask why he chooses this moment. It may be that, as we will see below, the festival's ceremonies of water and light gave him a good starting point (see 7:37–38). Whatever the reason, John reminds us again that Jesus is in control and he chooses when and where he wants to appear.

The courts of the temple were large and offered many shady porticoes where rabbis might teach any who chose to sit at their feet to listen. Clearly, people did stop to hear Jesus. The reaction of "the

Jews" is astonishment. They have questions about what and how he is teaching. The usual pattern was for a young man to attach himself to a rabbi to learn the law and the traditions for several years as a disciple or pupil. He might even attend a rabbinic school to further his education. When eventually he came to teach himself, he would cite other teachers as his authorities, those who had taught him, or quoting precedent from other rabbis: 'Rabbi X said this, but Rabbi Y said that' and so on. In the same way, although I have studied and taught John's gospel for many years, even now I am writing surrounded by some of the great commentaries which I consult constantly to see what these authorities have said before me. I do not write at my own whim. But not Jesus; he had never been a pupil, never 'learned his letters' and did not quote the authority of his respected predecessors (7:15).

Jesus' response to the crowd is typical: because his teaching is not his own, his authority is that of the one 'who sent me' (7:16). In both his previous debates after healing the lame man on the Sabbath and feeding the crowd, Jesus had stressed his utter dependence on God who sent him (see 5:30; 6:29). He is not interested in quoting others; to some this may seem like teaching his own ideas, but those who want to do the will of God will recognize the truth of what he is saying (7:17). He picks up both previous debates by this stress on doing the will of God (see 6:38) and seeking not other people's respect for his teaching, but only the glory of his Father (7:18; cf. 5:41–44). The way this chapter builds on the last two is another good reason for following the traditional sequence, for it shows how attention is increasingly focused on Jesus himself. The mixture of reactions to him directs our attention to the central question of his identity: who is this man who does not need others' authority? Where has he come from and what is his purpose?

PRAYER

Lord Jesus, I would sit at your feet;
teach me the will of the one who sent you.

JESUS' AUTHORITY & IDENTITY

Having answered the question about why he does not quote other authorities for his teaching, Jesus goes on the offensive by directing his hearers' attention back to the ultimate authority—Moses himself (7:19). We saw in chapter 5 how Jesus was accused of lawbreaking by healing on the Sabbath, but was content to have Moses as the judge in his case (see 5:30–47). Now he accuses his opponents of not keeping the law themselves by wanting to break the fifth commandment, 'Thou shalt not kill' (Exod. 20:13). This refers back to the opponents wanting to kill him after he had healed the lame man (5:18). The crowd, watching the debate between Jesus and the authorities, interject that he is mad to think that people want to kill him (7:20). So Jesus reminds them of his 'one work', the healing on the Sabbath which so amazed them (7:21).

Next, this 'uneducated' teacher shows that he is quite capable of proper theological debate by using an argument 'from the lesser to the greater', used by the rabbis. He notes that they are perfectly happy to perform one work on the Sabbath, namely to circumcise a baby boy. The rabbinic authorities are all clear that the command to circumcise infants eight days after they are born takes priority over the Sabbath command, particularly as this is to enable the child to fulfil the law. Circumcision only affects one of the 248 members of a man's body according to Jewish reckoning; therefore, says Jesus, making his 'whole body' well, in all its members, must be even more permissible (7:23).

Then Jesus sums up his argument: healing on a Sabbath might have had the appearance of work, but when it is assessed with a proper judgment, it can be seen as fulfilling the law (7:24). The problem is that this summary opens up further debate, for the one who will judge not by appearances, by 'what his eyes see, or his ears hear' but who will give a right judgment 'for the poor and for the meek of the earth' is none other than the Christ, the shoot from Jesse (Is. 11:3).

Can this be the Christ?

Thus Jesus' comment about the ability to judge aright makes the lame man's healing, like the miraculous feeding, into a Messianic claim. So the people of Jerusalem begin to speculate even more about Jesus' identity. After all, here he is, teaching openly in the temple, and the authorities seem to do nothing (7:25–26). The way the Jewish crowd refer to those who oppose Jesus as 'the authorities' confirms our interpretation of the phrase "the Jews", when used of his opponents, as indicating such leaders.

Furthermore, Jesus' identity and origins were well known: in a culture without surnames, places of origin, like fathers' names, were important as a way of identifying people—hence 'Jesus of Nazareth'. There was a Jewish tradition that the origins of the Messiah would be unknown, and he himself unrecognized until the moment of his revelation. This may have been based on Malachi's prophecy that the Lord would come to his temple 'suddenly' (Mal. 3:1). So Jesus *of Nazareth* cannot be the Christ (7:27). Like Nathanael (1:46), the Jerusalemites would never think that God might come into our world in such an ordinary way; are we any different?

Jesus' reply, which is best translated as a statement rather than a question, accepts the point that they do know about him—at the earthly level at least (7:28). But as always, there is a deeper level beyond earthly things. John has made it clear time after time since the heights of the Prologue that Jesus' true origins are to be found in the God who sent him (7:28). This has been the constant theme throughout the dialogues of the last two chapters, and now it is summarized in stark simplicity: 'I know him, because I am from him, and he sent me' (7:29). By now the pattern is clear: such a claim is followed by another attempt to arrest him which is not successful because 'his hour had not yet come' (7:30). While this may be the moment, *kairos*, for him to make such a public claim as his brothers wanted (see 7:6), the final hour, *hora*, of both glory and passion still lies several months in the future (see 2:4 and 13:1). For the present, we have a division among the people again; while the authorities plot and scheme, 'many in the crowd' do believe and accept him as Christ because of the signs he is doing (7:31, cf. 2:23).

PRAYER

Jesus of Nazareth, grant me a right judgment
that I may know your true origins
and believe that you are the Christ.

COME *to* ME & DRINK

Jesus chose his moment to start teaching in the middle of the Feast
of Tabernacles. He provoked mixed reactions, with some seeking to
arrest him while others believe (7:30–31). John describes the debate
within the crowd as 'complaining' or 'muttering', using *gongus-* again
(7:32, see 7:12; 6:41). Jesus' opponents are identified as the
Pharisees, who were centred around the Law and the synagogue, and
the chief priests, who were responsible for the ritual sacrifices and
the temple; the two groups were not natural allies. However, right
from their early questioning of John the Baptist (1:19, 24), they have
been united in their opposition to this Christ-movement; now they
send the temple police to arrest Jesus. Down through the church's
history, and even in our own day, it is as remarkable as it is lamen-
table how often opponents from different ends of the ecclesiastical
spectrum seem to unite only in their desire to stop something new
happening—and how often that new thing turns out to be of God!

Seeking and finding

John stresses Jesus' control of times and places. Now he says that he
will only be there 'a little while' before returning to the one who sent
him (7:33). In fact, the 'little while' will be about six months from this
autumn's Tabernacles to next spring's Passover when he will return to
his heavenly Father through the crucifixion and resurrection. Over this
time, Jesus repeats this phrase to warn both the crowds and the disciples that time is getting ever shorter (8:21; 12:35; and throughout
chs. 13—16). Now is the time to search for him, not to arrest him,
but to find out what he has to say and to offer; the time will come soon
enough when they will not be able to follow where he goes (7:34).
This enigmatic comment is greeted with typical misunderstanding.
Just as they think they know Jesus' origins, but actually know only the
human level (7:27–29), so now they speculate that his destination is
among the Jews dispersed in the Graeco-Roman world and do not
understand why they cannot follow him there (7:35–36). The deeper
level is that he has come from his Father and soon will return there.
Ironically, by the time the gospel is written, Jesus' followers will have
spread far and wide among the Greeks, while the temple and the

priests will have been destroyed. How easy it is to miss God's 'little while'; we must seek him 'while he may be found' (Is. 55:6).

Rivers of living water

Having chosen his moment to go to the festival, and to teach in its middle, now Jesus picks the last day, when people were packing up their booths, to make his proclamation. Water, so important in this gospel, was central to the festival. The harvest celebrations included prayers for rain; the rainy season began soon afterwards and it was believed that if rain fell during the festival it would continue abundantly. Every day water was taken from the Pool of Siloam in a golden flagon in solemn procession through the Water Gate into the temple, as the people sang, 'With joy you will draw water from the wells of salvation' (Is. 12:3) and chanted Psalms 113—118. In the temple, the water was then poured around the altar. Now Jesus no longer sits down to teach; he stands up to issue his ringing invitation for the thirsty not to go to the ceremony, but to come to him (7:37).

Some Bibles punctuate 7:38 differently, but the invitation to come to Jesus and drink is clear. However, the scripture quotation could mean that rivers of living water will flow from the heart of Jesus or from the believer's heart. The quotation's source is unclear. Psalm 78:24 was behind the text about 'bread from heaven' debated in 6:31–59; the same psalm describes how God 'made streams come out of the rock, and caused waters to flow down like rivers' (Ps. 78:16). The waters will flow out of his heart or belly, *koilia*; Jerusalem was thought to be the *koilia*, the centre of the world, from which living water would flow (Zech. 14:8). Nicodemus used the same word when he misunderstood being 'born again' to mean climbing again into his mother's *koilia*; then Jesus told him to be born of water and the Spirit (3:4–5). Now this living water is identified with the Spirit, to be poured out after Jesus is glorified through his Passion (7:39).

As Jesus was superior to the healing water and the Sabbath in chapter 5, and to the bread and the Passover in chapter 6, so now he transcends the temporary booths and the water ceremony of Tabernacles with his offer of the living water of the Spirit.

PRAYER

Lord Jesus, let your living waters flow
from my heart to a thirsty world.

No One Ever Spoke Like This Man

Jesus' claims to transcend the Sabbath and feasts like Passover and Tabernacles and to replace their perishable bread and water with his living bread and water have provoked speculation among his hearers. Throughout this chapter, some people have believed him (7:31), while others have been dismissive (7:27); the authorities, however, have tried to arrest him (7:32). All these reactions are now repeated, following his climactic invitation to come to the living waters at the end of the festival.

Prophet or Christ?

Some who heard him concluded 'This is really the prophet' (7:40). When the Pharisees and the priests questioned John the Baptist at the start, he denied being 'the prophet' (1:21, 25). Both the woman of Samaria and the five thousand recognized Jesus as the prophet (4:19, 6:14). Since the prophet was expected to be like Moses (Deut. 18:15), it is not surprising that Jesus' offer to give bread and water, as Moses did in the wilderness, should be so acclaimed.

Others go still further and decide 'This is the Christ' (7:41). This stimulates the third debate about where Jesus is from: there has already been discussion about his parentage (6:42) and his origins, contrasting them with the supposedly unknown origins of the Christ (7:27). Now Jesus' background in Galilee is debated (7:41–42). Micah 5:2 (quoted in Matt. 2:6) suggests that the Messiah would come from Bethlehem. However, for John both places are still only on the earthly level; throughout his gospel, he stresses Jesus' real origins with his heavenly Father who sent him.

This debate produced yet another division in the crowd about Jesus. This has been happening through all the recent dialogues (6:52; 7:12, 30–31). This time John uses the Greek word, *schisma* (7:43). The 'schism' between the early church and the synagogue centred around exactly the same questions as here: whether Jesus was an ignorant law-breaker, or an authoritative teacher from God; the contrast between his humble origins and the Messianic claims being made for him; whether he replaced or fulfilled Jewish faith and worship, or had been rightly executed for 'leading the people astray'. Once again, this division leads to another futile attempt to arrest him (7:44).

Acceptance or rejection?

The arresting party now return empty-handed to the chief priests and the Pharisees and their report shows again the division of reactions to Jesus. The temple police, like the crowd, are amazed by Jesus' different way of teaching; they stress that no human being, *anthropos*, has ever spoken the way this person does (7:46; cf. 7:15). The Pharisees, however, are so convinced of their view that they miss the hint that Jesus might be more than human and simply dismiss the police report; anybody who differs from them must have been 'led astray' (7:47; cf. 7:12). After all, they assert with supreme self-confidence, none of the authorities nor the Pharisees have believed Jesus (7:48). It is only the rabble—the crowd, who know nothing of the law (7:49). The disdain of the religious leaders for the ordinary 'people of the land' is well documented at that time, and often enough since in our own history, regrettably. Since those who do not uphold the law are accursed (Deut. 27:26), the truly religious would avoid them.

In fact, they do not all take this view. Nicodemus, described as one of the authorities and a Pharisee when he 'went to Jesus before', is still called 'one of them' (7:50; see 3:1). He refutes both their points by showing that some of the authorities have been to Jesus and that they do not have sole control of the law. Far from the people being ignorant of the law's demands, the Pharisees are acting against the law in judging Jesus without a fair hearing (7:51). Earlier, Jesus had suggested that his accusers did not keep the law by wishing to kill him (7:19); now one who had previously only talked to him 'by night' redirects their attention to the law's provision for a proper hearing with witnesses (see on 5:30 above). But Nicodemus' point is dismissed even more contemptuously than that of the police; the absurdity of taking Jesus' side must indicate that he is a Galilean too! Their metropolitan self-confidence that no prophet, still less a Messiah could come from Galilee, is such that they conveniently forget that Jonah came from only a few miles north of Nazareth (7:52; see 2 Kings 14:25; Jon. 1:1).

For REFLECTION

What is our response to Jesus? Are we so convinced of our point of view that we dismiss or despise what others tell us about him?

41 JOHN 7:53—8:11

The WOMAN TAKEN *in* ADULTERY

This famous story is not without problems. Some Bible versions put it in a footnote, while others include it, but note that it interrupts the flow of the story. In 7:53 'they all go home', only to return in the morning with the woman (8:3); in 8:9 they all leave except the woman, who also then departs (8:11). Thus Jesus is left on stage alone, but in 8:12 he starts speaking 'to them' again and carries on with the interrupted debate at the Feast of Tabernacles. It looks as though 7:52 should run straight into 8:12. This is what we find in most early manuscripts and in the earliest gospel commentaries by the Fathers. Later manuscripts include it here, but mark it separately, while others place it after 7:36, 7:44, or at the end of John, or even after Luke 21:38, since there is some evidence of different style here, not unlike Luke's.

John 20:30 refers to other things Jesus did which were not included because of space. Perhaps God wants this one in the Bible somewhere, even if we are not sure where! Certainly, the story reflects John's account of Jesus being sent not to condemn the world but to save it; furthermore, it fits John's motif of Jesus being on trial and yet still in control. Its position here illustrates Jesus' statement 'I judge no one' (8:15).

The trap is set

Early in the morning, Jesus is sitting down to teach in the temple in the outer Court of the Women, where 'all the people' could come to him (8:2). The Pharisees enter, with their scribes. As experts on the Law, they call Jesus 'Teacher' and make a woman stand 'before all of them' (8:3). Presumably, the poor thing is rather dishevelled, having been 'caught in the very act of committing adultery' (8:4). This means that Jesus cannot give her the 'benefit of the doubt', as the law allowed for someone raped where no one could hear her shout for help (Deut. 22:25–27). No, the law is clear: both she, and the man, must die (Deut. 22:22–24). But where is the man? People do not normally commit adultery in public view, and to have caught her 'in the very act' suggests a trap with the man being allowed to escape, hopping around Jerusalem half-clad!

Our suspicions are confirmed when these lawyers ask for Jesus' opinion, appealing as so often to Moses and the law as judge (8:5). It is not so much the woman who is on trial here, as Jesus himself, as they seek to test and trap him (8:6). The legal and political trap is that if Jesus forbids stoning her, he is breaking the law of Moses, while if he encourages stoning, he is breaking Roman law, which reserved the death penalty to Roman courts. Then there is the religious trap: if he decides against Moses' law of stoning, Jesus would forfeit any claim to be a teacher in the temple, whereas to advocate killing would contradict all his teaching about receiving and saving people. The woman is just a pawn, being used more than any sexual act can have used her.

The trap is sprung

Jesus averts his eyes and begins to write in the sand, like a teacher with a blackboard (8:6). Many speculate about what he may have written; a list of their sins, perhaps, or a text like Exodus 23:1, prohibiting false witness. When pressed further, he suggests that the one 'without sin' should throw the first stone (8:7)—the task of the witnesses (Deut. 17:6–7). But Jesus writes again in the sand, maybe continuing with Exodus 23:7, warning people not to join a false accusation. As he writes, the older ones, conscious of their own sin and their implication in this trumped up charge perhaps, slip away, until the woman is left alone with the only one who is 'without sin', Jesus himself (8:9). Instead of throwing stones, Jesus asks where her accusers are; are none left to judge? (8:10). In reply, this woman is remembered for two brief words, 'none, Sir' (8:11). Then the one to whom the Father has given all judgment (5:22), but who was himself accused by this charade, delivers his verdict: there is neither condemnation nor commendation: she is to go, but not to 'keep on sinning'. The use of the present continuous here is a challenge to her, and to us, to lead a new life.

Like all the passages around this story, once again Jesus has been put on trial, only for his accusers to be judged and found wanting, while we who read it are forgiven and invited to respond to God's love letter written in the sand of our lives.

For REFLECTION & PRAYER

Recreate the scene in your imagination—and join in.
Are you one of the accusers, an onlooker, or the woman?
What does Jesus say to you?

I Am *the* Light *of the* World

Jesus chose his moment to go to Jerusalem and teach at the Feast of Tabernacles. During that Feast's ceremony of drawing water, he announced that he is the source of the living water. His claims have provoked arguments about his authority and identity. As the discussion continues from 7:52, another of the symbols from the festival intensifies the debate further.

As well as the water procession recalling drinking from the rock in the wilderness, Tabernacles also included a light ceremony. On the first night, four very large golden lamps were lit in the Court of Women, where both men and women could gather—and where the woman taken in adultery would have been brought to Jesus. It is said that this light was so bright that every court and area around was reflected in it. Then, led by some exuberant priests, the people danced all night. Once again, this ceremony recalls the wilderness wanderings when the Israelites were led by a pillar of fire at night 'to give them light' (Exod. 13:21). Just as Jesus claimed to be the real bread and water, so now he takes over this symbol of light with his second 'I am' statement: 'I am the light of the world' (8:12). Light was another central image for the Jews. Not only did God lead them with light at night, but it could describe his very self: 'the Lord is my light' (Ps. 27:1). As with bread, light could also be a symbol for the law: 'Your word is a lamp to my feet and a light to my path' (Ps. 119:105). Light was also an image for the divine wisdom, while Israel's enemies were kept in darkness (Wis. 7:26; 18:1–4).

Electric light means that we have too easily forgotten what darkness meant to ancient people. It never really gets dark in cities like London, because of our so-called 'light pollution'. We have to go deep into the hills or moors to find thick darkness for star gazing. The darkness of wandering in the wilderness was very real for the Jews, so Jesus invites his hearers not to walk in darkness, but to follow him in the light of life as he fulfils and surpasses another symbol, central to both Judaism and John's thought (8:12; cf. 3:19).

A witness to the light

This claim leads us into a difficult chapter as the conflict between

Jesus and his opponents becomes more intense, with abuse on both sides. It is a chapter which has been much misused, especially in the Nazi persecution of Jews. But John is not 'anti-Jewish', since he himself, Jesus, and all those involved are Jews. For him, it is the battle of light against darkness, with those who think they are in the light gradually going into darkness after the healing of the blind man (see on 9:39–41).

Thus we find ourselves in debate about familiar themes again. Jesus' opponents, identified as Pharisees as in the previous chapter, reject his statement about himself as the light on the grounds of self-witness (8:13). This reminds us of the previous discussion about the need for two other witnesses (see on 5:31 above). But, as the incident with the woman taken in adultery showed, witnesses can be fixed. So this time, Jesus is not afraid to admit his own self-witness, because he knows it is true and valid, arising out of his own knowledge of his true origins and his eventual destination (8:14). Although his opponents think that they know about him over the last chapters, in fact they only 'judge by human standards' (8:15), by the appearances he warned them against in 7:24. When asked about the adulterous woman, Jesus refused to judge, even though his judgment is true and supported by the Father (8:16). The law's requirement for two witnesses is met by the testimony of Jesus and of his father (8:17–18). Significantly, for the first time here we have the phrase 'your law' as the polarity between Jesus and the Jewish authorities deepens.

Since Jesus has appealed to his father as a witness, his hearers want to know where he can be found to cross examine him. This is another typical 'misunderstanding'. They are thinking at the earthly level, by 'human standards'; if they realized the truth about Jesus, they would know his father also (8:19). This introduces another topic into the debate for the rest of this chapter: who is Jesus' father, and who is the father of the Jews?

But first we are reminded that Jesus is teaching by the temple treasury, in the Court of the Women, where the great lamps are burning. The true light of the world teaches in the light, and none can arrest him, for his hour has still not come (8:20).

PRAYER

Light of the World, grant that I may not walk in darkness,
but rather know you and your Father in the light of life.

WHO ARE YOU?

Jesus' claim to be the light of life has sparked another round of debate about his identity, his origins and parentage. Now we move to his final purpose and destination. It is the end of the festival and people are packing up to go home; so too Jesus announces that he is 'going away' (8:21). He had already warned his hearers that the time would come when they would not be able to find him since they do not know where he is going (7:33–36; 8:14). This theme of seeking is repeated now with a stronger warning that time is running out. To refuse the light is to stay in darkness; since Jesus offers water which is 'living' and the 'light of life', not to accept life leads to dying in sin and not being able to follow him.

As before, the conversation proceeds on several levels. We know that Jesus means that he is going back to the Father. Last time, his hearers mockingly suggested that he might be going to the Greeks, with the irony that the gospel would indeed spread there (7:35). Now they pick up the hint about death and wonder if Jesus is going to kill himself to stop them following him (8:22). Of course, as readers, we know that Jesus will die. This time the irony is that it is not Jesus, as a suicide, who will go below, under the earth. Quite the reverse: it is his accusers who are the ones 'from below'; throughout all these dialogues, Jesus' origins 'from above' have been stressed consistently (8:23; cf. 3:31; 6:38). He is not 'of this world', but has been sent by his Father into this world. The repeated 'I am' from above and 'I am' not of this world prepares the way for the stronger use of this phrase without any description: his hearers will remain in darkness and death 'unless you believe that I am' (8:24). With John's usual levels of meaning, we, as readers, notice the divine claim which is being implied, but it is not yet obvious to Jesus' hearers.

The Father who sent me

Thus, they ask for the description—'I am who?', 'I am what?'—and so we are back to the fundamental question of Jesus' identity: 'who are you?' (8:25). Jesus' reply is difficult to translate. Some versions, such as the RSV, NIV and AV, interpret it as a answer to the question, I am... 'what I have been saying from the beginning.' Others, like the

NEB and NRSV, see it as an exasperated question, 'why do I bother?' Whichever we read, Jesus' frustration with their failure to understand is clearly growing. He has more to say, which will result in judgment as he seeks to declare to the world the words of the one who sent him, who is true (8:26). But even this repeated stress on Jesus' dependency on his Father is again misunderstood, as the evangelist makes clear to the reader (8:27).

Final realization will have to wait until Jesus has been 'lifted up' (8:28). The earlier use of this phrase compared Moses, lifting up the bronze serpent in the wilderness to bring life to the dying Israelites, with Jesus being 'lifted up' (3:14). Even this has a double meaning, referring both to Jesus' exaltation and to the way he will be exalted, through his death on the cross (12:32–4). His hearers' earlier guess was partly right; they will not be able to follow him for he will die, but it will not be a suicide. These opponents will bring it about when they lift him up on the cross. This will be the moment when people will 'realize that I am'—and again the 'I am' phrase stands alone (8:28). Yet Jesus stresses that this is no claim to divinity in himself. He can do nothing on his own; he is totally dependent on his Father for all he does and says. His relationship with the one who sent him is such that God is always with Jesus and Jesus always does what is pleasing to his Father (8:29). A closer relationship than this is hard to imagine.

So the question, 'who are you?' with all the issues about Jesus' identity, origins and purpose, is answered with several claims of 'I am', together with an emphasis that his identity and purpose are only to be found in his dependency upon his Father who sent him. This is a clear response and so 'many believed in him' (8:30). This debate will soon become more polarized. As John has frequently pointed out, Jesus is causing a division among his hearers, with some believing and others opposing him.

PRAYER

Lord Jesus, help me to realize who you really are,
that I may live in the light
of your relationship with your Father.

The TRUTH WILL MAKE YOU FREE

The debate at the end of the Feast of Tabernacles continues between Jesus and "the Jews". As often, his hearers are divided. Many of them have come to believe in him and he now addresses those believers (8:30–31). As the dialogue continues, it becomes clear that not all his hearers are believers; some question him and become more opposed as the chapter progresses. Some commentators try to explain this apparent change by distinguishing between those 'who believed *in* him' in 8:30 and those who simply 'believed him' in 8:31, but then lapse into opposition later. The distinction in the Greek is hard to maintain, and most translations do not note it. The situation is better explained by a mixed crowd of believers and opponents—and probably a good number of observers waiting to see how things turn out! John has noted such a divided context frequently in the previous dialogues. Jesus' words, then and now, elicit a reaction in people, which can be either faith or rejection.

This point is amplified by the comment that it is those who 'continue in my word' who are truly his disciples (8:31). This means to remain or abide, *menein*, and the same word is used for abiding in Jesus the true vine (15:4–10). Discipleship is not a single event, an instant reaction to someone speaking; it is a life of constant listening and learning. Such a life will enable us to know the truth and 'the truth will make you free' (8:32). This would have been recognized both by Jews, who believed that the truth seen in the law made people free, and by Greeks, who were liberated by truth discovered through reason and philosophical debate.

Descendants of Abraham

Thus, Jesus' hearers do not see why they need to be set free. Indeed, they take great pride in being 'descendants of Abraham' (8:33). After all the appeals to Moses in recent chapters, this shift back to the father of Judaism is significant. It was through God's promise of descendants to Abraham that their nation came into being (Gen. 22:17–8) and they used his name to define themselves (Ps. 105:6). But the proud boast of freedom is somewhat hollow. Years after Abraham, they were slaves in Egypt and needed the light of the pillar of fire to guide them to freedom across the wilderness. Centuries of independence may have followed, but this ended in the captivity in Babylon. More recently, they had been absorbed into various near eastern empires, of which Roman rule was only the latest.

Slaves, sons and fathers

But Jesus has a different slavery in mind, the bondage to sin (8:34). He illustrates this with an image which is like a parable, the difference between a slave and a son where only the son 'abides' in the father's house (8:35). It is the same word as 'continuing in my word' (8:31). After the mention of Abraham, this image would remind his hearers of the contrast between Ishmael, the son of Hagar the slave-woman, and Isaac the legitimate son (Gen. 17:20–21). Only the freeborn son could stay in father Abraham's house forever (Gen. 21:9–21). Thus, says Jesus, 'if the son makes you free, you will be free indeed' (8:36). The move from 'the son' in the story to 'the son' who sets us free is one of John's typical shifts of level. The Greek words are the same, with no different punctuation or capital 'S' as in our translations. But the meaning has changed to a deeper level, as 'the Son'—one of John's favourite ways of referring to Jesus—claims to 'make you free' in a way superior to both Jewish law and Greek reason.

Jesus initially accepts his hearers' claim to be 'descendants of Abraham' (8:37). However, a son should reflect his father's character, but these 'descendants of Abraham' seek to kill him. Instead of 'continuing in my word', his word finds no place in them. Relying on the past is never enough. No matter how illustrious our spiritual parentage or how wonderful the time when we first 'believed in Jesus', it is the reality of our present action which reveals whose children we are. Jesus speaks what he has seen with 'the father', and his opponents do what they have heard from 'the father' (8:38). It is the same phrase in Greek, with no capital 'F' or possessive pronoun 'my' or 'your' to indicate that they have different fathers. But the separation of the two is revealed by their different characters and activity, saving life or seeking to kill, just like two children growing up in the same family but revealing different paternity by their contrasting appearances.

PRAYER

Lord Jesus, set me free by your truth
that I may live in your house forever and reflect our Father's glory.

WHO IS YOUR FATHER?

The debate between Jesus and his opponents has moved beyond Moses to the father of Judaism, Abraham. A son remains in his father's house forever and his paternity is revealed in his actions. Thus the opponents' desire to kill Jesus conflicts with their claim to be descended from Abraham. After all, Jesus only says and does what he has learned from his father—so where have his opponents learned what they say and do? The debate shifts away from Jesus' origins to those of his hearers: who is their father as revealed by their actions?

Abraham

Jesus' hearers are confused by his comments about doing what they heard from the father (8:38); so they assert once again, 'Abraham is our father'. Jesus says that, if so, they would do 'what Abraham did' (8:39). In fact, they want to kill him even though he brings a true message which he 'heard from God' (8:40). This is not behaviour to be expected from Abraham. In the famous story at the beginning of the Jewish faith and nation, God visited Abraham with three messengers; Abraham fed and received them so well that God promised him a son and debated his intentions about Sodom with Abraham (Gen. 18). Thus their rejection of Jesus as the one sent by the Father must reveal that his hearers are following the example of a different father (8:41a).

God

Their immediate response is that they cannot have a different father because they are not illegitimate (8:41b). This may be an allusion to doubts about Jesus' paternity. The crowd wondered whether the one who feeds multitudes and makes such claims could be the 'son of Joseph, whose father and mother we know' (6:42; see 1:45). John does not mention anything about the virgin birth or Jesus' earthly paternity. Later Jewish debate with the early Christians quickly included the charge that Jesus was illegitimate, born of Mary and a Roman soldier called Panthera, and this may be the first hint of this claim.

However, if Jesus is right to suggest that they have another father and not Abraham, then they claim it must be God (8:41c). The Hebrew scriptures are full of this idea, from God calling Israel his firstborn son out of Egypt (Exod. 4:22) to Isaiah's assertion that even 'though Abraham does not know us ... you, O Lord, are our Father' (Is. 63:16). Jesus replies that if God were their father, they would love Jesus, since he has been sent from God (8:42). The fact that they do not understand him and cannot accept his word implies that they must have a different father (8:43).

The devil

Because they seek to kill Jesus, the awful reality must be that their father is the devil, for they are doing what he desires (8:44). As a 'murderer from the beginning', he inspired Cain's murder of Abel, which John's first letter contrasts with Jesus' sacrificial death (1 John 3: 12–16). Later Jesus will stress that it is really the devil who wants his death (12:31; 14:30). As well as being a murderer, there is 'no truth in him'. The word 'devil', *diabolos*, means slanderer. His lies from the time of Eve and the serpent (Gen. 3:1–5) speak 'from his own nature' as a liar. Jesus, however, does not speak from himself, but only what God has sent him to say, the truth to make us free (8:45). No one can convict him of sin (8:46). He has rebutted the charges of Sabbath breaking and their other accusations, and avoided the trap with the adulterous woman. Unlike the others who went away, aware of their sin, he was the only one to remain with her (8:7–9). He speaks the truth, the words of God. Those who are of God recognize him, so the only conclusion must be that these opponents are not of God (8:47).

The use of this passage, especially 8:44, by the Nazis to claim that all Jews were of the devil is clearly false. The section began with 'the Jews who believed', while both Jesus and John are Jews, like the rest of the disciples. The chapter describes an internal 'family feud' between two Jewish groups, one that accepts Jesus and another that rejects him. Jewish or Irish jokes can be funny when told by their own comedians, but seem racist when repeated by others. This debate, however, is no joke, for family feuds and civil wars are always the most bitter. There is no doubt that there was real conflict between Jesus and the authorities of his day, but some of the strong language here also reflects the pain and bitterness of the Jewish believers in Jesus who were thrown out of the synagogue later (see Introduction, p. 19).

For PRAYER & REFLECTION

What do my actions reveal about my spiritual parentage?

46

BEFORE ABRAHAM WAS, I AM

This dialogue is set at the end of the Feast of Tabernacles, with its ceremony of light and Jesus' claim, 'I am the light of the world' (8:12). Debate has concentrated on Jesus' identity and authority, his origins and destination, which he says come from the Father who sent him. Some Jews have believed, but others have become more opposed. This led to speculation about their origins since the desire to kill Jesus indicated that their father is neither God nor Abraham, but the devil himself. Now it climaxes with three questions from the opponents back on Jesus' claim and identity.

You are a Samaritan and have a demon

"The Jews" respond to Jesus' suggestion that the devil is their father in similar terms (8:48). To call him 'a Samaritan' was to go beyond the hint that he was illegitimate; the Samaritans were seen as the illegitimate offspring of Jews and pagan oppressors and religiously impure (2 Kings 17:24–41; see on 4:4). Thus it is Jesus who is inspired by the devil, not themselves. Again, all these charges were part of later argument between Jews and those who accepted Jesus, when, as here, the insults went both ways. Jesus replies that he cannot be a demon because he is honouring God, which demons could never do (8:49). The insult dishonours him, but since he does not seek his own glory, it does not matter to him. It is God who matters as he has maintained throughout the chapter. But God is concerned about his Son's glory (see 8:18), and he is the ultimate judge (8:50). However, those who keep Jesus' word need not worry about judgment since they will not see death (8:51; cf. 8:31). All his sayings about the bread of life, living water and the light of life have been offers of life, not death.

Are you greater than Abraham?

"The Jews" repeat the charge of demon possession and interpret Jesus' offer of not seeing death on a literal level as usual. After all, even Abraham died and all the prophets likewise (8:52). Jesus' statement is preposterous, pretending to be greater than Abraham. Previously, they asked Jesus, 'who are you' (8:25); now this claim makes them ask, 'who do you think you are? (8:53).

Jesus responds again that what he thinks about himself does not matter. He glorifies the Father, not himself. As always, he is totally dependent on his Father who in turn glorifies his Son (8:54). As we know, this glory will be through his suffering and passion (see 12:23, 28; 13:31). Jesus' opponents may claim his Father as their God, yet they do not know him. Jesus has constantly stressed his knowledge of God through this debate and does so again (8:55; see 7:28–29; 8:19). To deny it now would make himself into a liar like them (see 8:44). This reference back to the earlier debate recalls their claim to be children of Abraham; if Abraham is their father, they should know that he rejoiced to see Jesus' day (8:56). This may allude to rabbinic belief that Abraham's vision of Gen. 15:12–16 showed him all his future descendants, including the Messiah. Alternatively, it suggests that Abraham is in the presence of God now, rejoicing at Jesus' ministry.

I am

Once again, "the Jews" misunderstand his comment at an earthly level: a young man like him cannot have seen Abraham (8:57). 'Not yet fifty' does not tell us anything about Jesus' actual age; since fifty was the age when the Levites retired (Num. 8:24–25), it means in his prime. (Lk. 3:23 suggests Jesus was about thirty.)

Jesus' reply is truly staggering: 'before Abraham was, I am' (8:58). This balances how the debate began with his claim 'I am the light of the world' (8:12). After the other 'I am' sayings here with their hints and levels of meaning (see 8:23, 28), this time it is an absolute and unmistakable claim to exist in the eternal being of God. The attempt by his opponents to pick up some of the stones lying around for the building work on the temple to stone him is itself recognition of what he has said (8:59). It is not about stoning an adulterous woman any more, but someone guilty of the much more serious blasphemy, according to the penalty in Lev. 24:16. Jesus' accusation that they wish to kill him is thus proved true. Yet, somehow, Jesus leaves the temple, hidden 'in secret' as he came to the temple 'in secret' at the start of the Feast (7:4, 10). After this debate, the hour for his suffering is much closer, but it is still not yet.

PRAYER

Eternal 'I am', search my heart
that I may rejoice in your day and glorify the Father.

47 JOHN 9:1–5

The LIGHT COMES *to a* BLIND MAN

The story of how the light of the world comes to heal a blind man is beautifully written. Although it is self-contained in chapter 9, its part in the development of the gospel is significant. Chapters 7 and 8 take place during the Feast of Tabernacles, with its rituals of water and light. Both of those symbols recur here also. Jesus' claim to be the 'light of the world' (8:12) led to debate about his origins and identity, causing divisions and antagonism. The accusations and counterclaims culminated in charges of demonic inspiration and an attempt to stone him. Now those symbols of darkness and light are translated into physical terms as a blind man is healed. It happens 'as Jesus passed by' (9:1); in the narrative, Jesus has just left the temple (8:59), so perhaps he passes the blind man at the temple gate, a favourite spot for the sick and the destitute to lie, beseeching help from entering pilgrims (see Peter and John at the gate, Acts 3:2).

The stress on light at the Feast of Tabernacles and Jesus' claim to be even greater as the light of the world are reflected in this chapter's key words which are repeated many times, such as 'blind' (9:1, 2, 13, 17, 18, 19, 20, 24, 25, 32, 39, 40, 41), 'eyes' (6, 10, 11, 14, 15, 17, 21, 26, 30, 32), and 'to see' (7, 8, 11, 15, 18, 19, 21, 25, 37, 39, 41). The actual healing from blindness to seeing happens early (9:7), but it leads rapidly to another debate about Jesus' identity which causes division. As the blind man comes more fully into the light, so we discover that 'there are none so blind as those who will not see'. As the blind man journeys not just out of physical darkness, but also from ignorance to a growing faith, Jesus' opponents travel from certainty through increasing doubt to rejecting the light. And all the while others are watching—the disciples, the man's parents, the bystanders, and even us, the readers. What will be our journey be, into light, or darkness—healing, or rejection?

Sin and suffering

In the Old Testament, to 'open the eyes of the blind' is the work of God (Ps. 146:8), a sign of his coming (Is. 29:18; 35:5) or of his anointed servant (Is. 42:7). It is remarkable therefore that no one blind is cured anywhere in the Old Testament, yet now Jesus comes to this blind man. What is more, he has not gone blind recently, but was born like that (9:1). Jesus' disciples ask their rabbi, 'why?' (9:2). It is a common human reaction to suffering, especially of the innocent, to ask, 'why me? why her?' In fact, the disciples assume it is *not* undeserved, and want to know whose fault caused it, the man's or his parents? Faced with this situation, they see not a person in need, but a theological problem—is this the result of sin? The Old Testament suggests that the sins of parents could be visited upon their children (e.g. Exod. 20:5), and some rabbinic commentators also thought it possible for a foetus to sin (when discussing Esau and Jacob's behaviour in the womb, Gen. 25:22). Belief in the reincarnation of souls, which would have been known in first-century Palestine among followers of both Greek philosophy and Eastern religions (and which is increasingly common today), also suggests that people can be punished in this life for their former sins. Against all these views, the Book of Job argued that suffering is not necessarily caused by sin, and Jesus endorses this here.

Darkness and light

Where the disciples see a problem, Jesus sees a person in need, and an opportunity for works of God 'to be revealed', to be made manifest in the light (9:3). In this gospel, Jesus' miracles are 'signs', pointers to the glory of God. His comment does not mean that this is the reason for the man's suffering, but that his situation can result in God's work. Jesus must 'work the works of him who sent me' while he can, 'while it is day' (9:4). Jesus knew his time was limited, and he had to 'seize the day', *carpe diem*, as the Latin proverb puts it, for night, the time of darkness, was soon coming. Here John picks up the theme from the Feast of Tabernacles, that Jesus is the 'light of the world' (9:5; see also 8:12). The man has spent his existence in darkness, but now he meets the one 'in whom was life, and the life was the light of men', as the Prologue made clear (1:4). Regrettably, there is still much death and darkness in our world, which we struggle to understand; but if we are to 'work the works of God', we must never just discuss it, but seek to bring light and life.

PRAYER

Jesus, light of the world, shine in our darkness
and bring us your healing life.

48   JOHN 9:6–12

The BLIND MAN IS HEALED

As with Nicodemus, the Samaritan woman and the paralysed man, so the blind man is led by Jesus away from understanding things on a simple physical level to a deeper spiritual reality. In particular, there are a lot of links to the story of the paralysed man in chapter 5. Both have been suffering for many years (9:1; 5:5) but are healed by Jesus by a pool in Jerusalem (9:7; 5:2) on a Sabbath (9:14; 5:9) which causes problems with the authorities (9:16; 5:10, 16) who question the men (9:15, 24; 5:12); Jesus is absent (9:12; 5:13) and the men do not know anything about him (9:12, 25; 5:13), but he comes to find them and reveal himself to them (9:35; 5:14). This similarity is not accidental, but part of John's artistry in painting his picture of Jesus to reveal his loving concern and divine identity through his miracles, the 'signs'. In both cases, the physical healing must lead onto a revelation of who Jesus is.

'Sent' for healing

True to his comment about doing the works of God while there is time (9:4), Jesus turns his words into action for the man's healing. As soon as he finished speaking, he spat on the ground and mixed his saliva with the earth to form a clay to put on the man's eyes (9:6). Some early church Fathers link this action to God's creation of Adam (whose name in Hebrew means 'earth') out the dust of the ground in Genesis 2:7; other commentators compare the use of saliva by the emperor Vespasian to cure a blind man at Alexandria, described in Tacitus' *Histories* IV:81. Saliva was highly regarded in the ancient world, and it certainly makes a better eyesalve than the honey and cock's blood a blind Roman soldier called Aper wore on his eyes for three days at the instruction of the healing god Aesculapius! (Dittenberger's *Greek Inscriptions* 1173:15–18).

Whatever the reason for Jesus' impromptu eye ointment, he tells the blind man to go and wash in the Pool of Siloam (9:7). This is the pool from which water was drawn for the procession at the Feast of Tabernacles (see on 7:37 above). It is a marvel of ancient Jewish engineering. The Gihon spring is one of Jerusalem's main water supplies, but it was in the Kidron valley outside the old fortified city. Therefore, when Jerusalem was threatened with attack in 701BC, Hezekiah cut a tunnel through the solid rock for over 500 metres to 'send' the water to a basin inside the walls, called Siloam or 'sent' (see 2 Kings 20:20; 2 Chron. 32:2–4,30; Is. 22:9–11). Now this man is sent to the pool of 'Sent' by the one who is himself sent by God to bring light and healing. Because the man is healed of being blind from birth by washing in the pool, many in the early church saw a reference to baptism in this story, and it would often be depicted as a baptism in art in the catacombs, as well as in the writings of people like Tertullian and Augustine. Whether John intended an allusion to baptism is not clear, but what is vital is that, unlike Naaman refusing to wash in the Jordan (2 Kings 5:10–12), the blind man obeyed his instruction: he was told to go and he went—and as a result he came back seeing (9:7).

Who, how and where?

The miracle, however, is not the end of the story—merely its beginning. Now the questions really start. The first is, 'Who is this man?' The blind man has been so changed, even transformed by his encounter with Jesus that his old neighbours are not sure if it is him (9:8–9). People do not expect change—and those who have been brought out of darkness through baptism into Christ are sometimes not recognized by their former acquaintances.

Some, though, will keep asking how it happened: 'how were your eyes opened?' (9:10). All the man can do is to tell his story of being anointed with mud and told to go and wash, and how his obedience led to receiving his sight (9:11). He does not know anything about his healer yet, as is shown by his reference to him as 'a man called Jesus'.

Naturally, people want to know where someone who can do this can be found, but the man is not afraid to admit, 'I don't know' (9:12). He has much to learn, but all he can do now is bear witness to what happened to him and confess his ignorance: Jesus has slipped quietly away again, and will not reappear until 9:35. In the meantime, as so often after a new spiritual experience, the man will have to face some questioning and opposition, yet through this he will grow in understanding what has happened to him.

PRAYER

'Man called Jesus', let me obey your instructions,
and wash me in your love, that I may see.

HEALING BRINGS OPPOSITION

The blind man's healing is only the start of this story. More important is what happens next, and everyone's reactions. After the bystanders' initial questioning, 'they lead him to the Pharisees' (9:13) as Jesus himself will be led to the authorities later (18:13). Their investigation forms the centrepiece of the whole story.

The man is now described as 'formerly blind' (9:13), but the problem is that he was healed on 'a Sabbath day', as when Jesus healed the paralysed man (9:14; see 5:9). Last time the paralytic's offence was to carry his mat on the Sabbath, and Jesus' was the work of healing. This time not only did he heal, but his actions breached various regulations. Ancient Jewish writings on the Sabbath forbid many things, including the work of kneading, carrying water, anointing eyes, and using saliva. Jesus' mixing of earth with saliva (a form of water), making clay, and putting it on the man's eyes would all have been unacceptable. So the Pharisees investigate carefully which rules were broken. The man, however, sticks to the simple facts of his story: 'he put clay on my eyes, I washed and I see' (9:15).

Division of opinion

Unfortunately, the 'simple facts' cause an immediate division. For those who concentrate on the importance of keeping the Sabbath, such unlawful actions show that Jesus cannot be 'from God' (9:16). Others look not at the Sabbath, but at the miraculous sign and disagree, using Nicodemus' earlier logic (see 3:2), for a sinner cannot do such things. Earlier there was a division, *schisma*, among the people at the Feast (7:43); now the same word appears, with a schism among the religious leaders (9:16). They ask the blind man's opinion, given that his eyes have been opened. He has moved from seeing his healer as 'the man called Jesus' to describing him as 'a prophet' (9:11, 17), like the Samaritan woman at the well when Jesus correctly identified her situation (4:19).

Out of the synagogue

While the man is making progress in his faith, the authorities are going the other way: 'the Jews did not believe' (9:18). The Pharisees are called "the Jews", as so often in John for Jesus' religious opponents. While they seemed to accept the healing (9:17), now they 'do not believe' and even doubt his blindness. Perhaps he was never blind or is lying—and so they check the story with his parents (9:19). There are indeed 'none so blind as those who will not see'. When our cherished views are threatened we will believe anything to avoid the terrifying consequences of change. The man's parents seem curt and frightened by the question; they confirm that he is their son and was indeed born blind (9:20), but they have 'no comment' on how it happened. They pass the buck: 'he's a big boy now—ask him' (9:21).

The writer explains that 'they were afraid of the Jews' (9:22), which is curious since the parents, the man, Jesus and everyone else involved are all Jews. Furthermore, these frightening "Jews" have 'already agreed' that anyone who 'confesses Jesus as Christ' should be put 'out of the synagogue'. This word, *aposynagogos*, occurs only here and in John 12:42 and 16:2 in the New Testament. Yet it did not stop Jesus and his disciples going to synagogue regularly in the gospels and in Acts. The threat makes more sense after the Jewish War and the destruction of Jerusalem and the temple by the Romans in AD 70. After Jewish faith and practice was regrouped around the synagogue at the Council of Yavneh in AD 85, 'the blessing against the heretics' in the services made it difficult for Jews who confessed Jesus as the Christ (see Introduction, p. 19).

Some scholars believe that John (like Matthew) is writing for people who have suffered the traumatic experience of being excommunicated, perhaps while their parents or families stood aside. This followed the opposition to Jesus and his followers in his own day (see Lk. 6:22). Perhaps, therefore, John is using this later technical term here to console those who have been healed by Jesus and come to faith in him—and who, like their master, suffer rejection from family, friends or religious community. This explains why this interrogation is at the centre of this story: as Christ was rejected so will all those like this man who were blind, but now can see.

PRAYER

Jesus, who suffered rejection for our sake, bless all who are rejected by their families or friends because of faith in you.

I WAS BLIND *but* NOW I SEE

The Jewish leaders' interrogation of the blind man's parents has not given them any answers, but it has confirmed their suspicion and doubts. Now, therefore, they call the man in for a second interrogation. It begins with their opening statement, 'Give glory to God' (9:24). In fact, they are not interested in giving glory to God for the man's healing. It is like Joshua's cross-examination of Achan: 'My son, give glory to the Lord God of Israel and make confession to him. Tell me now what you have done; do not hide it from me' (Josh. 7:19). In other words they are ordering the man to tell the truth, and stop lying about being blind and having been healed. Instead of being divided (9:16), now they are sure: the man is a liar, and 'we know' that Jesus is 'a sinner' (9:24).

The paradox of this chapter is that the more they push the man, the more he seems to understand about Jesus and what has happened in his healing. He has already moved from calling him a man to 'a prophet' (9:11, 17). Now he refuses to be drawn into a theological argument with them. He may not know much—but he wants really to give glory to God: 'one thing I do know: though I was blind, now I see' (9:25). This simple statement is the testimony of Christians down through the ages and across the world.

Whose disciples?

Faced with the man's continuing assertion of his healing, they go back to the same questions—what happened and how? (9:26). They follow the age old police method, getting him to repeat his story in the hope of catching him out. The man, however, gets exasperated and refuses to tell the story again, replying instead with some wonderfully sardonic comments. He pretends not to understand why they want to hear it again, unless it is because 'you want to become his disciples' (9:27). Not surprisingly, this suggestion leads them to abuse him but in their opposition they inadvertently take him a step further in his pilgrimage: it's you who are that fellow's disciple—the 'his' is very dismissive (9:28). They contrast his poor discipleship with their pride as 'disciples of Moses'. The argument about Jesus' healing of the paralytic soon became a contrast between Jesus and Moses (see on 5:45 above), and the same happens here. After all, they note, 'we know' that God spoke with Moses (9:29), as the Old Testament says, 'face to face, as one speaks to a friend' (Exod. 33:11; see also Num. 12:8). In contrast to what 'we know' about Moses, they know nothing about Jesus, not even where he comes from, as in the previous debate about Jesus' origins at the Feast of Tabernacles (7:27; 8:14).

Cast out

As the opponents' view of Jesus goes down even further, so the man grows in both faith and confidence. With marvellous irony, he applauds this 'astonishing thing'—that Jesus can open a blind man's eyes and the religious authorities don't even know where he comes from! (9:30). He reminds them of what he and they both know, that 'God does not listen to sinners' but only to those who worship him and obey his will (9:31). This is common right across the Old Testament: 'the Lord is far from the wicked, but he hears the prayer of the righteous' (Prov. 15:29, see also, Pss. 34:15; 66:18; 145:19; Job 27:9; Is. 1:15). What has happened is unique; as we saw on 9:2 above, no one in the Old Testament heals blindness from birth (9:32). Therefore, reasons the man, 'the man called Jesus' is not just 'a prophet' (9:11, 17), but must be someone 'who worships God and obeys his will' (9:31). And so he concludes, 'if this man were not from God, he could do nothing' (9:33). This is all too much for the leaders; they are quite certain about what 'we know', and are not about to tolerate lessons in basic theology from someone like this. In their downward journey, they have reached the position the disciples assumed at the start (see 9:2), that the man was 'born entirely in sin'—thus tacitly admitting that he is not lying and was born blind. As such, they refuse to be taught by him, but reject him and cast him out from the synagogue and community of faith (9:34).

So this blind man becomes an example for John's original readers, who may have suffered a similar fate, and a challenge to us. Are we prepared to stand up for what Jesus has done for us—even under hard questioning and threats of rejection?

PRAYER

*'Amazing grace, how sweet the sound, that saved a wretch like me
I once was lost, but now am found, was blind, but now I see'.*
John Newton, converted slave trader (1725–1807)

51

JESUS BRINGS *both* SIGHT & BLINDNESS

The extraordinary thing is that Jesus has been missing for most of the story, ever since he told the man to wash in the Pool of Siloam (9:7). But, although Jesus has been off stage, his presence has been very real as the characters on stage—the Pharisees, blind man and parents—have all been discussing him. Now that is all over, and the blind man is left alone, abandoned at the edge of the empty stage—precisely when Jesus chooses to reappear, having heard that the man had been excommunicated, 'cast out' (9:35). Someone 'cast out' should be shunned and ignored by others for the punishment to work—but not by Jesus. In his divine compassion, he comes and finds the man rejected by his community and abandoned by his parents (cf. Ps. 27:9–10).

In this way, Jesus fulfils his earlier promise that 'anyone who comes to me, I will not cast out' (6:37), where the words 'cast out' are the same as what the religious leaders did to this man (9:34). This, too, is the testimony of others rejected for Christ—such as the Romanian pastor, Richard Wurmbrand in solitary confinement in a Communist prison, or Dietrich Bonhoeffer in a Nazi camp—that Jesus comes to find those who remain loyal to him. He did exactly the same for the paralysed man after he had been investigated for carrying his mat on the Sabbath (5:14). However, after Jesus came and revealed himself to that man, he promptly went and 'shopped' Jesus, telling the authorities who he was (5:15). The blind man, however, has had more than enough of them already—and now he is ready for the final stage of his journey into the light of faith.

Lord, I believe

When he has found him, Jesus asks the man if he believes 'in the Son of Man' (9:35). Again, the verb, *pisteuein*, does not mean 'believe in the existence of', but to trust in Jesus. The man has progressed towards faith, but now needs more explanation to believe and trust—who is he? (9:36). He can see physically and is beginning to make out spiritual things—but he is not quite able to see spiritually yet.

This time Jesus does not need to 'send' him anywhere else to open his eyes, but only to reveal himself. In fact, the man has seen him with his newly opened eyes—it is 'the one speaking to you' (9:37). This phrase is the same as Jesus used to reveal himself to the Samaritan woman (4:26). As she progressed from seeing Jesus as 'a prophet' to wondering if he might be the Christ (4:19, 29), so now the blind man finally realizes who has healed him. From calling Jesus 'a man' (9:11), through 'a prophet' (9:17) to 'a worshipper of God' who has come 'from God' (9:31–33), now he proclaims 'Lord, I believe', and he worships him (9:38). Here is the real miracle, the real giving of sight. Physical sight may have come at the Pool but spiritual insight comes from the one who created eyes in the first place.

Light and darkness

After Jesus revealed himself to the paralytic, the debate centred on judgment (see on 5:19–29 above). So now Jesus warns that his coming into the world brings judgment (9:39). The divisions among the authorities are only a foretaste. Jesus' coming may enable those who do not see to be able to see, but the inevitable corollary is that those who refuse to see become blind. Some Pharisees wonder about this: 'Surely we are not blind, are we?' (9:40). The Greek construction is a question expecting the answer 'no'. They may be being sarcastic, but perhaps it is a genuine enquiry. If so, says Jesus, then they have no sin or guilt. Genuine blindness can be excused—but a deliberate, perverse refusal to see is culpable (9:41). To claim to see, to keep stressing, as they have done, that 'we know' everything while refusing to see what is front of our eyes is to put ourselves beyond help, for only those who know they are blind can receive healing, and only those who admit their sin can accept forgiveness.

In many ways, this encounter sums up all the others with Nicodemus, the Samaritan woman, the paralytic, the crowd—for here we have a full response, unlike the partial ones so far. To the ignorant and blind, Jesus can bring light. The more 'we know', the more we cling to our way of seeing the universe, the deeper into darkness we fall. The coming of light into darkness creates shadows. It is not his purpose, for Jesus was not sent to condemn the world, but it is an inevitable result when people love darkness rather than light (3:17–19).

PRAYER

Lord Jesus, I believe;
heal my blindness and bring me into your light.

52

I AM *the* DOOR

The first half of John's gospel, chapters 1—10, covers Jesus' miraculous 'signs', his teaching and the debates which followed in Galilee and Jerusalem. After an interlude at Bethany (11:1—12:11), Jesus comes to Jerusalem for his last week, arrest and death (12:12—20:31). This chapter draws together the threads from the first half and prepares us for the shift towards Jesus' passion.

Since John the Baptist first identified Jesus (1:29), Jesus has met various people—the first disciples, people in Cana and in the temple, Nicodemus, the Samaritan woman, the lame man, the hungry crowd in the desert, the worshippers at the Feast of Tabernacles in Jerusalem, the woman taken in adultery and the blind man. Sometimes these meetings have been accompanied by signs, but they have all discussed who Jesus is. The people Jesus met and the bystanders have had differing reactions, with some believing and others dismissing him, but increasingly these discussions have brought him into conflict with the religious leaders. In the last story, the blind man came to full faith in Jesus, but the authorities have excommunicated him.

Is this what true leadership of God's people means—casting them out? Who are the right leaders anyway, those who believe in Jesus or those who oppose him? As events have unfolded, we have gone through various Jewish feasts, and now the Feast of the Dedication is near, when the Jews celebrated the leadership of the Maccabeans (see on 10:22). The typical Old Testament image for the people and their leaders is that of sheep and shepherds (e.g. Ezek. 34). So this chapter picks up this image as its theme to bring to a climax all the issues of the first half about Jesus' identity, his witnesses, and what it means to believe in him.

Most of ancient Israel-Palestine was rough stony pasture land, rather than rich agricultural fields, so the wandering shepherd and his flock was very common. Sheep were kept more for their wool than for meat, and the shepherd would herd them over several years, caring for them, feeding them and protecting them from dangers. All of these images appear here.

The door to the sheepfold

We begin with a 'figure of speech' (10:6), an image involving a door or gate, some sheep and a shepherd in 10:1–5, each of which will feature in turn through the chapter. It is more of a word-picture than a story but it is the nearest John has to the parables in the other gospels, which often feature sheep and shepherds. In our society, the shepherd and his flock is not a common sight, yet pastoral imagery is used a lot, especially in caring professions such as the church and social services, and in 'pastoral care' found in universities, colleges and schools.

We begin with the entrance to 'the sheepfold', the *aule*, a yard or enclosure where the sheep are kept, especially at night. Doors and gates are for those who have the right to enter, as when the Psalmist sings of the 'gates of righteousness ... the gate of the Lord' through which 'the righteous shall enter' (Ps. 118:19–20). However, thieves and robbers do not use the door, but climb in some other way (10:1–2). The door of a sheepfold admits only sheep and shepherds.

Protection from danger

The door thus gives protection for the sheep. The gatekeeper only opens it to the shepherd and the sheep are not frightened by his entry. They know his voice. Because he kept them for years, the shepherd would identify them by names like 'black-ear', 'whitey' and so on. Even today, travellers tell stories of shepherds calling their sheep by name and by the sound of their voice out from a fold where several different flocks are together. Also, in the east, the sheep follow the shepherd, rather than being driven from behind (10:4). Like good school-children, they will not 'go with strangers', but only those they know (10:5). The blind man, who could not see at all, had to respond to the voice of Jesus and follow what he said, but the religious leaders thought Jesus was just a stranger whom they did not know (9:7, 29). Not surprisingly, therefore, they do not understand this figure of speech (10:6). So Jesus has to spell it out, 'I am the door of the sheep'; he is the way to safety and salvation (10:7). Unlike the thieves and robbers, and the false leaders, he will not cast out, but save and protect all those who hear his voice and respond.

PRAYER

Lord Jesus, door to salvation, may I hear your voice;
call my name and enter through you to eternal life.

I AM *the* GOOD SHEPHERD

In a pastoral society like ancient Israel, sheep and shepherds were used to describe the relationship of God with his people: 'the Lord is my shepherd' and 'we are his people, the sheep of his pasture' (Pss. 23:1; 100:3). Good leaders were 'shepherds of the people', such as David (2 Sam. 5:2; Ps. 78:71) but when he had Uriah killed and took his wife, he was exposed as a bad shepherd by Nathan the prophet (2 Sam. 12:1–7). The prophets denounced Israel's leaders as bad shepherds who do not care for their sheep (e.g. Ezek. 34; Jer. 23:1; 50:6; Zech. 11).

Pasture and life

So when the Jewish leaders treat people as they did the blind man, casting them out rather than caring for them, Jesus turns to the image of the shepherd. At Passover he used the bread of life (6:35, 51) and at Tabernacles, the living water and the light of life (7:37–38; 8:12). In this 'I am' saying, he calls himself the door for the sheep (10:7). 'All who came before me', the religious leaders, 'are thieves and bandits', and the sheep, like the blind man, will not listen to them (10:8). Thieves and robbers come to steal, but Jesus comes to provide: whoever enters through him as the door will find safety inside and they can go in and out to feed (10:9). A shepherd would lie across the entrance to a fold, to allow only his sheep to go in, and to watch them when they came out. So Jesus is the entrance to life, to 'preserve your going out and your coming in forever' (Ps. 121:8). While thieves come to kill the sheep and destroy life, Jesus comes to bring life 'in all its abundance' (10:10). The leaders rejected the blind man, destroying his hopes of life within their community, but Jesus gave him new life of physical sight and faith.

The shepherd's sacrifice for his sheep

The focus moves from the door to the shepherd, as the next 'I am' follows immediately: 'I am the good shepherd' (10:11). The word for good, *kalos*, included notions of beauty and loveliness. The good shepherd not only gives life instead of stealing it, but the life he gives is his own, laid down for the sake of the sheep. This is a contrast with the behaviour of a hireling: since he does not own the sheep, he does not care about them when danger threatens (10:12–13). The behaviour of the leaders to the blind man when they were threatened by his healing shows that they are only hirelings at best, not shepherds.

Jesus, however, is the good shepherd, who knows his own sheep as they also know him (10:14). Shepherds called their sheep out of the fold by their names and the flock followed their voice (10:3–4). The Greek word for church literally means 'called out', *ec-clesia*, from which all our 'ecclesiastical' words are derived. Jesus' knowledge of his sheep is rooted in his knowledge of his Father and his Father's knowing him as his Son. And because the nature of God's love is always self-giving, the good shepherd lays down his life for his sheep (10:15). What is more, God's love is universal, so the shepherd must also be concerned for 'other sheep ... not of this fold', who also will hear his voice and be brought together into one flock (10:16). In contrast to the religious leaders' concern to maintain their pure group and throw the blind man out, the good shepherd wants to include all people. While Jesus' debate has been mostly with "the Jews", the Samaritans have already realized that this is 'the Saviour of the World' (4:42) and the universal implications of the death of the shepherd will soon be stressed (11:52; 12:32). As we move towards the Passion, the inevitable result of his clash with the authorities, Jesus emphasizes that he lays down his life willingly, out of sheer love for his people, a love which flows even from the heart of God (10:17–18).

This is a challenge to all involved in the pastoral care of God's people. It takes time and effort to know everyone individually, even as God knows us, and caring for them as Christ laid down his life for us may demand the ultimate sacrifice. The ordination charge for priests in the Church of England says 'as servant and shepherd ... set the Good Shepherd always before you as the pattern of your calling ... to search for his children in the wilderness of this world's temptations ... the treasure now to be entrusted to you is Christ's own flock'. This is true whether we are an Archbishop or a bible study group leader, a minister or just visiting an elderly person around the corner—we love others as the good shepherd loves us.

PRAYER

Good shepherd, bless all those in pastoral care, that
they may live out your self-sacrificial love for your sheep.

135

TELL US PLAINLY

The words of the good shepherd once more cause a 'division' among "the Jews" (10:19). Again we have the word for *schism*, which happened first to the people and then the leaders (7:43; 9:16). And so this division sums up so many attitudes throughout the first half of this gospel. On the one hand, some oppose Jesus and accuse him of having a demon and being mad, so people should not listen to him (10:20). This accusation of demon possession has been made both by the people and by the Jewish leaders (7:20; 8:48, 52). On the other hand, others point out that neither his words nor his miraculous actions are demonic (10:21). This argument from what Jesus says and does was first noted by Nicodemus, and repeated by the Samaritan woman, by the five thousand, by the crowd in Jerusalem, by some Pharisees and the blind man (3:2; 4:29; 6:14; 7:31; 9:16, 33). The two sides are clear—so now the question must be answered plainly.

Dedication and light

The showdown takes place as we come to the Feast of the Dedication, or Hanukkah (10:22). While all the other feasts reflect the early history of the Jews, this was relatively recent. During the Graeco-Syrian control of Israel in the second century, Antiochus Epiphanes desecrated the temple in 167BC with a pagan altar and sacrifices of pigs in his attempt to impose Hellenistic culture and end Jewish faith and practice. After the successful rebellion led by Judas Maccabeus, the temple was rededicated with proper sacrifice on 25 Khislev 164BC and the Feast of the Dedication was thus instituted (see 1 Macc. 4:36–59; 2 Macc. 10:1–8). It was kept for eight days at the winter solstice and the custom of putting eight lights in the window, still observed by Jews today, gives it its other name of the Festival of Lights.

The festival's stress on the zeal of good leaders, like the Maccabees, contrasts with the bad shepherds' treatment of the blind man (9:34), while the Lights remind us of Jesus, the light of the world (8:12; 9:5). The setting in the temple porticoes (10:23) recall the other debates in the temple (2:13–22; 7:14–44; 8:12–59), as well as the healing of the paralysed man and the woman taken in adultery (5:14; 8:1–12). In this final confrontation, John brings all that has happened to a climax. In the darkness of winter, Jesus, the Light of the World and the Good Shepherd, the true leader of God's people, comes to the temple, not just to rededicate it, but to replace it as he offers the ultimate sacrifice of laying down his own life. Later, this connection was strengthened by celebrating the birth of Jesus on 25th December, the same month as Khislev.

The identity of Jesus

The stage is set: "the Jews" can stand the suspense no longer and want to know if Jesus is the Christ (10:24). 'Tell us plainly' uses the same word, *parresia*, as Jesus' brothers' request to show himself 'openly' (7:4). The debate about Jesus' identity has been going on from the Pharisees' first questions to John the Baptist (1:19–28) to their discussions of 7:25–31, 40–42. In fact, Jesus has revealed himself to the Samaritan woman and the blind man (4:25; 9:35). However, in answer to the authorities' direct questions (8:25, 53), he referred them to how his works witness to who he is (see on 5:30–47; 7:14–44; 8:12–59). He reminds them of this now; if only they had had faith, they would have believed and realized who he is (10:25). That they do not know him or recognize his voice shows that they do not belong to his sheep, picking up the earlier shepherd image (10:26–27).

Those who hear Jesus' voice, follow him and receive the gift of eternal life (10:28). In the figure of the shepherd and the door, Jesus offered protection to his sheep (10:3, 9). He demonstrated this by shielding the woman taken in adultery from stoning and by going to find the blind man when he had been cast out (8:7; 9:35). Thieves and robbers come to destroy life and wolves 'snatch' sheep (10:10, 12), but no one can 'snatch' Jesus' sheep or cause them to perish (10:28; see 6:37–39). This is because their security is based on the greatness of God the Father himself and none can snatch anything from him (10:29). Thus the sheep's protection is rooted in the relationship of Jesus and his Father, as was his knowledge of them (see 10:15 above). And that relationship is so close that it alone can provide the answer to the question of "the Jews" about Jesus' identity, as he finally replies 'plainly': 'the Father and I are one' (10:30).

PRAYER

Lord Jesus Christ, revelation of the Father,
help me to hear your voice and keep me safe in your hand.

The FATHER & I ARE ONE

The debates between Jesus and "the Jews" about his identity have revealed much about his relationship with God. After healing the paralysed man, Jesus called God his Father, saying that he could only do what his Father wanted; in turn, the Father shares with the Son his authority to give life and exercise judgment (5:18–47). Similarly, during the Bread of Life discussion, Jesus stressed his origins with God the Father (6:37–40). The argument at the Feast of Tabernacles concerned whether Abraham, the devil or God was the Father of either Jesus or "the Jews" (8:39–59). The desire of the Good Shepherd to lay down his life for the sheep comes from his Father (10:17–18). Thus it is no surprise that the first half of the gospel comes to a climax with Jesus' ringing declaration, 'the Father and I are one' (10:30).

The word 'one' is the neuter pronoun, *hen*, implying something like 'the Father and I are a unity'—in action, purpose, power, authority—rather than the masculine personal pronoun, *heis*, meaning 'one and the same person'. This interpretation is borne out in 10:38, 'the Father is in me, and I am in the Father'. This verse was used in the third and fourth century controversies about the exact nature of the relationship of the Father and Son, but philosophical debate was not John's concern here. At the end of the first half of his gospel, he stresses the unity of the Father and the Son as the basis for all Jesus says and does. In the second half of the gospel, this unity will be the basis for the relationship of believers with each other and with Jesus himself, 'even as we are one' (see on 15:9–10 and 17:11, 21–23). The sheep's relationship with the Good Shepherd depends totally upon the Shepherd's relationship with God his Father (10:29–30).

Stoning for blasphemy

Having asked for 'plain speaking', "the Jews" find this revelation of Jesus' relationship with God too much, and they 'took up stones to stone him' (10:31). Previous debates also ended in attempts to kill Jesus (5:17–18; 7:19–20; 8:59), so this response to a direct claim is predictable. Nonetheless, the Good (*kalos*) Shepherd asks which of the many 'good' (*kala*) works he has done 'from the Father' has prompted this response (10:32). Before, Jesus' offence, officially at least, has been things he has done, and when he has done them, on the Sabbath (5:16; 9:14–16). "The Jews" reply that things have moved beyond that, from what he has *done*, to who he claims to *be*: for 'a human being to make yourself God' is to commit blasphemy (10:33). The penalty in the Law is death by stoning (Lev. 24:16), so they have no alternative.

Jesus' defence against the charge

Jesus' defence is in two brief parts. First, he notes that other human beings are called 'gods', 'written in your law' (10:34). Human judges are called 'gods', even though they are unjust and failing in their task (Ps. 82:6). If they can be termed 'gods' by the 'word of God' because judgment is entrusted to them by God, how much more can one whom the Father has sent into the world? Secondly, Jesus is not 'making himself God'; it is God, who has 'consecrated' him. At this Feast of the Dedication, is it blasphemy for the 'dedicated one' to call himself 'the Son of God'? (10:35–36). Of course, words are easy, but his actions, the works of the Good Shepherd in protecting, healing and feeding God's people, show his relationship with God, which can only be described as 'the Father is in me and I am in the Father' (10: 37–38). The works witness to Jesus' identity *and* his relationship with God.

Withdrawal across the Jordan

The previous attempts to arrest or kill Jesus failed because 'his hour had not yet come' (7:30, 44; 8:20, 59). So now, this final stoning comes to nothing, as Jesus slips away (10:39). However, the time for his arrest is drawing near, and now that his public ministry has reached its climax, he withdraws 'across the Jordan', back where it all started (10:40). This balances the beginning of the gospel with John the Baptist (1:28; 3:26) and brings the first half to a close. John did no miraculous signs, but through all these intervening chapters, Jesus has demonstrated that the Baptist's witness was true. Despite the 'schism' in the people, nonetheless many do believe (10:42). After all the opposition of the authorities, the last note is one of faith, that Jesus and the Father 'are one'.

PRAYER

Father God, may I believe 'all that John said is true'
and share in your unity and love with your Son.

56

The ONE YOU LOVE IS ILL

Chapter 10 finished Jesus' public ministry back across the Jordan, where it all began with John the Baptist, and ended all the debates with the religious leaders. Since the division between those who believe and those who oppose Jesus is clear, we might expect to go straight into the passion narrative, Jesus' last week in Jerusalem, his arrest, trial and death. In the other gospels, this is exactly what happens, as the temple episode provokes the hostility of the leaders.

John, however, has already used the temple incident at the start of Jesus' ministry to show him replacing Judaism (2:13–22). Instead, therefore, he has an interlude at the centre of his gospel, a 'hinge' around which everything turns from the ministry to the passion, with one final sign to add up to the perfect seven. So far we have had six: water into wine, healing an official's son, healing the paralysed man, the miraculous feeding, walking on water and healing the blind man (2:1–11; 4:46–54; 5:1–14; 6:1–14, 16–21; 9:1–12). This seventh sign has links to the others, especially the first, but it is also different. Unusually, the person is named, while all the others are anonymous. The miracle only happens at the end of the story, and any discussion takes place en route, unlike the usual pattern of the sign described briefly first, leading into debate about its meaning and Jesus' identity. All of that is now taken for granted. Instead, John gives us his longest single story before the passion narrative itself—a beautiful preparation which raises the question of death. As the use of the story in funerals shows, it has the theme of life from death, but only at the cost of Jesus preparing to move from life to death, to lay down his life for his sheep.

God is my help

After all the unnamed people, the names 'Lazarus of Bethany' are significant. Lazarus is the Greek version of the Hebrew Eleazar, meaning 'God is my help' (a son of Aaron, see Exod. 6:23–25), while Bethany means 'house of affliction'. The affliction is that Lazarus is ill (11:1). John expects his readers to know Lazarus' sisters, Mary and Martha. Mary is identified in a 'flash forward' as 'the one who anointed the Lord with perfume', but that story is yet to come (12:1–3). The sisters send a simple message for 'God to help': 'Lord, the one whom you love is ill' (11:3). It is enough to identify their brother, and the evangelist stresses this love (11:5). Some commentators identify Lazarus with 'the disciple Jesus loved', mentioned several times later (see 13:23; 19:26; 20:2; 21:7, 20). This is unlikely, since Lazarus is named and appears only here, while the unnamed disciple is part of Jesus' central group (21:2).

Notice how they simply tell Jesus the problem, that Lazarus is ill, and leave it at that. No requests are made, nor instructions given, just as the mother of Jesus told him 'they have no wine' (2:3). Many of us find it difficult in prayer just to tell Jesus the situation—and how easily we instruct God what to do! Jesus' response is again unexpected, like the apparent rebuff he gave his mother (2:4). Now he states that this illness is not fatal, but 'for the glory of God' (11:4). This does not mean that God is sadistically causing it for his glory, but that his Son will be glorified through it, as happened with the blind man (9:3). However, for Jesus 'to be glorified' entails suffering and death (see 7:39), and this phrase will recur several times (12:16, 23; 13:31).

Love and absence

Finally, John says that 'Jesus loved Martha and her sister and Lazarus' (11:5), which is necessary because of what happens next. Our reaction to such news would be to rush straight there—yet Jesus delays for another two days (11:6). John even connects these two verses with a 'therefore', which many translations omit because it seems so strange to wait when someone we love is ill. Some scholars explain this delay by referring either to Jesus' own three days in a tomb, or to the rabbinic belief that the soul waited around the body for three days before finally departing, but this does not help much. What John shows is that, as with Mary's request about the wine (2:4) or Jesus' brothers' suggestion about revealing himself in Jerusalem (7:2–10), so here too Jesus takes his own initiative in his own time and acts when he is ready, hard though that may be for us to understand. How do we cope when someone we love is ill? Can we find the courage to tell God about them, and then be patient when he seems to do nothing?

PRAYER

O God our help, when those we love are ill
give us courage to pray and patience to wait with you.

57

LAZARUS IS ASLEEP

After the unexplained delay for two days, Jesus tells his disciples that they are returning to Judaea (11:7). Not surprisingly, they are rather taken aback by this—they have all just escaped from there. As they remind Jesus, 'the Jews were just now trying to stone you', referring to the outcome of the final debate with the religious leaders (11:8; see 10:31, 39).

Walk in the day

Jesus' reply seems rather odd at first since it has nothing to do with Lazarus. It is another 'figure of speech', about walking in the day or in the night. Jesus said something similar to the disciples when they asked him about the blind man's condition; then he reminded them that he had work to do as the 'light of the world' (9:4–5). The ancients divided the day from sunrise to sunset into twelve hours. Jesus says that this gives plenty of light to walk in and no need to worry about stumbling; it is those who walk around at night, in the pitch darkness of a society without street lighting, who trip over (11:9–10). This is all very well, but how does it answer their concerns about being stoned? At the surface level, Jesus is reminding them that God's timing is sufficient. The fact that there are twelve hours means there is no need to rush or panic, but also that there is only a fixed time, with none to waste for God's work. At the spiritual level, however, the disciples are still blundering around in darkness of not understanding what is going on, while Jesus is walking in the light of God's day and sees all too clearly the darkness of his final struggle with evil coming soon. He must act, and act now.

Sleep, death or life?

Therefore he explains why they must leave the safety of their refuge across the Jordan and go back into the dangers of Judaea: 'our friend Lazarus has fallen asleep' (11:11). Here Jesus is using a euphemism for death which was common in the ancient world, and is still used today. The Greek word used here gives us our word 'cemetery', the 'sleeping place', for those who sleep in Christ (see 1 Cor. 15:6; 1 Thess. 4:14). As so often in John, the disciples take this simply at the surface level; if Lazarus is asleep, he does not need Jesus to wake him, for he will recover by himself (11:12). Once again we are reminded of previous misunderstandings like Nicodemus talking about wombs (3:3–8), the Samaritan woman asking about buckets for water (4:10–15), or the multitude wanting bread from heaven (6:32–34). In each case, they were thinking on the surface at the physical level, and had to be helped by Jesus through to the deeper, spiritual meaning. This is only the first of several misunderstandings in this chapter, and so Jesus has to spell it out for them 'plainly', using the same word as he was asked to speak by "the Jews" in 10:24: 'Lazarus is dead' (11:14).

To die with him

After breaking the news of their friend's death first euphemistically, then bluntly, Jesus seems to fall back into the apparent callousness which made him wait two days when he first heard of Lazarus' illness: 'for your sake I'm glad I was not there' (11:15). The obvious reason for this is that he would have then been asked to cure Lazarus when he was ill, whereas now the bigger miracle of raising him from death will help the disciples to 'believe'. Hard though this may be for us to understand, let alone the disciples, we seem to be back to the mystery of God's timing again.

However, the disciples have not even got that far. They are still thinking that to return to Judaea is simply suicide, as Thomas' remark demonstrates (11:16). Thomas' character as the one who wants it all explained at the basic level before he will believe will emerge more and more through the next few chapters (see 14:5; 20:24–29). For the moment, he sounds more like a donkey, depressed and stubborn —like Winnie the Pooh's friend Eeyore: 'let's go and die with him'. At least this wonderfully morose comment shows that he is committed to the end—even if he thinks it is to die. The irony, of course, is that only Jesus will die—and his death will mean that they will all live, including Thomas and Lazarus and all who 'sleep in Christ'.

PRAYER

Lord, when I am asleep wake me,
and when I misunderstand, tell me plainly.

YOUR BROTHER WILL RISE AGAIN

It would probably have been a two day journey back across the Jordan to Bethany, a small village on the edge of Jerusalem. Jesus' delay of two days plus the journey means that when he arrives Lazarus is not only dead and buried, but has been in his tomb for four days (11:17). This may be another allusion to the rabbinic idea that the soul would wait for three days until it saw from the change in colour of the face that decomposition had started, and then depart. The evangelist is making sure that there is no doubt about Lazarus being really dead—no nonsense about him having been ill and merely revived in the cool of the tomb!

The two mile journey from Jerusalem to Bethany is quite easy, and today many pilgrims and tourists travel to this little village, now called El 'Azariyeh, after Lazarus. Lazarus would have been buried on the day of his death, as is the custom in hot climates, and the usual mourning rituals would have followed. Thus 'many of the Jews' came to console Mary and Martha (11:19). Here the phrase does not mean the religious opponents of Jesus, but probably inhabitants of Jerusalem, given its proximity. After the processions to the tomb with public displays of grief and the burial, the family would keep the practice of sitting in the house mourning, accompanied by friends and well wishers.

Martha confronts Jesus

Now John gives us a little glimpse of the two bereaved sisters. They are known also from Luke 10:38–42, where Martha was busy with her domestic tasks while Mary sat at Jesus' feet listening like a disciple. So now, Mary is 'sitting in the house' keeping the mourning. Martha, the active one here also, wants to do something and as soon as she hears of Jesus' approach, she stops sitting mourning to go and meet him (11:20). However, it is not so easy to leave her loss behind and her first words are typical of someone in grief: 'if you had been here, my brother would not have died' (11:21). 'If only I hadn't' ... 'if only she had' ... are common comments from the bereaved—then my loved one would still be alive. In the initial stages of the shock, we still cannot believe it and want it all to have been different. This may manifest itself as guilt, blaming oneself for doing or not doing something. Alternatively, it may be anger, blaming someone else instead, as here. Martha rushes not to greet Jesus but to reproach him. Why didn't he come earlier and cure Lazarus? Perhaps she has even worked out that he must have delayed somewhere (11:6). In her pain, her first words are those of anger and criticism.

Resurrection—now or then?

As so often with grief, her mood quickly changes, to a wistful expression of hope, or even faith; 'even now', she believes, whatever Jesus asks, 'God will give you' (11:22). We are reminded again of the wedding at Cana and the instruction of Jesus' mother to the servants, despite his rebuff, that they should do 'whatever he says' (2:5). Jesus gives no answer to Martha's reproach, but offers her the promise 'your brother will rise again' (11:23). As often in John, it can be understood on at least two levels. Is this answering her half-expressed wish for a miracle, offering her some hope now, or is it just the sympathetic consolation of a conventional belief in a future resurrection which any Jew might offer?

John's usual multi-level approach would lead us to expect the conventional surface meaning to be understood first and then the other only later, and this is what happens. Martha certainly takes it as conventional sympathy and gives the automatic religious response, 'I know he will rise again in the resurrection on the last day' (11:24). Such a belief in a future resurrection on the last day begins to appear towards the end of Old Testament times (see Dan. 12:2) and was commonly held by groups like the Pharisees in Jesus' day, although not by the Sadducees (see Mk. 12:18, Acts 23:6–9). But behind her resignation in what is almost a platitude, we can almost hear her screaming, 'but what about *now*? It hurts too much to wait to the last day!'

For many of us, when faced with a grieving person's pain or anger, the temptation is strong to assuage it with conventional beliefs and expressions of sympathy when perhaps we should just be quiet. But it is much more worrying when God seems to offer some hope for us *now* in response to our prayers. Can we open ourselves to that possibility—or do we quash the idea quick with a religious platitude?

PRAYER

*Lord Jesus, help me to hope in you for the future
and open my life to you here and now.*

59 JOHN 11:24–33

I AM *the* RESURRECTION & *the* LIFE

Martha expresses her belief in the conventional view, that her brother 'will rise again in the resurrection on the last day' (11:24). According to this, everything to do with eschatology—judgment, death, life—all are in the future at the End of time. Such 'future eschatology' is clearly expressed in passages such as 5:25–29 (see notes above). Jesus' response both confirms and challenges that. In this magnificent saying, all the other 'I am' sayings now come together: Jesus can claim to be the 'bread of life', 'light of life', the 'door' and the 'good shepherd' who brings 'life in all its abundance' (6:35; 8:12; 10:7, 10–11) only because he can also say, 'I am the resurrection and the life' and thus give Martha some hope (11:25). The two words are not synonymous: the 'resurrection' is what will happen at the End, and 'life' is what we will be raised to, as well as what we experience now.

Suddenly, Martha's conventional belief in a future resurrection at the last day is turned inside out. The Resurrection and the End are here, now, in this person before her. Any resurrection in the future will be through Jesus—and will depend on people's belief in him: 'those who believe' in him will live, 'even though they die', and what's more, 'everyone who lives and believes in me' will have something even more amazing, they 'will never die' (11:26). All the verbs are still future—'will live'—yet there is a daring hint about the present with 'will never die'. Jesus has already promised that anyone who believes in him 'will not come to judgment, but has passed from death to life' and 'will never see death' (5:24; 8:51). This is a stupendous claim when death is all too present, with Lazarus four days in his tomb.

Yes, Lord, I believe

After this extraordinary statement, Jesus asks Martha, 'do you believe this?' (11:26). Martha's confession of faith picks up all the key descriptions of Jesus so far. After the gradual progress towards faith made by the other individuals leading up to the blind man's 'Lord, I believe' (9:38), now we have the full set: 'I believe that you are the Christ, the Son of God, the one coming into the world' (11:27). John began with the Pharisees' questioning John the Baptist to see if he is the Christ (1:19) and continued with Jesus' revelations to the first disciples, the Samaritan woman and the blind man (1:41; 4:26; 9:37). Equally, the phrase 'Son of God' has recurred regularly from John the Baptist's original witness and Nathanael's first steps of faith to the final debate with the religious leaders (1:34, 49; 10:36). The light and the prophet which were both 'coming into the world' (1:9; 6:14) are now here, Martha says. It is a most comprehensive expression of faith in all that Jesus is, the female version of Peter's confession (see on 6:69).

Mary at Jesus' feet

Mary, however, is still back in the house, sitting at her mourning ritual; Martha tells her 'privately' of Jesus' arrival, so that she can go for a quiet word with him (11:28). In Luke's story, Mary was sitting at Jesus' feet (Lk. 10:39); now she gets up from sitting alone in her grief and comes to fall at his feet (11:29, 32). Jesus is not yet at the house, or even the village; he is still where Martha met him, out on the road where the tombs would have been, since they were not allowed in towns or villages (11:30). When the Jews see her leave the house and the village, they follow, assuming she is going to the tomb 'to weep', to undertake yet more mourning (11:31). There will be not much chance of Mary's quiet word with Jesus! Undeterred by their accompanying stares, Mary comes to Jesus and 'kneels at his feet'. Perhaps she is taking up the disciple's position at the master's feet she adopted before; or maybe it is in an attitude of supplication or worship? Whatever is implied by her action, her words are the same as her sister's—the reproach of faith, 'if you had been here, my brother would not have died' (11:32). This time, Jesus does not respond with conventional expressions of sympathy or probing questions of faith, as he did with Martha. Mary's distraught position at his feet answers all those already. When he sees her grief, all Jesus can do is also to be 'deeply moved in spirit and troubled' (11:33). Sometimes, 'to weep with those who weep' is not only all we can do, but also the best we can offer.

PRAYER

Lord Jesus Christ, Son of God,
the resurrection and the life of all who put their trust in you
let me come to kneel at your feet and worship you.

LAZARUS, COME OUT!

When Jesus saw them weeping, his only response was to weep, as anyone who cared about Lazarus and his family might (11:33). Yet the words used to describe his emotions are much more than that. The first, *en-brimo*, is used in Greek of horses, 'snorting in the nostrils'. Elsewhere in the New Testament it conveys anger and indignation, when rebuking someone (Matt. 9:30; Mk. 1:43; 14:5). Some scholars wonder who Jesus can be angry with, and suggest he is rebuking the Jews or the others for a lack of faith, or even angry at death itself. Yet anger is part of grief, as we saw with Mary and Martha's reproach of Jesus (11:21, 32). The other word here, *tarasso*, means to be disturbed or troubled (used also of Jesus in 12:27, 13:21). Together, this phrase conveys the strength of Jesus' feeling; he was 'shuddering, shaking with emotions', grief, anger, pain, hurt, and a desire to do something. Like many bereaved people, he wants to see 'the one he loved', and asks where he has been laid (11:34). Then comes the Bible's shortest verse, 'Jesus wept' (11:35). Christians do not believe in a remote God, on a cloud where all is sweetness and light, without passions or feelings, as the Greeks did and many today still do. In Jesus, God has experienced the depths of the human condition, including pain, grief and love. Even the onlookers are amazed, 'see how he loved him!' (11:36). Yet others of "the Jews" doubt him; if he really cared, the Jesus who 'opened the eyes of the blind man' could have prevented Lazarus dying (11:37). Even here we have the usual division between those who believed Jesus and those who rejected him.

Roll away the stone

Jesus, still 'greatly disturbed' (*enbrimo* again) comes to the tomb, which like most Palestinian graves was a cave cut into the rock with a stone across it (11:38). He asks them to 'take away the stone', and the reader who knows the end of the story will think of a different tomb and another Mary coming to find another stone rolled away (20:1). Martha, however, despite her earlier confession of faith, is still thinking at the surface level. Presuming that Jesus wants to view her brother's body, she is afraid of the corruption inside and the 'stench from four days'. She has not realized that her faith that 'even now God will

give' whatever Jesus asks (11:22) will be answered, that the future resurrection in which she believes is breaking into the present. The future
belief that 'those in the tombs will hear his voice and come forth'
(5:28–29) is about to happen now. But if Jesus is to bring new life, we
must face the corruption within and roll away the stone for him.

The glory of God

Jesus gently reminds her of their conversation, and repeats his comment that this would all result in the 'glory of God' (11:40; see 11:4).
As the first sign in Cana 'manifested his glory (2:11), so now will this
seventh sign in Bethany, the 'house of affliction'. And so they take
away the stone, while Jesus turns to prayer (11:41). He addresses his
Father, the God with whom he is one (10:30). As with the loaves and
the bread of life, it is a prayer of thanks, *eucharisto* (see on 6:11). The
only petition is for the sake of others, those watching 'that they may
believe you sent me' (11:42). So we see clearly at last the christological nature of this miracle, the 'sign to God's glory' hinted at by Jesus'
opening words, the delay, and conversations on two levels (11:4, 6,
15, 23)—which have all brought us to this extraordinary moment.

Unbind him and let him go

Finally, Jesus shouts in a voice to wake the dead three words in Greek
with not even a verb, 'Lazarus! Here! Out!' (11:43). At this incredible
climax to all the grief and tears, the tragedy almost turns to comedy,
as the former corpse shuffles to the opening, still bound with the linen
cloths which held the limbs to the body and the head-cloth which
covered the face and held the jaw (11:44). Unlike Jesus' resurrection,
when the cloths are simply left behind (20:5–7), Lazarus shuffles into
new life still all tied up. Jesus, exhausted perhaps by his emotions and
the miracle, seeks others' help: 'unbind him and let him go'. The last
word, *aphete*, 'release', is the same word as to 'forgive our sins as we
forgive' in the Lord's prayer (Matt. 6:12–15). When we too hear the
Lord's voice and shuffle into new life, what are our grave clothes that
still bind us, the things we need to forgive or be released from? Who
are the people Jesus tells to release us, or whom we need to forgive?

PRAYER

Lord Jesus, when I am dead in sin and darkness
call me to come out, unbind me and release me.

ONE MAN *MUST* DIE *for the* PEOPLE

In a paradox typical of John, this chapter about giving life ends with the threat of death. In Chapter 9, Jesus took the blind man out of darkness to see the light, while the religious leaders went from seeing into self-imposed darkness. Jesus then described himself in Chapter 10 as the good shepherd in contrast to their bad leadership of God's people. Now all this is borne out as Jesus gives Lazarus the gift of life, but the leaders respond by plotting Jesus' death. The wonderful miracle, the 'sign' of God's glory, once again produces division. First many of "the Jews" believed 'therefore', i.e. because of what they saw Jesus do for Lazarus (11:45). However, as with the blind man's healing, others go to tell the Pharisees (11:46; see 9:13).

Cynical scheming or true prophecy?

At this time, the Pharisees were only one group in Judaism, interested in interpreting and keeping the law. Much of the power, both political and religious, was held by the chief priests, the Sadducees, who controlled the temple sacrifices at the heart of Jewish practice, and co-operated with the Roman authorities. Both groups, with their scribes and elders, belonged to the Sanhedrin, the council, which they now convene (11:47). Their concerns are immediately obvious. They accept that Jesus is doing 'many signs' which lead people to believe in him. While that alone would worry the Pharisees, the Sadducees are anxious about the possible consequences, if they 'let him go on like this' (11:48). Provided there was internal peace and stability, the Romans allowed local leaders, like the chief priests and Sadducees, to administer their own religion and home affairs. However, if there was unrest or trouble, they would intervene quickly. The leaders' concerns here reveal their true priorities. They are frightened that 'the Romans will take away our holy place and our nation' (11:48). They are not concerned about whether what Jesus says is true, or if God's glory is really with him, but with their own control. The temple of God has become 'our place' and the people of God are 'our nation'. The irony is that John began his account of Jesus' ministry with the prophecy that the temple would be destroyed and replaced with Jesus' body (2:19–21), while the Good Shepherd's self-sacrificial love for his sheep has exposed the leaders' treatment of God's flock as 'our nation' (10:11–14). Ultimately, their fears are realized in the destruction of Jerusalem and the temple by the Romans in AD70; with no temple and no power the Sadducees disappear, and the Pharisees are left to regroup Judaism around the law.

Caiaphas, High Priest from AD18 to 36, accuses them of 'knowing nothing' (11:49)—but then, neither does he. In his political scheming, he suggests that it is 'better for you' that Jesus should die than that 'the whole nation perish' (11:50). Again, John is writing on two levels: on the surface, Caiaphas' comment is just cynical plotting, but at the spiritual level it is a true prophecy. At another time when the people of God could have become 'like sheep without a shepherd', Moses brought Joshua as his successor before the High Priest Eleazar (the Hebrew for Lazarus) for God's guidance (Num. 27:16–23). After the good shepherd has given life to another Lazarus, this High Priest is unwittingly guided by God to prophesy how Jesus will lay down his life for the sheep (11:51). Nor will it be just for 'our nation'; the good shepherd cares for his 'other sheep not of this fold' (10:16) and his death will bring all the 'children of God' together into one (11:52; see 1:12). It is amazing how God can even take our cynical comments and turn them into his good purposes for the whole human race!

Hide and seek

Now, therefore, the leaders' plans for Jesus' death takes the gospel into its final stages (11:53). Jesus can no longer go around 'openly', 'plainly', as John uses *parresia* again (see 7:4; 10:24; 11:14). He withdraws briefly to Ephraim (11:54), a small town about 12 miles north of Jerusalem, near Bethel (2 Sam. 13:23; 2 Chron. 13:19). But soon the third Passover comes and everyone goes up to Jerusalem (11:55; see 2:13; 6:4). As with previous feasts, such as Tabernacles (7:11), the crowd debate about Jesus: 'surely he will not come to the feast, will he?' (11:56). And as they debate, so the two groups of religious leaders, the chief priests and the Pharisees, are planning his arrest (11:57).

PRAYER

Lord God, thank you that you can speak through our cynicism
and turn even our scheming to your purpose;
grant that we may seek the good
not just of 'our place' and nation, but of all your people.

ANOINTING *at* BETHANY

The Passover is at hand, and people come to Jerusalem to prepare (11:55). Six days before the feast, Jesus also arrives, for dinner back at Bethany, now identified as 'the home of Lazarus'. 'Six days' implies that this is Saturday evening, the end of the Sabbath at the start of this holy week leading to Passover, a week which will be Jesus' last. That hint of death is confirmed as John reminds us that Lazarus was the one 'whom Jesus had raised from the dead' (12:1). Jesus, the giver of life to those in the tomb, is setting out on the journey to his own death and burial.

At the end of this week, his crucified body will be anointed (19:39). To balance that event, it begins with a story of Jesus being anointed. Mark 14:3–9 and Matthew 26:6–13 describe Jesus being anointed on his head in Bethany two days before Passover at the house of Simon the leper by an unnamed woman; in Luke 7:36–38, he is anointed on his feet earlier in Galilee in the house of Simon the Pharisee by a sinful woman who wipes his feet with her hair. Whether these accounts describe two different events, or two versions of the same anointing, John's story has elements from both, while at the same time setting the scene beautifully for his account of the Passion.

Extravagance and fragrance

The story begins with dinner (12:2). Lazarus reclines at table with Jesus; the conversation between the one who had come out of the tomb and the other on his way to the tomb must have been interesting! Meanwhile, Martha is active, serving once more, while Mary again heads for Jesus' feet which she had clasped outside her brother's tomb; in both cases, they reflect the story in Luke 10:38–42 (see on 11:20 and 32 above).

Mary has 'a pound of costly perfume of pure nard' (12:3). The word 'pure', *pistikos*, occurs only here and may be connected with *pisteuo*, to believe or have faith, which has recurred throughout recent chapters; if so, it means 'faithful' or 'genuine' in quality, reflecting Mary's genuine faith and love for Jesus. 'Nard' is an oil derived from the root and spike of the nard plant, and the best examples were imported from as far east as India, hence its extreme expense. A 'pound' is an extraordinarily extravagant amount, recalling the vast quantity of wine created in Jesus' first sign at another dinner party (2:6). Yet she pours all this ointment, not on Jesus' *head*, where people wore perfume and kings were anointed, but on his *feet*, where the preparation of a corpse for burial would start. No wonder the whole 'house was filled with the fragrance'. Finally, she undoes her hair to wipe his feet. Jewish women kept their hair tied up in public, and only let it loose when undressing for a husband, or as a sign of distraction in mourning. Mary would have had her hair loose when she fell at Jesus' feet in her grief (11:32); now she does so again, in her unabashed love for him—but the hints of burial and grief are impossible to ignore.

Protests and the poor

Judas, however, has other thoughts. He protests at the waste: so much good perfume might have realized '300 denarii'; if a denarius was a worker's daily wage, this is a year's salary, even more than the cost of bread for the five thousand (see on 6:7 above). He claims to want to give it to the poor, perhaps in the Passover almsgiving as the group's treasurer. He has already been identified as the betrayer (6:70–71) and now he is called a 'thief', because he used to 'carry' the group's purse, a euphemism for 'steal', like the English 'lift' (12:6). The 'thief comes only to steal and destroy' and is recognized by the good shepherd (10:10), who now rebukes him and protects his sheep: 'leave her alone' (12:7). Jesus picks up the hints of the burial ritual in what Mary has done and reminds them of the death threats against him. Yes, Passover is a good time to remember that 'the poor are always with you' and obey scripture's instructions to be generous (Deut. 15:11). But it is also the week when 'you will not always have me', as Jesus heads resolutely towards his own death (12:8).

For REFLECTION & PRAYER

This is a good passage for meditation in prayer. Imagine the scene at the dinner party with everybody there—and join them.
Where are we? Perhaps we are sitting with Jesus like Lazarus or serving with Martha; do we show our love for Jesus at his feet, or complain with Judas?
What does Jesus have to say to us?

WHAT SORT *of* KING?

Although Mary's anointing Jesus' feet hinted at a burial, rather than anointing the head as for a king, the next scene looks like a coronation. Once again, John tells it differently from the other gospels with a particular focus on what it means to call Jesus king. In the Synoptics, it is Jesus' first visit to Jerusalem, his 'entry', while John has shown him at all the major feasts there over several years. Thus he is well known and his appearances usually provoke division among the people and the leaders. The crowd has been looking for Jesus since 11:56; when they heard that he had returned to Bethany, they came out to see him, but also to see 'Lazarus, whom he had raised from the dead' (12:9). So the chief priests plot Lazarus' death as well, partly out of fear of the Romans' intervention, but also to remove this embarrassing theological evidence. As Sadducees, the priests did not believe in the resurrection, so they need to prove that Lazarus would stay dead! Lazarus' new life was causing 'many to believe in Jesus', 'deserting' them and their religious control (12:11).

Hosanna to the King of Israel

Next comes 'Palm Sunday', although only John tells us about the day and the palms. 'The next day', after the Saturday evening dinner at Bethany, is the Sunday before Passover and 'the great crowd that had come to the festival heard that Jesus was coming' (12:12). Josephus says that over two million people would come to Jerusalem for Passover each year; no wonder the priests and the Romans were anxious about crowd control! Here, John refers to a crowd within Jerusalem who go out to welcome Jesus coming in from Bethany, waving 'palm branches' and shouting 'Hosanna' (12:13). The words for 'palm' (*phoinix*) and 'branches' (*baia*) are rare, but they occur in the accounts of greeting the successful Maccabean leaders. At the rededication of the temple after Judas Maccabeus' successful revolt in 164BC, the people greeted him with 'palm branches' (*baia*, 2 Macc. 10:7); when his brother Simon conquered Jerusalem's citadel in 142BC, the people entered it carrying 'palms' (*phoinix*, 1 Macc. 13:51). This recalls the Feast of the Dedication and the debate about good and bad shepherds (see on 10:22). The implication that the crowd is greeting a conquering hero is unmistakable. They sing Psalm 118, with its cry of 'Hosanna', meaning 'save us, Lord', to the conquering Messiah 'coming in the name of the Lord' (Ps. 118:25–26). After Jesus performed the messianic sign of feeding people in the wilderness, they wanted 'to make him king by force' (6:15). Now comes the coronation victory parade, and it all looks political, military and exceedingly dangerous.

In lowly pomp ride on to die

Jesus, however, has consistently refused political kingship and withdrew into the desert last time to hide from them. Now he finds, not the conqueror's mighty horse, but a young donkey, a symbol of peace and lowliness (12:14). John uses Zechariah 9:9, about a king on a donkey, but he omits Zechariah's shout of triumph 'rejoice greatly', and replaces it with 'fear not, O Zion', a promise that God will save Jerusalem from disaster (Zeph. 3:16). Yes, Jerusalem's king is coming, and can 'ride on, ride on in majesty' as the Palm Sunday hymn puts it. However, he comes not to conquer by military revolt, but 'in lowly pomp ride on to die'. Jerusalem need not fear disaster from the Romans, for this one man comes to die 'for the sake of the people'.

The response

This amazing drama of the people's offer of a revolutionary kingship turned into humility by Jesus provokes different responses from four groups. The 'disciples did not understand at first', but John has a flash forward to their look back after he had been 'glorified', crucified; only then did it make sense (12:16; see also 2:22). Then there are the two crowds: the crowd coming in from Bethany with Jesus continue to 'witness' to Lazarus' raising (12:17). The mob which came out of the city to greet the conquering hero react to what they heard about the sign (12:18). The Pharisees are exasperated and can only say to one another in resignation that 'all the world' has gone after him (12:19). At the surface level they just mean 'everyone', like the French *tout le monde*; but the deeper spiritual reality is that, far from a military campaign for one nation against another, the Good Shepherd is bringing his sheep from all the world into one flock.

PRAYER

Lord Jesus, lowly and suffering King, grant that 'all the world'
may renounce violence and seek your peace.

WE WANT *to* SEE JESUS

John's account of Jesus welcomed into Jerusalem by the crowd showed how he rejected violent revolution for just one nation, responding with a humility which caused 'all the world' to go after him. Both universalism and humble suffering are developed further in these next sections.

Greeks come to Jesus

First, John says that among the Jerusalem crowd 'were some Greeks' (12:20). Many Greek-speaking Jews would return to Jerusalem from all over the Mediterranean for festivals, but these are usually called 'Hellenists' (e.g. Acts 6:1). Thus, these 'Greeks' are not Jews; they might be proselytes, non-Jews interested in the Jewish faith, but they may just be visitors. The Greeks were renowned for their inquisitive nature, travelling around in search of something new. At Jerusalem, they would have been allowed into the Court of the Gentiles in the temple. Here, they are part of 'the world' which has gone after Jesus (12:19), some of the 'other sheep not of this fold' who hear the good shepherd's voice (10:16). As they watch this procession welcoming Jesus, the Greeks too want to see Jesus. They find Philip, a disciple with a Greek name (meaning 'horse-lover') from a mixed Greek-Jewish town, Bethsaida (see 1:43–44). Philip goes to find Andrew, from his home town with a Greek name also, and together they go to Jesus, thus repeating what happened with the little boy with the loaves and fishes (12:22; see 1:40–42; 6:5–8). If Philip and Andrew's behaviour provides a pattern for all who wish to bring others to Jesus, the Greeks' request is the classic text for all who speak, teach, preach, or listen: 'we want to see Jesus' (12:21). It is so easy to be seduced by our own eloquence, but the message is more important than the messenger and the one spoken about is greater than the speaker. The Christian's task is to communicate such that people see Jesus.

The interest of Gentiles helps Jesus realize the moment has come. After his ministry in Galilee, Judaea, Samaria and Jerusalem, now 'the world' is seeking him. He told his mother and the Samaritan woman that his 'hour is not yet' but 'coming' (2:4; 4:21–3) and he has often evaded capture because 'his hour had not yet come' (7:30, 8:20).

But now, 'the hour has come for the Son of man to be glorified' (12:23). The whole story has been leading towards this—and we might expect it to be glorious.

A grain of wheat must die

However, as he tried to show the welcoming crowd, Jesus' glory is not human triumph. He uses another 'figure'—the 'grain of wheat', reminiscent of the other gospels' seed parables. It is a simple truth that a grain of wheat must fall into earth and be buried; its external husk has to be broken open for the life within to come out. Only if it 'dies', will it bear 'much fruit' (12:24). Lazarus' death and burial is now bearing fruit as the celebrations attract the attention of the world. But supremely Jesus is talking about his own forthcoming death. It would be so easy to avoid it, to choose the path of human glory and follow the crowd to revolution. But if the seed is not placed in the earth, 'it remains alone'. If one seed reproduces itself forty-fold in the ear of corn which grows from it, and these are all replanted, and so on each year, it would only take just over six years before that one seed results in as many seeds as there are human beings on this planet—all from one seed buried in the ground. Jesus' path to glory will also put him in the ground before he can bring his fruit to his Father.

As far too many human conflicts show, those who fight to preserve their lives end up losing them. Jesus teaches that those who sacrifice their lives in this world will find eternal life (12:25). The good shepherd is on his way to lay down his life for the sheep, and those who serve him must follow him. The paradox is that in such self-denial we find that we are with Jesus, being honoured by his Father (12:26). Although this is all expressed in John's distinctive language, it is exactly the same message found at the heart of the other gospels (see Mk. 8:34–35; Matt. 10:38–40; Lk. 17:33). Jesus taught consistently and repeatedly that the way to life is through self sacrifice and the path of glory found only in crucifixion. The Greeks coming 'to see Jesus' means that now is the 'hour to be glorified', the time to put the words into action.

PRAYER

Father God, we want to see Jesus,
to lose ourselves in him
that we might find ourselves in you.

LIFTING UP *the* SON *of* MAN

The coming of the Greeks to see Jesus meant that the 'hour for the Son of Man to be glorified' had finally arrived. Jesus is clear that the way to glory lies only through his self-sacrificial death. No one can face imminent death without some pause. Jesus may have been the Son of God, but he was also incarnate fully as a human being, and here John gives a brief insight into Jesus' human emotions: 'now is my soul troubled' (12:27). The word 'troubled' is *tarasso* again, as in his feelings at Lazarus' grave (11:33). Jesus' prayer reflects how the Psalmist often describes his inner turmoil (e.g. Pss. 42:6; 55:4). In the other gospels, such agony in prayer happens in the Garden of Gethsemane before Jesus' arrest. John, however, has no agonized prayer at that point, when Jesus is in control and heading for his destiny. In many ways, then, this passage serves as the Gethsemane experience for John.

As in Gethsemane, Jesus' first thought is to pray for God's deliverance: 'Father, save me from this hour'. Yet after so many times when the 'hour was not yet', how can he avoid its final arrival? He has come for this hour and the whole story has led to this point (12:27). He must remain true to his purpose: 'Father, glorify your name' (12:28). His miracles have been 'signs' of God's glory, such as the water into wine, healing the blind man, or raising Lazarus (2:11; 9:3; 11:4, 40) and he has refused to exchange it for 'glory from men' (5:41–44).

The voice from heaven

In response to Jesus' decision to put the glory of God ahead of his own apprehension comes 'a voice from heaven'. Not only does John not describe Gethsemane, but also he has no account of the Transfiguration. He prefers to show how Jesus reflects and shares God's glory not just on one occasion, but always. Here, we get a voice from heaven as in the other gospels' accounts of the Transfiguration, as God confirms that he is being glorified in Jesus. The crowd is divided as usual, as some think it is merely 'thunder', while others assume it is an 'angel' (12:29). In the *Chronicles of Narnia* by C.S. Lewis, the voice of Aslan, the great lion, seems only a terrifying roar to those who oppose him, but gentle words and strength to the children who love him. So now, Jesus says the voice is not for his benefit, but for the bystanders'; whether they understand it or not, it is a sign to them that God is with him (12:30; see also 11:42).

Cast out and lifted up

This moment is also 'the judgment of this world' (12:31). In the raising of Lazarus we saw how the future resurrection could happen now; judgment also takes place, as the End breaks into the present. John describes the devil, or Satan, as the 'ruler of this world' (see also 14:30; 16:11). It has been the 'rulers' in this world, Caiaphas, the priests and Pharisees, who have been opposing Jesus, to keep their power here and now. But behind them is the 'ruler of this world' who will now be 'cast out', suffering what the human rulers did to the blind man (12:31; cf. 9:34). However, as Satan is cast down and out, so Jesus is 'lifted up' (12:32). We have already seen the double meaning of this word, *hypsoun*, to 'exalt' and to be 'lifted up' on a cross (see on 3:14 and 8:28), and its use for death by crucifixion is now made explicit (12:33). Also, the universal implications of the 'other sheep' and the Greeks coming to Jesus are brought out; Jesus' death on the cross will be how he will draw 'all people' to himself (12:32).

The Son of Man and the light

The crowd, however, are confused by these hints of death. They are still caught up in the Messianic fervour aroused by the welcoming demonstration. Scriptures like Pss. 89:29–37 or 110:4 suggest that the Christ will 'remain forever'. So what does Jesus mean about the Son of Man being 'lifted up'? (12:34). Jesus gives to them the same response as to the disciples about the blind man and Lazarus, to 'walk while you have the light' (12:35; see 9:4–5; 11:9–10). Light and darkness have been key words since 3:19–21, but now Jesus' warning of judgment is more urgent: 'the light' is with them for only 'a little longer' (12:35). The hour has come and time is short for them to become 'children of light'. They must believe while they still have the light, and with this saying he departs from the crowd for the very last time (12:36).

PRAYER

Father, glorify your name and draw me to your Son
lifted up on the cross to make us all the children of light.

BELIEF, BLINDNESS & FEAR

We have suggested that John's gospel is a two-act drama, with this section as an interlude (see on 1:19 and 11:1 above). The central actor, Jesus, is working very hard! He was not merely on stage for most of Act One, but at the centre of the action. A couple of times he disappeared briefly into the wings while the other characters discussed what to do about him, as in the story of the blind man (Jesus off stage from 9:7 to 9:35). Now this final dialogue with the people in Jerusalem after their procession of welcome has brought the interlude almost to an end. Warning that they will only have the light for 'a little while longer', Jesus left the stage and 'hid from them' (12:35–36). He will not appear in public again until the crucifixion. The light is temporarily eclipsed.

The evangelist, as narrator, turns to address his audience directly for the first time since the Prologue. Here, he reflects on what has happened, and tries to understand and explain it. Throughout the first act, Jesus has done seven great 'signs', discussing their significance with the people and the authorities. The problem is that so many still do not believe in him (12:37).

Blind eyes and hard hearts

The early Christians found it very difficult to understand why the people of God did not believe the one God sent to them. It was not a new problem. Even Moses, with whom Jesus has often been compared in this gospel, experienced something similar and complained that although the people saw 'signs and great wonders', they did not understand, or see or hear, despite having minds, eyes and ears (Deut. 29:2–4). John has wrestled with this since the Prologue, when he warned us that, although Jesus came to his own people, they did not receive him (1:10–12). Now he quotes from one of Isaiah's poems about the Servant of God, which had such an influence on the early church's thinking about Jesus. This fourth 'servant song' describes how the servant is 'despised and rejected ... wounded for our transgressions' and how he bore the sin of all who 'like sheep have gone astray' (Is. 52:13—53:12). John quotes from the start of this song to show that no one has 'believed our message', despite 'the arm of the Lord being revealed' (12:38, quoting Is. 53:1).

Having noted the fact of unbelief in Isaiah, the evangelist looks at its start for an explanation. In his vision of the glory of God in the temple in the 'year King Uzziah died', Isaiah describes how he responded to God's call to go to his people. Like Moses, however, he had to realize that people's eyes could be so blinded that they could not see, and their hearts so hard that they would not understand (Is. 6:10). In their attempt to understand why the people of God could not see what God was doing in Jesus, the early Christians recognized their experience in Isaiah's words. So now John quotes this verse here to explain why Jesus has not been accepted (12:40). This verse is similarly used to explain people's blindness in the other gospels (Matt. 13:13–5; Mk. 4:12; Lk. 8:10) and to conclude the book of Acts (28:26–27).

The glory of God or human praise?

Neither John, nor Isaiah, endorses a naked determinism where human beings have no choice but are condemned in advance not to believe. This is seen in John's earlier idea of 'none so blind as those who will not see' after the opening of the blind man's eyes was met with disbelief from the Pharisees, who thought they could see (9:39–41). The blind man's parents were afraid of being put 'out of the synagogue', and now John suggests that the same fear holds back even those leaders who believed (12:42; see on 9:22 above). He has already shown that one of them, Nicodemus, having come to Jesus first 'by night', has begun to travel to the light (3:1; 7:50) and he will be joined by at least one other, Joseph of Arimathea (19:38–39). But the others, says John, are held back by the fear of what people might say or think. Isaiah's vision in the temple of the glory of God included seeing Jesus' glory as well (12:41), but these leaders prefer the glory which comes from other human beings to the glory of God (12:43; see also 5:44). We cannot come to the new life when still wrapped up in our old ways. Like Lazarus shuffling out of the tomb, we need to be set free from all that binds us and holds us back. For many of us, says John, fear of what others might say or do blinds our eyes, hardens our hearts and keeps us trapped in death.

PRAYER

Lord, open our eyes and melt our hardened hearts
that we may behold your glory and reveal you to others.

67

LIGHT SENT *to* SAVE *the* WORLD

The 'hour' has arrived. Jesus has been anointed for burial and welcomed with great rejoicing. He refused the path of violent revolution,
but stressed instead that he will be glorified through a self-sacrificial
death for everyone, including non-Jews, like the Greeks. While his soul
may be troubled, he has been strengthened by the voice from heaven
and he has made his exit from public view. As the stage cleared, the
narrator addressed the audience about the inability of God's people to
see what he is doing. Everything is ready for Act Two, when suddenly
we have this little section of Jesus' teaching. John provides no setting
for it, but it stands free and independent. Some scholars provide a context by moving it elsewhere in the gospel. Yet, curiously, it fits well
here, even without any context. It summarizes the key themes of Jesus'
teaching and prepares us for the next Act. It is introduced simply by
'Jesus cried out in a loud voice' (12:44). Using our image of the
theatre, it is like a reprise over the public address system of the main
melodies from the first half before the curtain goes up for Act Two.

The one who sent me

The first melody is 'the one who sent me'. For John, God is the God
who sends. The gospel begins with 'a man sent from God', John the
Baptist (1:6). However, he is only the one who has been 'sent ahead'
(3:28). Now Jesus declares that 'whoever believes in me, believes not
in me, but in him who sent me' (12:44). Whoever sees Jesus, sees
'him who sent me' (12:45). Jesus calls God 'the one who sent me'
over thirty times in John. His awareness of being sent by God is the
heart of all he says and does. It is, literally, meat and drink to him as
he explained after talking to the Samaritan woman: 'my food is to do
the will of him who sent me' (4:34). As the bread of life, he has come
down from heaven 'to do the will of him who sent me' (6:38). His
teaching at the Feast of Tabernacles is not his own 'but his who sent
me' (7:16). His concern for the blind man was to 'work the works of
him who sent me' (9:4) and he prayed that the raising of Lazarus
would enable the crowd to 'believe that you sent me' (11:42). John
ended his prologue before Act One with 'no one has ever seen God'
(1:18); in this reprise before Act Two he declares that to have seen

Jesus is to have seen the God who sent him (12:45).

Light and judgment

The second theme is now introduced. Jesus, whom God has sent, has come 'as light into the world' (12:46). The Prologue called Jesus 'the light of men, shining in the darkness' (1:4–5). At the Feast of Tabernacles, with its light ceremonies, Jesus proclaimed, 'I am the light of the world' (8:12) which he demonstrated by healing the blind man (9:5–7) and raising Lazarus (11:9–11). No one need remain in darkness, for Jesus came not to condemn the world, but to save it (12:47). This is a reprise of the marvellous passage after Nicodemus came to Jesus 'by night' and learned that God so loved the world that he sent his only Son (3:16–17). But the coming of light into darkness creates shadows, and 'this is the judgment, that the light has come into the world and people loved darkness rather than light' (3:19). Over the intervening chapters, Jesus' opponents moved more and more into darkness by refusing to accept his light (e.g. 9:40–41). He came to save, but his coming brings judgment even now for those who reject him, a judgment which will be confirmed on the last day (12:48).

The Father and the Son

The third motif in this recapitulation is the relationship of the Father and the Son. Jesus has consistently insisted that 'I can do nothing on my own' but only the will of his Father who sent him (5:30). His stress on his relationship with God as his Father was even more unacceptable to his opponents than his healing on the Sabbath, and made them want to kill him (5:18). All the debates about Jesus' identity and origins in chapters 5 to 8 centred around this claim, building to a climax with 'the Father and I are one' (10:30). Now he declares that all this teaching has not been his own, but what the Father commanded him 'to say and speak', and this alone brings eternal life (12:49–50).

Thus in these few verses, John reminds us of the key themes throughout the first half, that God the Father sent Jesus as light to save the world. The reprise dies away, the audience are quiet and the curtain is ready to rise on the second half.

PRAYER

O God our Father, thank you that you sent your Son as light to save the world; open our eyes that we may do your will.

68

JESUS WASHES *the* DISCIPLES' FEET

The curtain rises on Act Two of John's drama, yet slowly. Now that the 'hour' has finally come, time slows down. Act One and the interlude (chs. 1—12) have taken over two years, with two previous Passovers (2:13; 6:4). Act Two (chs. 13—19) covers just 24 hours: John is making a meal of it—literally! The dinner lasts until Jesus' arrest, so it is the last supper on Thursday night before the crucifixion. The other gospels imply that it was a Passover meal, but Jn. 18:28 suggests Passover is not eaten until the next day. John portrays it like an ancient dinner party or *symposium* (literally 'drinking together'), where people discussed ideas over food and drink, which gives us 'symposium' to mean an academic gathering for debate.

Jesus, knowing that the hour has finally come, gathers 'his own' to show them the 'full extent of his love' (13:1). Jesus came to 'his own', but 'his own did not receive him' (1:11); the good shepherd, however, knows 'his own' sheep, and calls 'his own' out of the fold (10:3–4). Now that Jesus has been rejected by "the Jews", he calls 'his own' out to nourish them for the difficulties ahead. Not only will their shepherd return to his Father, but 'the thief' who comes to destroy is a disciple, Judas Iscariot (13:1–2; see 10:10; 12:6). Unlike the unwitting disciples, the author and his readers know what will happen and we have several warnings of the devil inspiring Judas' betrayal, like a funeral bell tolling somewhere in the background.

The servant

The start of the 'Passion narrative', when Jesus 'suffers' (the meaning of 'passion'), has nothing 'passive' about it. Jesus knows everything, including his origins and destiny, that 'he had come from God and was going to God' (13:3). Jesus' knowledge has been stressed (e.g. 1:48; 2:24–25; 6:6; 8:14) and, secure in that knowledge, he can undertake what the insecure disciples would not. He rises from table and 'lays down his clothes', like the good shepherd 'laying down his life' (10:11–18). With those clothes, he lays down his dignity and takes up the role of the servant (13:4). Walking in open sandals on unsurfaced roads, dusty or muddy in wet weather, made everyone's feet dirty. Water would always be provided for new arrivals to wash their feet, and, if you were lucky, a servant to do it. However, so menial a task could not be required of a Jewish male servant, only from women, children or non-Jews. On special occasions, it might be done as a sign of great love and respect to a superior, such as a disciple for his rabbi, or a wife for her husband. But in Jesus, the usual order is reversed. Jesus does for us what none of us are prepared to do for each other. Like someone nursing a dying spouse for whom even the most menial tasks are an act of love, so Jesus takes the water basin and the towel and starts to wash the disciples' feet (13:5).

Washing Peter

Jesus comes to Peter, who is flabbergasted and splutters a protest all out of order in the Greek, 'Lord, you—my—wash—feet?' (13:6). It is bad enough to be shown up for not having done the menial task—but ten times worse if your master does it for you! Often we hold back because we are too proud to let Jesus do something for us. It is all right for us to serve God, but to let him serve us costs our total surrender; sometimes we can only understand it later, as Jesus tells Peter (13:7). With his characteristic bluntness Peter refuses ever to let Jesus do this lowly task (13:8). Jesus gently explains that this is necessary if Peter is to have any 'share' in him. Impetuous as ever, the old 'Simon' comes out and wants the total experience—feet, hands and head! (13:9). Simon has always been 'all or nothing'. Jesus reminds him that people bathe all over before leaving home, and just need their feet washing from walking (13:10). Both ancient and modern commentators see hints of baptism here. Through baptism, we are 'made clean' and given a 'share' in the body of Christ. Walking in the world, we all get dirty feet through sin, but we cannot be re-baptized over and over again; we need simply to let Jesus cleanse us and forgive us, and let him feed us at his table. But some will accept Christ's loving ministrations while still plotting against him. Jesus would have washed even Judas' feet, despite knowing that he would soon betray him—and we hear another clang from the funeral bell (13:11).

PRAYER

Lord Jesus, Servant King,
thank you that you laid down so much for me;
give me grace to lay aside my pride and let you make me clean.

69

I HAVE GIVEN YOU *an* EXAMPLE

Jesus has washed the disciples' feet and returned to the table (13:12). From our experience of church services and the other gospels we expect the institution of the holy communion next—but it is completely missing. Instead, Jesus begins to explain things to his disciples and continues through the long discourse of chapters 14—17. Some argue from this curious absence that John was not interested in communion, or even opposed sacraments all together. However, we noted that John used the '*eucharist-*' word when Jesus 'gave thanks' over the loaves and fishes (see on 6:11) and that the discourse which followed talked of eating his flesh and drinking his blood (see on 6:51–59). Not only does chapter 6 look forward to the last supper, but this section has several links back to ch. 6. So John could not have been uninterested in communion and its omission here is even stranger.

One answer may be that John assumed that his audience already knew about the institution of the communion and so he took it for granted. If the gospel was originally read aloud at communion services, the account of its institution would be heard later, so was not needed here. However, his audience may not have known the other gospels, and the gospel would have been read on other occasions. Another possibility involves the practice of keeping 'holy knowledge' secret from the uninitiated. In the early church, people who were not baptized left after the readings and sermon, before the communion; there was even speculation outside the church about what exactly happened at the eucharist. Thus, the communion seems absent on the surface level of John, but for those 'in the know' who look deeper, there are hints and allusions everywhere. Whatever the reason, here the foot washing is followed by a typical 'farewell speech', looking ahead to what will happen when the speaker has gone, with hopes for the future, warnings about betrayals or fighting, and prayer for the disciples' success without their leader (see the farewells of Jacob in Gen. 49; Moses, Deut. 31; Joshua, Josh. 23—24; David, 1 Kings 2).

The master's humility

As earlier 'signs' led into dialogues to explain them, so now Jesus moves from the sign of foot washing to ask his disciples if they understand what he has done (13:12). He is their master: they came to him first as a teacher but then realized that he is also their Lord, and Jesus does not refuse those titles (13:13). What he does reject is the 'pecking order', equally beloved of chickens and human beings! If our Lord and master treats his followers like this, we cannot stand on our dignity, but must treat each other similarly (13:14). He challenges all human systems of management, control and hierarchy. The religious leaders have proudly expected service and obedience in this gospel (1:22; 7:47–49; 8:33, 39; 9:34). But Jesus, the humble good shepherd of the people has been out seeking the shunned Samaritan woman, the abandoned paralysed man or the rejected blind man. The foot washing is not just a symbolic action, but a way of life which Jesus' example expects us to follow (13:15). We may act this out at a Maundy Thursday service, but such humble service must characterize all Christians' lives, doing good and helping others (see 1 Tim. 5:10).

Masters, servants and messengers

If Jesus is our 'lord and teacher', his servants cannot act as if we are greater than our master. Equally, messengers, those who run errands, are not greater than 'the one who sent' them (13:16). 'The one who sent' reflects Jesus' understanding of God as 'the one who sent' him, while the word for 'messengers' in Greek is *apostles*, those who are sent. 'Apostles' are not 'top of the Christian tree'; they, and we, are just God's messengers—and when we really understand this and are set free from jockeying for position, then we are truly blessed (13:17). Of course, there will always be at least one person who wants to play it differently, and so we hear another clang from the funeral bell, as Jesus looks ahead to Judas' betrayal (13:18). What is worse, he is one who 'ate my bread', quoting Ps. 41:9, which uses the same word, *trogo*, to 'munch' Jesus' flesh, as in the bread discourse (see on 6:55). That discourse also ended with Jesus' knowledge about his betrayer (6:70–71), so now he gives them another warning (13:19). Finally, the apostles, 'messengers', are told that people who receive those he sends, not only receive Jesus himself, but also God his Father, 'who sent me' (13:20, see 5:23; 12:44).

PRAYER

Lord Jesus, thank you for feeding me and washing my feet,
give me courage to follow your example.

BELOVED *or* BETRAYER?

After Jesus has explained the footwashing as an example of humility, the hints of 'eating the bread' and knowing the betrayer cause him to be 'troubled in spirit' (13:21). This is *tarasso* again; so far, Jesus has been 'troubled' by the death of Lazarus and by the prospect of his own death (see 11:33; 12:27 above). Now, however, the constant tolling of the bell through the supper has become too much to ignore, so he explains the previous allusions: 'one of you will betray me' (see 13:2, 10–11, 18). Despite the hints, the disciples are shocked, looking at each other uncertainly and wondering.

The disciple Jesus loved

Before we come to Judas, John draws our attention to the person reclining at dinner next to Jesus (13:23). He identifies him as 'the disciple Jesus loved', lying 'close to Jesus' bosom', as he earlier told us that Jesus was in 'the bosom of the Father' (1:18). Being next to Jesus might suggest that he is the host, the owner of the house, who has invited Jesus to hold his meal here; but he is clearly personally close to him also, a 'bosom friend'—yet he is unnamed. This 'beloved disciple', as he is usually called, is also entrusted with Jesus' mother at the cross (19:26–27); outruns Peter to the empty tomb (20:2–8) and recognizes the risen Jesus on the shore (21:7). He may also be the 'other disciple' who knows the High Priest and gets Peter into his house (18:15–17). The description 'whom Jesus loved' reminds us of Lazarus (11:3, 36), but since he has already been named, he cannot be this anonymous disciple. The gospel concludes that he has been the authority, if not the author, behind the story (21:20–24). This clue has traditionally identified him with John son of Zebedee, who was in the boat at Jesus' final appearance (21:2) and so John is thought to be the founder of the church behind this gospel. While that is the most likely identification, we must take seriously the anonymity of the beloved disciple. He is like an 'ideal' disciple, close to Jesus and staying loyal, even outdoing Peter, who now asks him to find out who the traitor is (13:24). Given the author's liking for levels of meaning, whoever he was at the physical level, we are all invited to become disciples 'whom Jesus loved' and to stay close to him.

Judas goes into darkness

To answer Peter's enquiry, the beloved disciple 'leans back' to ask Jesus, 'Lord, who is it?' (13:25). Jesus identifies the traitor as the one to whom he will give some bread which he has dipped in the sauce on the dish (13:26). This is a mark of respect, used by Boaz to invite Ruth to his meal (Ruth 2:14). It would be easy to do if Judas, perhaps in his capacity as the group's treasurer, were sitting in the other place of honour, on Jesus' left. Yet the left side is also where the good shepherd will put the goats and the lost at the end, according to Matthew's parable (Matt. 25:33, 41). So it is here also, for after Judas has received the bread from Jesus, 'the Satan', the deceiver who inspired the betrayal (13:2) 'entered into him' (13:27). This does not absolve Judas of responsibility. At the human level, there have been several appeals to him during this meal, the tolling of our symbolic bell. But now the inner conflict of considering betrayal while letting Jesus wash his feet and feed him, proves too much for Judas, who has a spiritual break-down. Similarly, those who are washed in the waters of baptism and fed with the bread of the eucharist cannot plan to betray Jesus without being in grave danger of spiritual darkness.

Recognizing what has finally happened, Jesus tells him to do it quickly. Once again, John writes on two levels: the others at the table misunderstand why Judas is leaving, and assume he is going out as their treasurer for supplies or to undertake the Passover alms giving, after his protest about Mary's ointment (13:28–29; see 12:4–6). This may have been the surface appearance, but the spiritual level is tersely described: having received the bread, he went out—'and it was night' (13:30). The hour of darkness, which Jesus has warned about when people stumble (9:4; 11:10), has finally arrived. Nicodemus came to Jesus 'by night', but he has gradually journeyed out of the darkness (3:2; 7:50). Judas, however, despite having been chosen to sit with 'the light of the world', is going the other way. 'And this is the judgment, that the light has come into the world, and people loved darkness rather than light because their deeds were evil' (3:19).

PRAYER

Lord Jesus, lover of all your disciples,
grant that I may be fed by you
and give me the courage never to betray you.

LOVE ONE ANOTHER

When Judas has 'gone out' to begin the events leading to Jesus' arrest and death, Jesus starts talking to his disciples. This introduces several themes which will recur through the Farewell Discourse of chapters 14—17. There is no clear structure, but the themes are mixed together, returning and repeating as the conversation progresses. It is more like a symphony, weaving several motifs together than a logical sequence. As often in John, we have misunderstandings and levels of meaning which develop what he is saying. So it is better understood through prayerful meditation than by analysis. As it progresses, several parts of a farewell speech emerge again (see on 13:12). However, the main point is crystal clear: Jesus is going away and he wants to comfort and prepare the disciples, warning them and reassuring them that everything will be all right in the plan of God.

Judas has gone out and it is now 'night', but the hour of darkness is also the hour of glorification. Jesus begins with how he and God are glorified in each other (13:31). Jesus' signs and words have revealed God's glory (1:14; 8:54; 11:4, 40). John has used 'to be glorified' to refer to Jesus' passion and his return through death to his Father (see 7:39; 12:16, 23). So if God has been glorified like this in Jesus, then, in response, Jesus will be glorified in God himself (13:32). Jesus knows that his departure and death will be a great shock to his disciples, but stresses right at the start that he is on his way to glory. This motif will be developed further in his prayer at the end of the Discourse in Chapter 17. After this reminder of glory, Jesus breaks the news gently to his 'little children'; this is a farewell speech because 'I will be with you only a little longer' (13:33). They will look for him, but as he told "the Jews", now he tells the disciples that they cannot come with him (see 7:33–34). "The Jews" did not understand what he meant (7:35–36; 8:21–22), nor will the disciples, so this theme will also reappear later.

A new commandment

If the first two themes reveal that Jesus' way to glory involves going away, then thirdly the disciples need a new way of living without him physically present, to love each other 'as I have loved you' (13:34).

The chapter began with Jesus loving his disciples 'to the end' and demonstrating this by washing their feet (13:1–5). In one sense, this is not 'a new commandment' at all. The heart of the Jewish law is to 'love your neighbour as yourself' (Lev. 19:18) and it forms part of most moral codes. On the other hand, it is also a universal human experience that it is not so easy to put into practice, such is our selfishness. What is 'new' is that Jesus gives us a new motive and power. We do not love others simply to fulfil an ethical demand, but in response to Jesus, 'as I have loved you'. 'God so loved the world that he gave his only Son', and he loved the disciples to the extreme of washing their feet and going to die for them. Such extreme love is the mark of the Christian life, by which others will know 'you are my disciples' (13:35). In the centuries of poverty and persecution which followed, this was one characteristic which the world could not ignore: 'see how these Christians love one another', says Tertullian (*Apology* 39.7). Today, when we truly follow Jesus' example, people say the same. Unfortunately, these words are all too often hurled as a sarcastic taunt at churches when we fight among ourselves! It all depends on whether we keep the new commandment, which Jesus introduces here and which will be replayed in the next chapters.

Death or denial?

The three themes of the symphony have been introduced but Peter is still trying to grasp the basic point: what is Jesus talking about? 'Lord, where are you going?' (13:36). Jesus gently repeats that Peter cannot come with him now; Jesus' hour has come, but not Peter's yet. A second-century story (turned into a Hollywood epic) describes how Peter, fleeing Rome to avoid being killed, meets Jesus going towards the city. Peter repeats his question, 'Lord, where are you going?'—*quo vadis?* in Latin. Jesus' reply, that he is going to Rome to die for Peter, makes the apostle turn around and face his own martyrdom. The impetuous Peter, as at the foot washing, wants to go the whole way now, to do the same as the good shepherd and lay down his life (13:37). Jesus' answer shows how little Peter is really ready to die; before cock crow he will have denied his master three times (13:38).

PRAYER

Thank you, Jesus, for loving us even to the extremes of the cross; grant that I may love others and so come to be with you.

72

I Am *the* Way, Truth & Life

People often start reading the Farewell Discourse here, but this section runs straight on from chapter 13. Starting here misses those opening themes about glory and loving each other, because Jesus is going away. Peter wanted to know where he is going and the disciples began to panic. Jesus rebuked Peter and warned him of his denial, so they are bound to be troubled and upset. As Jesus reassures them, there is a crucial change in the verbs. He began speaking to them all as 'you-plural' with 'little children' (13:33), but dropped into 'you-singular', thee/thou, when talking to Peter alone. Now Jesus returns to 'you-plurals' to address all the disciples, and most modern translations (unlike the AV or KJV) have 'your hearts' here to make the point (14:1). There is a constant temptation to apply all these wonderful promises of the Farewell Discourse to an individual believer's relationship with Jesus. However, remembering that the promises are to 'you-plural' enables us to appreciate better the corporate nature of our life together in Christ.

In my father's house

Jesus looks at the worried faces around the table, wondering what all this talk of going away means, and moves to comfort them: 'let not your hearts be troubled' (14:1). Again the word is *tarasso*, recalling Jesus being troubled at Lazarus' grave and his feelings about his own death (11:33; 12:27; 13:21). Thus it is appropriate to use this passage at funerals. We comfort each other in bereavement as Jesus comforted his disciples, that there is hope in death because of Jesus' own death for us. Therefore he tells us to 'believe in God, believe also in me'. Both verbs could also be translated as statements, 'you believe', but the sense is clear: we can comfort our troubled hearts through our belief in God and so believe and trust in Jesus also.

Then comes the much-loved image of 'many mansions in my Father's house' (14:2). The word, *monai*, comes from the verb *meno*, to abide or remain, which occurs often here. So it means 'abiding-places', rooms to stay in a travel lodge, stopping places on our way to God. Its Latin equivalent is *mansio*, giving us the English 'mansions'. Jesus is going to 'prepare a place for you-all (plural)'; the word 'place', *topos*, was used by the priests for 'our place', the temple (11:48). Through Jesus, his disciples find rest and a place in the eternal worship of God. This is why he will 'come again' for us, 'that where I am, you may be also' (14:3). Does this 'coming again' mean when he returns to them after the Resurrection, or after each Christian's death, or his final coming at the end of time? Since they all bring us to be with Jesus, probably all are included. He has made it clear that the 'way to the place where he is going' is through his glorification on the cross (14:4, see 12:23, 32–33; 13:31).

The way to the Father

Again, Thomas misunderstands, thinking at the earthly level. When Jesus was going into Judaea to wake Lazarus, Thomas morosely went to 'die with him' (11:16). Again, he has not realized what Jesus means, and does not know the way to this wonderful place (14:5). Jesus replies that we do not have to *go* anywhere—we have to *be* with him: 'I am the way, the truth and the life' (14:6). As with the other 'I am' sayings, these are all key Jewish terms which Jesus is claiming to fulfil. To be the 'way' is similar to 'I am the Door' (10:7–9), while the 'truth' is what Jesus has been talking about throughout the gospel. All the other 'I am' sayings involve 'life', 'bread of life', 'resurrection and life' and so forth. Now they all come together. As the Jewish law and scriptures brought people to God, now Jesus is claiming to be the way to the Father, where all truth and life is to be found.

The exclusive claim of 'no one comes to the Father except through me' (14:6) is much debated. What does this mean for people of other faiths? Certainly, no other religious teacher claimed actually to *be* the way, the truth and the life, but rather to have pointed people *to* the way, the truth and life of God. Only one who has come from God, from the infinite, can become the bridge whereby finite human beings come to God. Whenever anyone, of whatever belief, finds truth and life in God they come through the way of Jesus, whether they realize it or not. But those who do know it and know Jesus as the way, do not just find God, but they know him as Jesus reveals him, as our Father: 'if you (plural) know me, you will know my Father also' (14:7).

PRAYER

Lord Jesus, grant me to walk in your way, to know your truth and to experience the life you share with your Father.

SHOW US *the* FATHER

Thomas misunderstood Jesus' claim to be 'the way, the truth and the life' as a physical way to God. Jesus took him deeper into the spiritual relationship between himself and his Father, so that to know Jesus is to know the Father (14:6–7). Now Philip responds superficially. One of the first disciples, he brought others like Nathanael and the Greeks to Jesus (1:43–48; 12:21–22). He tends to look at the physical level, as in his pessimism that feeding the five thousand would cost over half a year's wages (6:5–7). To such a literal thinker, Jesus' comment that 'you know and have seen the Father' (14:7) would seem odd. If only Jesus would 'show us the Father', then we would all be satisfied and life would be clearer (14:8).

Seeing God in Jesus

The desire to see God is a basic religious instinct. Moses, the 'friend of God', asked to see his glory, but had to be content with a view of his back (Exod. 33:18–23). The Psalmist longs to behold the face of God (e.g. Pss. 13:1; 27:8; 42:1–2). However, as John's prologue put it, 'no one has ever seen God' (1:18). Philip's request is so simple, yet so profound—but it also reveals how little he has understood what he has seen. There is resigned sadness in Jesus' reply that even one of the first he called still does not see, as he addresses Philip directly: 'have I been with you-all (plural) so long, Philip, and yet you (singular) still do not know me?' (14:9). 'How can *you* say…' and 'do *you* not believe?' continue as you-singular. It is incredible that Philip, who brought others to Jesus, can still talk like this and not realize that 'whoever has seen me has seen the Father … I am in the Father and the Father is in me' (14:9–10). John depicts the incarnation as the Father 'dwelling' or 'abiding' in Jesus, (using *meno*, the word which gave us 'dwelling places', 14:2). To see Jesus heal the paralysed and blind men and to raise Lazarus was to see God at work; to watch Jesus turn water into wine and feed the crowd was to marvel at the abundance of God; to hear Jesus speak was to see God pleading with his people. So Jesus changes back to the you-plural and appeals to them all: 'believe me that I am in the Father and the Father is in me' (14:11). And if that is too hard, they should believe 'because of the works themselves', not because they are magic but because they are 'signs' that Jesus has come 'from God' (see 3:2; 9:33; 10:37–38).

Greater works

In farewell speeches, the person about to leave looks ahead to what will happen when they have gone. So now Jesus lifts his horizon beyond Philip's lack of insight to describe what those 'who believe in me' will do in the future. Not only will they 'do the works that I do' but they will also do 'greater works' (14:12). What does this promise of 'greater works', also mentioned earlier (5:20), mean? The early church did many miracles, as is seen in the stories in Acts and the lists of spiritual gifts (e.g. 1 Cor. 12:7–10). All our great spiritual reawakenings, from founding the monasteries to Wesley and beyond, have been accompanied by such 'works'. In recent years, a renewed expectation that God is active through his Holy Spirit has brought a resurgence of belief in miracles, and some people seek to do the 'greater works' than Jesus. Whenever someone is healed, or prayers are answered and God is glorified, we should rejoice, but this verse does not mean that we should 'out-perform' Jesus.

The 'greater works' are 'because I am going to the Father', and from his Father he poured out his Holy Spirit to send the church out in mission. In the incarnation, Jesus was limited by his human form; he could only travel within one locality and touch so many people. Since his return to the Father, he has sent his disciples across the whole world, to touch and heal millions. These are the prayers he longs to answer when we 'ask in my name' (14:13). The 'whatever' and the 'anything' (14:13–14) are sometimes understood that all our prayers can answered. Yet they have to be 'in my name'. This is not a magic formula, tacked onto the end of any outrageous request. Jesus could do nothing 'on my own' but only because the Father was dwelling in him (14:10). Similarly, we pray in his name only when we so dwell in Jesus that through the answer to our prayers, 'the Father may be glorified in the Son' (14:13). Then not only will we, and Philip, see the Father, but so will all the world, and 'be satisfied'.

PRAYER

'Christ has no hands but our hands to do his work today.
He has no feet but our feet to lead men in his way.'
From St Theresa

The PROMISE *of the* SPIRIT

Jesus continues to reassure his disciples as several farewell themes are woven together in this next section. He reinforces the main point that he is going away, and yet will still be with them; this leads into a discussion of the relationship of the Father and the Son, which picks up Philip's question about 'seeing the Father'. Because of the love of the Father and the Son, not only will we see God, but he will dwell with us. This is all made possible through the coming of the Holy Spirit, a new theme introduced here and repeated and developed in the coming sections.

First, Jesus moves from talking about granting the believers' prayers to how we keep his commandments (14:15). The word for 'keep' could be a future tense, 'if you love me, you will keep my commandments', so that obedience flows naturally out of our love for him; alternatively, it may be a command, 'if you love me, keep' so that we show our love by striving to obey him. Either way, the connection of loving Jesus and doing what he says is clear.

Another Helper

As a result of this, Jesus says that he will ask the Father to give us 'another Paraclete' (14:16). This is the first use of an important term in these Discourses. The Greek word, *Paraclete*, means 'someone called alongside' to help or assist. Its direct translation into Latin gives us the word 'advocate'. It is often used in the law courts to mean someone who is 'called in' to speak for someone on trial, either as their defending counsel or to intercede with the judge on their behalf. Thus two possible English translations are 'Counsellor' or 'Intercessor', both of which can be found in some Bibles. The second idea of interceding can be seen in 1 Jn. 2:1, where Jesus is our 'advocate (*paraclete*) with the Father'. Another greatly loved translation is 'Comforter'. This gives us the image of someone 'called in' to console someone in need or grief, as the disciples are here; but the original meaning of 'comfort' through the Latin is to give strength or courage. The Bayeux tapestry has 'Bishop Odo comforteth his men', where the good bishop is encouraging them by prodding them with a spear from behind! Thus the Paraclete is our counsellor, advocate, intercessor, comforter, strengthener—an all round helper.

He is further identified as 'another Paraclete', where the word 'another', *allos* in Greek, is another of the same sort, like the last one, rather than 'another, different one'. Since everything said about the Paraclete is also said of Jesus elsewhere in this gospel, he is 'another Jesus' to be with the disciples as Jesus goes away. Then he is finally identified as 'the Spirit of truth' (14:17). This description of the Holy Spirit as both 'Paraclete' and 'Spirit of truth' will be developed later (14:26; 15:26; 16:7; 16:13). At this point, Jesus stresses that the Spirit is coming for the disciples, to replace Jesus when he is taken from them. The 'world cannot receive' him; that which is opposed to God cannot recognize him, cannot see or know him. But if we know him, we will find that he 'abides' in us, using the word, *meno*, to dwell, linking us back to the 'many abodes' of 14:2.

I will come to you

Jesus will be with those first disciples and all who love and keep his commandments through the Holy Spirit, the Paraclete. Thus he can give us the marvellous promise 'I will not leave you desolate; I am coming to you' (14:18). The word here is literally 'orphans' and was used of children without parents or of pupils without a master, such as the followers of Socrates when he was executed. Again we note that, while this promise is to each individual Christian, the 'you' is still plural. It is in our relationship all together that we find Jesus coming to us. In 'a little while', the world will see him no longer; but we will see him: 'because I live, you also will live' (14:19). Jesus has already answered Philip's desire to see the Father by reassuring him that 'the Father is in me and I in the Father' (14:10–11). Through the Holy Spirit, Jesus will also be one with those who love him: 'you in me and I in you' and so we are caught up into the very life of the Godhead (14:20). Thus not only are those who keep Jesus' words loved by him, but by his Father also and through this he is able to reveal himself to them, even when he has physically departed from them (14:21).

PRAYER

Lord Jesus, thank you that you do not leave us desolate;
pour out your Spirit to strengthen, comfort and advise us
that the world may know you live in us and we in you.

75

A Parting Gift

Jesus explains to his disciples that, although he is going to leave them, he will still be with them through the Holy Spirit, revealing himself to them (14:21). Each time he has talked of going away, one of the disciples has asked a question for further clarification—Peter, Thomas, Philip (13:36; 14:5, 8). Now it is the turn of Judas, who is identified as 'not Iscariot', not the betrayer, who has gone out into the darkness of the night. We know nothing else about him, although Luke also mentions a 'Judas, son of James' different from Iscariot (Lk. 6:16; Acts 1:13). This Judas asks why Jesus will reveal himself to the disciples, but not to the world (14:22). Jesus' reply recalls his previous theme of loving him and keeping his commandments (14:15). Only those who love him and keep his word, which is not his anyway, but 'from the Father who sent me', can accept his revelation; those who do not love or obey him, will not recognize him, or his Father (14:23–24). Yet to those who do love him, not only will Jesus reveal himself, but he and his Father will come and 'dwell' with them. Jesus and his Father will 'make our home with them', using *mone* for 'home', like the many 'dwelling places' in the Father's house (14:2). Not only does Jesus prepare a place for us in God, but he also makes a place for God in us.

The Counsellor will teach you

This mutual indwelling of God in us and us in God is wonderful, but not easy to grasp. So Jesus reminds the disciples that he says all this to explain it to them, 'while I am still with you', before he goes away (14:25). This theme is repeated frequently (15:11; 16:1, 4, 6, 25, 33). But Jesus does not expect them to comprehend it all now. The task of the Paraclete, the Holy Spirit who will be sent by the Father, is to 'teach you everything and remind you of all that I have said to you' (14:26). 'Disciples' means learners and they have called Jesus their rabbi, teacher. Now the Holy Spirit will be their rabbi, 'another' Jesus teaching them. Christians need to go on 'lifelong learning' as we grow in our faith and discipleship. But the teaching we learn cannot be different from Jesus' words. The Spirit comes 'in my name', as we respond also 'in my name' in prayer (14:13). This is the test when someone claims a new revelation from the Spirit: is it consistent with

Jesus' words and commandment, and can it be done in his name?

Peace I leave with you

Jesus returns to his central theme of reassurance as he gives them his parting gift of peace (14:27). It is customary in a farewell to bequeath something 'to remember me by', like an inheritance in a will. Jesus' bequest, however, is 'not as the world gives', where peace is merely the absence of conflict. The Hebrew concept of 'Shalom' includes peace, health, and well being. It is a regular greeting and leave taking: live long and prosper. The 'shalom' of God is often promised in the Old Testament as a mark of God's coming in his glorious kingdom. Such a leaving gift of peace from Jesus means that the disciples must not let their 'hearts be troubled', as the word, *tarasso*, recalls the beginning (14:1). Why would they still be troubled? Jesus suggests that it is because they heard him say 'I am going away' (14:28). The grief this causes them shows that their love is possessive, concerned for themselves. If they really understood and loved Jesus, they would rejoice because 'I am going to the Father'. While they may be sad for their sake, they should be pleased for his sake as he returns to God. Since 'the Father is greater than I', Jesus can leave in perfect trust that God knows what he is doing. In later Christological controversies, the Arian heretics argued that this verse implied that Jesus is less than God. But the whole point of the Discourse is that to have seen Jesus is to have seen the Father (14:9).

The end is very near

Actually, the Father's greatness is what Jesus is returning to, and so he seeks again to reassure them: 'I have told you this before it happens' (14:29). This is to build their faith, so that his death is not a destructive disaster, but helps them to believe because Jesus has warned them about it. Time is very short for talking, for 'the ruler of this world' is coming, a phrase describing the devil (12:31). This would terrify the disciples, so we get more reassurance—'he has no power over me' (14:30). This final section weaves four key themes of going, obeying, knowing and loving together as Jesus goes to obey his Father 'that the world may know' his love. So it is time to be on their way (14:31).

PRAYER

Lord Jesus, calm our troubled hearts and grant us your peace.

76

I AM *the* VINE

The various themes introduced in chapter 13 were developed through chapter 14, including the key elements of a farewell speech. Finally, Jesus said, 'Rise, let us go from here' (14:31). However, they do not do this until 18:1. Some scholars suggest that chapters 15—17 were inserted later. However, even if 14:31 originally led into 18:1, the gospel as we have it today, and in every ancient copy, includes these chapters here. Others suggest that they set out at 14:31 and these three chapters are delivered by Jesus on the way to Gethsemane. Since these chapters develop many of the key themes, it is better to see Jesus' comment as giving some urgency to the Discourse. After all, it is not unusual at dinner-parties to say, 'we really must be going', several times before actually departing, such is the interesting conversation!

The true vine and the farmer

Jesus now introduces the last 'I am' saying: 'I am the true vine' (15:1). The vine, from which wine comes, reminds us immediately of the institution of the holy communion in bread and wine in the other gospels, but absent here. This may be a hint for those who are 'in the know' to look beyond the words to the deeper spiritual level, as Jesus prepares his disciples for his death.

He gives them another 'figure', or *mashal*, like the door and the shepherd (10:1–6). In the other 'I am' sayings, Jesus applied the great Hebrew images of bread, light, shepherds and so forth, usually used for the law, to himself. Here he takes the vine—the supreme image, not just of the law or faith, but the very people of God themselves. Israel was a 'vine brought out of Egypt' and planted by God (Ps. 80:8). Regrettably, most references suggest a lack of fruitfulness. Isaiah speaks of a 'vineyard on a very fertile hill … which only yielded wild grapes' (Is. 5:1–4; see also Jer. 2:21). None the less, the vine was an emblem on the coins of the Maccabean leaders, which recalls the good and bad shepherds (see on 10:22).

In contrast, Jesus is the 'true vine'. The eucharistic discourse after the miraculous feeding said that his flesh is 'true food' and his blood 'true drink' (6:55). He has been called the 'true light' and the 'true bread from heaven' (1:9; 6:32), other key Jewish images. Now, as the 'true vine', he is nothing less than the 'real' Israel. God his Father is the vine grower, *georgos*, the farmer who planted the vine. Again, Jesus is dependent on his Father: as the one who sends precedes the one who is sent, so the vine grower precedes the vine. And it is the farmer, 'George', who prunes the barren branches from the vine (15:2). He 'cleans out' the small shoots budding with growth and using up precious nutrients, but not producing fruit. To have something 'nipped in the bud' can be painful, but it is the only way to promote healthy growth. The verb used for 'pruning', *kathairo*, means to 'clean out'; so Jesus remarks that the disciples need not fear since they have been 'made clean', *katharos*, by his word (15:3). This refers back to the foot washing when they were all made 'clean', *katharos*, except for Judas, who, like a dead branch, has fallen away (13:10).

Abide in me

Branches can only survive as an intimate part of the vine. So Jesus tells them, 'abide in me as I abide in you' (15:4). The word 'abide', *meno*, links us to the 'abodes' in the Father's house and the way the Father and the Son dwell in each other and make their home in believers (14:2, 10, 23). Now this word occurs ten times in these few verses. The lesson is applied both negatively, that branches cannot bear fruit by themselves (15:4) and positively, that branches remaining on the vine bear 'much fruit' (15:5). When branches are pruned from a fruit tree, they can remain lodged in the tree, looking as healthy as the others; but as time goes by they turn brown, fall out and are fit only for the bonfire (15:6). Christians who have severed their connection with Christ may remain caught up in the church, but eventually they fall away, fruitless. To keep our life rooted in Christ's, we must protect time for prayer and worship. If we do this, we will so abide in Jesus that we will only pray that which is his will (15:7; see 14:13–14). When such prayers from our abiding in Christ are answered, they produce not just fruit, but also glorify God the Father (15:8; see 13:31–32; 14:13).

PRAYER

You are the vine and we are the branches;
keep us abiding in you and prune us clean
that we might bear much fruit to your glory.

ABIDE *in* LOVE

Jesus uses the image of the vine to describe his relationship with his disciples, even when he is physically absent. He is the 'true' or 'real vine', and we are branches which must remain in the vine to bear fruit, the fruit of love, one of John's key themes. Jesus has been dependent upon his Father in everything. Now he shows that the Father is the source of all love: 'as the Father has loved me, so I have loved you' (15:9). The Greek tense of these verbs are aorists, depicting definite and concrete events in the past, affecting us now. Jesus was so secure in his Father's love that he could show his love for his disciples by washing their feet (13:1–5).

We are to 'abide' in Jesus' love, using *meno* again, just as he 'abides' in his Father's love, by keeping his commandment (15:10). The earlier theme of remaining in love through obedience (see 14:15, 21, 23–24) is now linked to joy. Jesus is explaining all this so that 'my joy may be in you' and our joy might be 'fully complete' (15:11). He has already told the disciples that they should rejoice at his going to the Father (14:28) and this theme of joy will be developed later (16:20–33). Since the fruit of the vine is wine, which brings joy to 'gladden our hearts' (Ps. 104:15), we may have another hint of communion here.

Love one another

As the Father has loved Jesus, and Jesus has loved us, so we are to abide in his love (15:9). Thus the church is to be a community of love where the new commandment is lived out. Jesus reminds them of the foot washing: 'this is my commandment, that you love one another as I have loved you' (15:12, picking up 13:34). The past tense of 'I have loved you' is to result in our present love for one another. Jesus' specific act of love is his self sacrifice, to lay down his life 'for his friends' (15:13). This was foreshadowed in the good shepherd laying down his life for the sheep (10:11) and now he prepares them for his sacrificial death. The word, 'for', *hyper*, means 'on behalf of', that his death is for our benefit. The same word comes in the institution of the communion, 'this is my body, given *for* you' (Lk. 22:19–20; 1 Cor. 11:24), so here we have another hint of the eucharist. If we are to love each other as Jesus has loved us, then we must be ready to pay the ultimate sacrifice. Peter offered to lay down his life, and although only Jesus is to die now, we know that Peter's time will also come (13:37; 21:19).

Beloved friends

Talking of laying down his life 'for his friends' moves Jesus to call his disciples not 'servants', but 'friends', *philoi*, which comes from the verb 'to love' and indicates 'dear ones', 'beloved'. We show that we are his 'beloved' by our love for him, in keeping his commandment as was seen earlier (15:14; see on 15:10). There is, of course, nothing wrong in being 'God's servant'. Many Old Testament prophets, priests and kings were glad to be called this, including Joshua and David (Josh. 24:29; Ps. 89:20). Jesus himself took the servant's role when he washed their feet but, as their master, accepted them as his servants (13:13–16). But now he calls them his 'loved ones', as Moses was the 'friend' of God (Exod. 33:11). The Roman emperor's inner circle of 'friends' were his principal advisers. So Jesus wants to 'make known' everything to his beloved disciples (15:15). Christians are often so busy being God's servants, 'working for Jesus', that we forget he wants us to be his friends, to love him and to be loved by him.

Rabbis did not usually look for disciples. Young people seeking a teacher would 'shop around', visit several and choose the one they wanted. But not Jesus, who reminds his disciples that he chose them, and did so for a purpose, that they should 'go and bear fruit' (15:16). This fruit is to 'last', 'abide' (*meno* again) and results in the Father answering their prayers, picking up another theme (14:13; 15:7). Then he repeats his final command, 'love one another' (15:17). Farewells typically include some last words or instructions, and we take them very seriously and try to do them. Thus Jesus' disciples are his 'beloved', loved by him as he is by his Father and he wants them to be a community of love, loving each other. This is not in order to be an introverted, cosy warm church but so that we might 'go and bear fruit that will last', reaching out in love to the world around us.

PRAYER

Lord Jesus, thank you that you call us your beloved friends
inspire us to love one another as you have loved us
and send us out to bear much fruit that will last.

NOT *of the* WORLD

In a farewell speech the speaker may talk of the terrible things which will happen after they have gone: as Madame de Pompadour put it before the French Revolution, '*après nous le déluge*'. Jesus' teaching about the coming end times includes the persecution of his followers in the other gospels (Mk. 13; Matt. 24—25; Lk. 21). Here in John, Jesus looks ahead to the persecution and opposition coming for the disciples, first from 'the world' and also from "the Jews". This is an important new theme for the next chapters.

First, however, we must consider how the phrase 'the world' is used in this gospel. Already in these discourses the 'Spirit of truth' is not seen or known by 'the world' and Jesus' parting gift of peace is 'not as the world gives' (14:17, 27). Over the next few chapters, 'the world' will be increasingly portrayed as 'hating' and opposing Jesus and his disciples, until finally Jesus tells Pilate 'my kingdom is not of this world' (18:36). So some scholars accuse John of being 'other-worldly', and some Christians withdraw from the world into isolationist sects to follow this teaching. The 'world' is seen as evil, the domain of thieves, robbers and wolves, while the good shepherd's followers are to save as many individuals as possible and protect them in the sheepfold of the church. While this is an exaggeration, it is not an unreasonable inference from some verses about the world in these chapters.

The word 'world' occurs nearly 80 times in 60 verses of John's gospel (see on 1:10). But only about twenty verses have this negative connotation, mostly occurring in these Farewell chapters. Nearly another twenty verses use 'the world' in a neutral way, to mean 'everyone', as the Pharisees complain that 'the world' had gone after Jesus (12:19). Finally, a third group of verses treat 'the world' positively as the object of God's love into which he sent his only Son (3:16). Jesus is the 'Saviour of the world', the living bread for 'the life of the world' and the 'light of the world' (4:42; 6:33, 51; 8:12; 9:5). Most of these 'positive' uses occur in the first half of the gospel where Jesus is calling the world to himself through his words and his miraculous signs. The 'world' only becomes negative in these final chapters after it has rejected Jesus—and the phrase now describes the human structures which oppose God.

The hatred of the world

John has stressed the intimate link of Jesus and his disciples: they are loved by him as he is loved by the Father and, as he was sent by the Father, so they are to go and bear fruit. Now we find the corollary is also true: the disciples will be hated by the world, as it hated Jesus (15:18). Jesus' identification with his persecuted church is also seen in Paul's vision on the Damascus road: 'Saul, Saul, why do you persecute *me*?' (Acts 9:4). In fact, the Graeco-Roman world was remarkably tolerant of different religions. Their belief in many gods meant that any new faith could be included in their pantheon—provided that believers were prepared to sacrifice in reverence to the emperor worship which was important in binding so many different peoples into one empire faithful to Rome. To stand out against that, as the early Christians had to, and declare that God alone is worthy of our allegiance was to be disloyal. Thus Jesus says that the world loves 'its own' (15:19). Jesus came to 'his own' and was rejected (1:11); the disciples became 'his own' whom he loved to the uttermost (13:1). He chose them (15:16)—and took them out of the world. The consequence is that the world hates them, as it does him.

Servants follow their master

The intimate relationship of Jesus and his disciples leads him to remind them that he said at the foot washing that 'servants are not greater than their master' (15:20; see 13:16). If they persecute the master, Jesus, then they will do the same to his disciples. But even here it is not all gloomy and negative. There is also the possibility that those who obey him, will also do what the disciples say. It all depends on their reaction to Jesus' name. 'Jesus' means 'Saviour', a title used by the Romans for the emperor and by the Jews for God; to call Jesus 'Lord' would offend both groups for similar reasons. So this is the motive for their opposition 'on account of my name, because they do not know him who sent me' (15:21). Because the world does not know God, they cannot recognize Jesus whom he has sent, nor his disciples who come in his name.

For REFLECTION & PRAYER

Pray for all the places in the world where Christians are persecuted because of Jesus' name. If it were a crime to be a Christian in your country, would there be enough evidence to convict you?

The SPIRIT *of* TRUTH

So far the opposition and the hatred has been predicted from 'the world'—every human system and structure opposed to God, anything or anyone who wants to be in the centre where only God can be. Into this world of darkness, God sent his only Son to bring light by his words and works, both of which testified that the Father had sent him. As we have seen, the coming of light into darkness inevitably brings shadows, and for those who will not see nor listen, the mission of Jesus and the disciples brings a *crisis*, a turning point of judgment.

"The Jews" reject Jesus' words and works

Jesus now moves from talking about 'the world' to discuss the fate of the people to whom he came and spoke. The first thing they have ignored is his words. Jesus was sent into the world not to condemn it but that it might be saved through him (3:17). However, there is another, awful consequence of Jesus' mission; if he had not 'spoken to them, they would not have sin'. But, since he has given them his words which they have chosen to ignore or reject, 'now they have no excuse' (15:22). This reminds us of the Pharisees who cast out the blind man while claiming that they were able to see; it was their wilful blindness to what Jesus was doing that caused their sin or guilt (9:41).

The links between the Father, the Son and the disciples in John usually means that whoever loves the disciples loves the Son, and whoever loves the Son loves the Father. Here we have the reverse: Jesus has already warned that the world will hate them because it hates him. Now it follows that those who hate him are also hating the Father who sent him (15:23).

Proof of their hatred was seen in their refusal to accept Jesus' words (15:22). Now he moves on to his 'works', the miracles which 'no one else had done'. John has called them 'signs' because they 'manifest his glory' (2:11). Jesus has appealed to both "the Jews" and the disciples to believe in him because of his works (10:37–38; 14:11). But once again, the converse is also true: since they have refused to accept his works as signs of God's activity, they have no excuse for their sin.

To see his works and reject them is the opposite of love, as was shown in their treatment of the blind man. Therefore 'they have seen and hated' both Jesus and his Father who sent him (15:24).

It has been obvious from Jesus' appeal to his words and works that he is not referring here to 'the world' in general, but to those who have seen and heard him, "the Jews" who opposed him. Now that is made explicit as he cites the Psalms as predicting that 'they hated me without a cause' (Ps. 35:19; 69:4). The sense of rejection is such that he can even talk of the Jewish scriptures as 'their law', despite being himself a Jew who revered these holy books. This picks up his earlier debates with "the Jews" where Jesus called the scriptures 'your law' (8:17; 10:34).

The witness of the Spirit

All this talk of hating and opposing brings back the court room imagery and the themes of witness from the debates of chapters 5—8. These arguments were like mini-trials of Jesus in advance about how to interpret his words and works. The crucial issue turned on what were his witnesses to prove that he was sent from God (see on 5:30–47). We have already noted that the 'Paraclete' is a legal term for either a defending counsel or for someone to speak or witness on a defendant's behalf, and the first mention of the Paraclete identified him as 'the Spirit of truth' (14:16–17). In a situation of accusation, defence and witness, one who can speak the truth is absolutely vital. So now Jesus says that he is sending the Spirit of truth to 'testify on my behalf' (15:26). The Spirit is described here as one who comes 'from the Father', yet also one 'whom I will send to you'. This verse caused endless debates in the early church, resulting in the phrase in the Nicene Creed that the Holy Spirit 'proceeds from the Father and the Son'. However, John was thinking more of the mission and witness of the church than eternal relationships within the Trinity! Not only will the Spirit witness to Jesus, but as the encouraging Comforter he will stir up the disciples also to testify what they have seen having been 'with me from the beginning' (15:27).

PRAYER

Holy Spirit of truth, comforter and advocate
grant me courage to witness
to the words and works of Jesus.

RETURNING *to the* FATHER

Throughout these farewell discourses, Jesus has been preparing the disciples for his departure. He has made it increasingly clear that there will be a major division after he has gone. On his side there will be those who remain in his love and in the Father's by abiding in the vine and loving one another with the Spirit as their 'helper'. On the other side, there will be opposition—from the world in general, from the Romans and from "the Jews". These same themes recur in this chapter as the discourse comes to an end, but in the reverse order: it begins with the certainty of opposition, and then moves through the assistance of the Spirit to Jesus' going away to his Father.

Out of the synagogues

Like most people trying hard to convey a difficult message, Jesus repeats himself. He has already said twice that the purpose of these discourses is to tell them these things while he is still with them (14:25; 15:11) and this refrain 'I have said these things' will repeat throughout this chapter (16:1, 4, 6, 25, 33). He is particularly concerned to stop them 'stumbling', or being 'scandalized', as the Greek puts it (16:1). The only other time this verb occurs in John is when Jesus asks if his teaching 'scandalizes' them when some disciples give up and fall away (6:60–66). So now he is trying to stop them 'stumbling' and 'falling away' when he is no longer there and opposition comes. None of us knows how we may react under persecution. Unfortunately, the history of the church has many periods where the pressures have been so great that some have given up while others have paid the ultimate sacrifice.

Here we have the painful separation of the followers of Jesus from their Jewish roots (16:2). The problem is once again being put 'out of the synagogue', *aposynagogos*, as was threatened to the blind man and the authorities who believed (9:22; 12:42). Even if this technical term refers to action taken at the time the gospel was being written, severe opposition was waged against the early church, as the former persecutor Paul testifies (see Gal. 1:13; Phil. 3:6; Acts 26:9). Here, Jesus warns that in some cases it will even bring martyrdom, as happened to Stephen and James (Acts 7:60; 12:2). The irony is that the persecutors think they are offering a 'service' to God. The irony of people killing others as a 'service to God' when the real worship is offered by the death of the martyr has regrettably happened all too often, not just for some early Christians at Jewish hands, but also as Christians have killed Jews and most often, their fellow Christians. In all these cases, says Jesus, they may think they are doing it for God, but such actions reveal how little they know God or Jesus (16:3). Then he repeats that he is saying it now, so that when it does happen, they will not be surprised, but remember his warning (16:4).

To your advantage

With this warning, Jesus reminds them of why and where he is going, returning to 'the one who sent me' (16:5). They are so sunk in their concern about this, that Jesus notices that this time no disciple pops up to ask, 'where are you going?', the *quo vadis?* question. Of course, both Peter and Thomas asked this earlier (13:36; 14:5). So some commentators suggest that these discourses are from separate sources, or delivered on separate nights. However, in the flow of the overall narrative, it is their lack of questioning now, in the present, which shows how they are too wrapped up in grief to ask about his joy at returning to his Father. Despite his repeated stress that their hearts should 'not be troubled' (14:1), 'sorrow has filled' them now (16:6).

Jesus makes another attempt to enable them to understand. It is 'to your advantage', using the same word as Caiaphas' prophecy that it was 'expedient' or 'better' for one man to die for the nation (11:50; 18:14). Jesus' departure means that he will be able to send them the Helper, the Paraclete, already promised earlier (14:26). If Jesus does not face death and 'go away', the Spirit cannot come (16:7, see also 7:39). Jesus is still limited in space and time by his physical body, but when he has returned to his Father, he will send the Spirit, 'another helper' to be alongside them, just as he was, but not so limited. This is indeed to their advantage, but at the moment the disciples are too absorbed to realize it.

PRAYER

Lord Jesus, send me your Holy Spirit,
to comfort me and keep me from falling away
and to stop me from being too wrapped up in my own anxieties
that I miss what you are trying to tell me.

81

The TASK of the SPIRIT

In this final farewell discourse, Jesus has described the two sides, those who are abiding in love with him and his Father and those who are opposed to them all. Although he is going away, this will enable the Holy Spirit to be 'called alongside', as the Paraclete, to continue the work of Jesus. He has a particular task to do with regard to both sides.

The conviction of the Spirit

The first area relates to the world, which we have seen means here those opposed to Jesus (see on 15:18–19 above). If the Spirit is 'another' Jesus, he will do what Jesus did. Jesus came into the world to save it, not condemn it; but when the light came into the darkness, there were those who refused him, preferring to stay in the shadows lest their evil deeds were 'exposed' (3:16–20). In a verbal echo of that passage, now the Spirit's task is the same: he will 'convict' the world (16:8). In both verses the word is *elencho*. As 'paraclete' is used for a legal counsel, so *elencho* means to 'prove wrong', 'convict', 'reprove', the work of cross examination in a trial. The three things the Spirit will 'convince' the world of are also legal words meaning 'crime', 'justice', and 'sentence or verdict' at this human level. As always with John, if we look closer, we will see that they have a spiritual meaning also.

The first word, *hamartia*, can mean 'mistake', or 'crime', which at the spiritual level means 'sin'. In the cross examination of Jesus after those who were going to stone the woman taken in adultery went away aware of their own sin, Jesus asked 'which of you convicts (*elencho*) me of sin (*hamartia*)?' (8:46). At his coming trial, they will 'convict' him and sentence him to death. It is the task of the Spirit to 'convince' the world that this was wrong; instead, they are guilty of the most basic sin, that God has come among them and they 'do not believe' in him (16:9). Jesus has already said that they are 'without excuse' for this sin because of their claim to be able to see (9:41; 15:22–24). It is still the first work of the Spirit to convince men and women of their sin and lack of faith in Jesus.

Secondly, he will convict them of 'justice', or 'righteousness', *dikaiosune*. This is the only time this favourite word of Paul's appears in John. At the human level, the Spirit will convince the world that Jesus' death was not a 'just' condemnation of a criminal. But what was a human injustice, God has made his 'righteousness'; through it Jesus has returned to his Father and his presence with God now is the final proof (16:10).

Finally, the Spirit will 'expose' the 'verdict', *krisis*. It looks as though evil has triumphed and Jesus has been condemned. In fact, the coming of Jesus brought the 'critical moment', the 'judgment' that people loved darkness rather than light (see on 3:19). So the third task of the Spirit is to convince the world that Jesus' death on the cross is actually the 'judgment' when the 'ruler of this world' is condemned (16:11; see 12:31).

Guidance into all truth

If the Paraclete comes as a cross-examining counsel to convince the world of the truth, so he comes also to the disciples to 'guide you into all truth' (16:13). As Jesus was their teacher, so now the Spirit will be also. But what he teaches will not be his own teaching; instead he will continue the teaching of Jesus. Jesus still has 'many things to say' to the disciples which they are not yet ready for (16:12). We must always beware of thinking that we know it all, or even are ready for all that Jesus longs to show us. Christian discipleship is a journey of life-long learning in the guidance of the Spirit of truth. It is his task to speak 'whatever he hears' from Jesus and the Father, to 'declare what is to come' (16:13). As Jesus glorified the Father by doing the will of the one who sent him, so the Spirit will glorify Jesus, by taking 'what is mine' and declaring it to us (16:14). And because of the unity of love within the Holy Trinity, 'what is mine' is actually 'all that the Father has' (16:15). Thus we are back to our key themes of glory given and received within the Father, the Son and the Spirit in the unity of love into which we are invited by the Paraclete to share and abide.

PRAYER

Come Holy Spirit,
convince the world
of sin, righteousness and judgment
and guide us into all truth.

82

SORROW WILL TURN *to* JOY

Now that Jesus has warned his disciples of the coming persecution and the presence of the Spirit to convince the world and guide them into truth, he returns to his main theme. The whole point of these 'Farewell Discourses' has been to prepare them for his departure—but they are still having problems grasping it.

A little while

So Jesus repeats again that 'a little while' and they will not see him, but after 'a little while' they will (16:16). He used this phrase to warn the crowd and "the Jews" that his ministry among them would only be for a limited time (7:33; 12:35). Equally, the disciples have been told twice that in 'a little while' he would be leaving them (13:33; 14:19). Now this phrase is repeated seven times in these few verses. No wonder it eventually stirs up the disciples, who have not said a word since Judas' question in 14:22, to discuss it with one another. What is Jesus talking about? What is all this about 'a little while and 'going to the Father'? (16:17–18). Obviously Jesus means that he is leaving— but because that is so unthinkable, they cannot grasp it. When pupils or students are having problems understanding something, a good teacher will let them bounce it around between them. So Jesus lets them debate it for a while, and then asks them what they were discussing (16:19). Earlier, the questions of Peter, Thomas, Philip and Judas helped to move the discussion on. Now their general questioning brings us to the final section and its key point of Jesus' departure.

Birth pangs

Since Jesus is trying to warn them about his coming death, now he says that they will 'weep and mourn'. We noted the ancient customs of loud weeping at Lazarus' death (11:31, 33, 35), and, apart from here, John uses 'weep' only there and for Mary weeping at Jesus' grave (20:11, 13, 15). This is the strongest suggestion that Jesus is going to die, reinforced by 'the world will rejoice' after his opponents' previous attempts to arrest and kill Jesus (16:20). This will cause the disciples the pain of grief, but there is the comfort that their 'pain will turn into joy'. It is unclear when this joyful transformation is meant to take place. Is the 'little while' when they will see him again at the resurrection appearances? On the other hand, much of this discourse has interpreted Jesus' coming back to the disciples as the arrival of the Spirit as Paraclete, to be with them and guide them as another Jesus. Thirdly, it could mean the joy at his final coming on the last day at the end of all things.

These possibilities of pain being turned into joy are developed by the image of a woman in labour, experiencing birth pangs when 'her hour comes'. However, the outcome of bringing a new human life into the world gives her great joy (16:21). It is not that the 'anguish' is forgotten; I still remember the difficulties of the births of my children and the physical effects on my wife afterwards! But it is outweighed by the joy of the new life. So, says Jesus, the disciples will have pain now—the pangs of grief and the anguish of persecution by the world—but 'I will see you again', and the joy of that new life will fill their hearts with rejoicing. Furthermore, it will be a joy which 'no one can take away' (16:22). Such a joy will be experienced by them both at the resurrection and when the Spirit comes upon them, and it will fulfilled at the End—and it is likely that John, with his use of many levels of understanding, intends all three here.

Asking questions and praying

'On that day' of great joy all their questions will cease as they finally understand (16:23). But now, instead of asking all these questions, Jesus would prefer them to turn to the Father in prayer, as is shown by the change in Greek to a different verb of asking. The disciples have been used to asking things of Jesus. Now that he is leaving they need to 'beseech the Father in my name' and he will grant it. This is why throughout the discourse Jesus has encouraged them to pray (14:13–14; 15:7). However, they have not done so yet; they need to look up from their grief and beseech the Father, so that he might answer their prayers and their joy may be 'completely full' (16:24). How often do we miss out on joy, because we are too wrapped up in our concerns even to pray about them to our heavenly Father in Jesus' name?

PRAYER

Father God, draw close to all who suffer pain and persecution;
bring your new life out of our birth pangs,
and grant us all the fullness of your joy.

GOING *to the* FATHER

The disciples are still discussing among themselves what Jesus means by all his allusions to 'a little while'. At the end of the discourse the time has come to be blunt.

Plain speaking

Jesus says that he has been speaking to them 'in figures of speech', the word used to describe his image of the door and shepherd (10:6). We noted then that this was the nearest John has to the parables so frequent in the other gospels. There was also the riddle, or *mashal*, about destroying the temple as a way of referring to himself (see on 2:19). In these discourses, we have had the image of the vine and the branches, and finally the recent passage about the woman giving birth. The time is coming, says Jesus, to put aside such 'figures' and talk 'plainly of the Father' (16:25). His brothers wanted Jesus to show himself 'plainly' to the world, and "the Jews", frustrated by the 'figure' of the shepherd, asked him to speak 'plainly' (7:4; 10:24). The disciples got equally confused by Jesus' way of speaking: he had to tell them 'plainly' that Lazarus was dead (11:14) and he uses the same bluntness now for his own death. After years of asking him for what they wanted, now they must ask the Father 'in my name'. Through his death, they will have direct access to the Father who loves them. Such will be their relationship with the Father that Jesus does not need to be a *paraclete* for them, interceding on their behalf (16:26). Special pleading is not needed, for 'the Father himself loves you', because of their love for Jesus and their faith in him (16:27).

The disciples' relationship with the Father is a direct result of the whole of Jesus' mission, which is summed up sublimely in a single sentence: Jesus came from his Father into the world, and now that he has achieved the purpose for which the Father sent him, he is leaving the world to go to the Father (16:28). You could not get much plainer speech than this nor a clearer summary.

I have overcome the world

The disciples think that they have finally got it, clearly, 'plainly', not in a 'figure of speech' (16:29). His knowledge of what they were discussing and the way he answered their question without waiting for Peter or Thomas or anyone to ask him is proof enough for them: 'by this we believe that you came from God' (16:30). Now they are buoyed up with renewed enthusiasm—which just shows how little they have understood, particularly of the 'figure' of the woman in birth pangs. Jesus' reply has a hint of exasperation about it: 'so *now* do you believe?' (16:31). His return to the Father is not a matter for complacency; it will mean a lonely death for him, while the disciples will all 'be scattered, each to his own', abandoning Jesus (16:32). This echoes the prophecy of Zechariah, 'strike the shepherd, that the sheep may be scattered' (Zech. 13:7). Interestingly, John does not record the desertion of the disciples in his account of Jesus' arrest and death and the Beloved Disciple will be at the foot of the cross (19:26). Nonetheless, Jesus will be abandoned by all human support; but the Son can never be completely alone, for his Father is always with him, as he had previously told "the Jews" (see 8:16, 29).

After such a dire warning of desertion, Jesus' final word is to renew his parting gift of peace. He will not be surprised at their falling away and assures them of his knowledge now so that they may not be troubled when it happens, but find his peace (16:33). In the world there will be persecution, 'anguish', the same word as the birth pangs of the woman (16:21). In that anguish they are to 'be of good cheer', to 'take courage'. So the discourse which began with 'let not your hearts be troubled' (14:1) ends with similar reassurances, because, although Jesus is going to his death, this will be how he finally overcomes the world.

Like all good composers, John has ended these discourses with the same theme which opened his final symphony. As the chapters have progressed, he has deftly woven together motifs about how abiding in love for each other and for God gives confidence in prayer, under the guidance of another Helper, the Spirit of Truth, who will encourage them through the various trials and persecutions—and over it all the main theme is still heard: the 'hour' has finally come for Jesus to leave them and return to his Father.

PRAYER

Lord Jesus, thank you that you have overcome the world;
speak to me plainly and give me your peace,
that I may abide in love with you and your Father.

84

FATHER, GLORIFY YOUR SON

We now come to one of the most sublime passages of the New Testament. It was common at the end of a farewell speech to pray and pronounce a blessing over the listeners. Thus Jacob blesses his sons after his farewell, and Moses breaks into a song of praise and prays for each of the tribes (Gen. 49:28; Deut. 32—33). So now, after his farewell discourses, Jesus prays to his Father. This chapter reveals years of prayer and reflection by the evangelist under the guidance of the Holy Spirit, but at its heart there are three simple petitions all addressed by Jesus to God his Father:

'Father, glorify your Son' (17:1).
'Father, protect them in your name' (17:11).
'Father, may they be with me' (17:24).

These three simple prayers are developed into the three sections of this chapter when Jesus prays for himself (17:1–5), for his disciples (17:6–19) and for the whole church (17:20–26).

It has been known since the early fathers as a 'high priestly prayer', referring to the intercession the High Priest made before God for the whole people, or as a 'prayer of consecration', reflecting the way Jesus consecrates both himself and his disciples. At the same time, it echoes the Lord's Prayer: it is addressed to our 'Father', whose 'name' is stressed throughout the prayer (17:6, 11, 12, 26); his work 'on earth' has been done as he returns to heaven (17:4–5), praying that the disciples would be 'delivered from evil' (17:15).

The key themes of the prayer, which weave around the simple three petitions, are the same as in the farewell discourses, since it is praying for those same disciples Jesus has just been trying to encourage and teach. Therefore we will not be surprised to hear Jesus stress the unity of the Father and the Son with all those who believe; that Jesus is going to be glorified, but only through his death; that it is in knowing God and keeping his word that we find life; that as God sent Jesus into the world, so he sends us, but we must expect opposition from the world; and that through and over it all is the song of love.

Glory and eternal life

The time for Jesus' talking to his disciples is finished, so now 'he looked up to heaven' and addresses God with a simple 'Father', just as at Lazarus' grave (17:1; 11:41). The 'hour' so long expected has finally come (see 12:23, 27; 13:1). There is no doubt or hesitation, but just a prayer for God to be glorified in his Son, as he had prayed before (12:28; 13:31). In Jesus, God's word became flesh and 'we have beheld his glory' (1:14). All his signs have shown the glory of God, from the water into wine to the blind man and Lazarus (2:11; 9:3; 11:4, 40). Isaiah looked forward to when the glory of God would be revealed to 'all flesh', to everyone—and now not only will 'all flesh' see God's glory in Jesus, but he has authority to give them eternal life (17:2; see 1:12 and Is. 40:5). Then we have the famous definition of 'eternal life', the life 'of the ages', referring to its quality as much as to its quantity, 'to know you, the only true God' (17:3). To know is such an intimate word in the Bible, involving not just intellectual knowledge, but a physical, sexual, emotional, spiritual, total relationship. The prophets longed for when 'the earth shall be filled with the knowledge of the glory of God as the waters cover the sea' (Hab. 2:14; see also Hos. 6:3, 6). If we want to know the 'only true God', it involves knowing 'Jesus Christ whom you have sent'— John's typical phrase for the one in whom God's glory is revealed.

Returning to the Father's presence

So now Jesus can pray that he has 'finished the work on earth you gave me to do' (17:4). Because he has been sent by God, Jesus has always insisted that he has been doing the Father's work, not his own (4:34; 5:36; 9:4; 10:37–38)—but now this has been completed. All that remains for him is to return to the glory he had in God's presence 'before the world existed' (17:5). The gospel began with the wonderful prologue showing how Jesus existed with God 'in the beginning' (1:1–4). Its whole story has been about how Jesus brought that glory of God into our world through his words and works; now therefore he prays to be glorified again in his Father's presence.

PRAYER

Father God, may all people see your glory
in Jesus Christ whom you sent
and come to have eternal life in him with you.

85

JESUS PRAYS *for* HIS DISCIPLES

Having prayed to be with God in glory, Jesus turns to pray for his disciples who will be left behind. They are only a small frightened group, who still do not really understand what he is saying. At one level, it is not much to show for the fruits of three years of Jesus' labour. Yet these are the ones who will have to do the job and turn the world upside down.

Manifesting God's name

First, Jesus describes what he has done and to whom. The disciples originate from God, 'they were yours' but he gave them to Jesus 'out from the world' (17:6). God knows us and makes us his own, long before we think of coming to him. Jesus has manifested God's 'name' to them. Names were very important in ancient beliefs. To know a god's name gave you a certain power, to get what you were praying for. Altars to 'unknown gods' (as Paul found in Athens, Acts 17:23) were an 'insurance policy' against offending gods by not knowing their names. Names convey something of the character and nature of both gods and human beings. The Hebrew scriptures stress the importance of knowing God's name; it enables people to trust in him (Pss. 9:10; 20:7) and God dwells where he has put his name (Deut. 12:5). God revealed his name to Moses as 'I am who I am' (Exod. 3:13–14), but the Jews considered it a blasphemy to pronounce his name. Thus the consonants YHWH are written in the scriptures with the vowels a-o-a, taken from *adonai*, 'the Lord' which was read instead. The mixture of Y(J)HW(V)H with a-o-a produced 'Jehovah' in early English Bibles.

The Lord's Prayer begins with 'hallowed be thy name'. In John's gospel, Jesus has used the phrase 'I am'—the bread, the light, the vine—not just to recall the great images of Judaism, but also to refer to the name of God. When he pronounced it by itself, 'before Abraham was, I am' they tried to stone him (8:58–59). Jesus has not just revealed God's name, 'I am', but also he has shown the disciples the nature and character of God. Now that the disciples have heard the Farewell Discourses, they 'have come to know' that everything Jesus has is from God (17:7). For all their inadequate understanding, their comments show that they realize that Jesus has come from God (16:30). Jesus has passed on God's words and truth to them; now 'they have believed that you sent me' (17:8).

Keep them in your name

Therefore, Jesus is now praying 'not for the world', but for those 'you gave me' (17:9). This does not mean that Jesus has no concern for the world. We have noted how 'the world' in John means those who oppose Jesus but is also the object of God's love (see on 15:18–21). At this point, Jesus' concern is for his disciples in the midst of a world which will oppose them as it opposed him. But his prayer is for them as he sends them into that world, which still shows his care for it. This verse cannot justify a sectarian, isolationist withdrawal from the world.

The unity of Father and Son means that 'all mine are yours, and yours are mine' (17:10). Thus as God was glorified in Jesus, so Jesus is glorified in his disciples. It is extraordinary that God is glorified in our stumbling attempts to live for him in this world, yet that is what Jesus says here. If this is to happen, his disciples need protection, so we come to the heart of his prayer. Since Jesus is no longer to be in the world with them, but is going back to his Father, he prays that God will 'keep them in your name' (17:11). This word 'keep' means to 'protect', literally to 'watch over' like a loving parent seeing their children about to launch into the world; they have to let them go, yet they are concerned to watch over them and save them from harm. So Jesus does not just call God 'Father' here, but also 'Holy'. To be 'holy' is to be set apart for God; we are to be holy as he is holy (Lev. 11:44). This also entails being 'one as we are one', picking up a major theme of the Discourse and anticipating Jesus' final prayer for the unity of all his disciples (see 13:34; 14:20; 15:9; 17:22–23).

Jesus has protected them in God's name, which is a safe refuge (Prov. 18:10). The good shepherd has been concerned that 'none be lost' (17:12; see 6:12, 39; 10:28). However, this gives us a final clang from the funeral bell, as Jesus remembers Judas, the one who went out into the night to be lost; but even this fulfilled scripture (see 13:18 quoting Ps. 41:9).

PRAYER

Holy Father, thank you that you have revealed yourself in Jesus protect and watch over us that we may glorify your name.

SANCTIFY THEM *in the* TRUTH

In his prayer, Jesus has described how he manifested the name of God to his disciples and has prayed for their protection in the world which he is leaving as 'I am coming to you' (17:13). Before he leaves, however, he speaks this prayer still in the world 'so that they may have my joy made complete in themselves'. Twice in the Farewell Discourses, Jesus said that he wanted the disciples' joy to be 'full' or 'complete' through his words and their prayers (15:11; 16:24). Their joy alone, in their sadness at his death, will not do this; Jesus must pray for *his* joy to be fulfilled in them.

In the world, but not of the world

Through the Farewell Discourses, the division between those who refused Jesus and those who received him has been increasingly clear. So now, the disciples are the ones to whom Jesus has 'given your word', while the world responds by hating them (17:14). Jesus repeats in his prayer the connection between himself and his followers which he made throughout the Discourses. Since a disciple is not greater than their master the world would persecute them as it persecuted him (15:20). Now we see that the disciples 'do not belong to the world, just as I do not belong to the world'.

The obvious temptation both for the church and for individual Christians is to withdraw from the world. When a small light is flickering in the darkness, the shadows can appear menacing. But removing the light consigns the place to total darkness. Instead, the light needs to know that the darkness cannot overcome it (1:5). So Jesus will not pray for God 'to take them out of the world' but asks rather for their protection from evil (17:15). In both the Lord's Prayer and here, the word is often translated in the neuter: 'deliver us from evil'. However, it could also be the masculine pronoun, meaning 'from the evil one', the source of evil, the devil. Because 'they do not belong to the world, just as I do not belong to the world' (17:16), all that is opposed to God—the world, the flesh and the devil—will seek to lure Jesus' disciples into one of two possible responses. On the one hand, there is the call to be pure, to come out from the world, to avoid being tainted. This leads to isolation—to be 'so heavenly minded' that we are 'no earthly use'. On the other, we can try so hard to avoid this mistake that we fall into the opposite extreme, so identifying ourselves with the world that we become 'worldly', and no different from everyone else. Either way, the light has been so withdrawn or quenched, that the darkness is unaffected. To be 'in the world, but not of the world' is a difficult balancing act for churches and individual Christians alike. How can we maintain that difficult balance?

Consecrated for mission

The answer is to be consecrated for mission. Jesus prays that God will 'sanctify them in the truth' (17:17). The 'truth' reminds us of 'the Spirit of truth' and 'sanctify' picks up the description of the Father as 'holy' (14:7; 17:11). To 'sanctify' or to 'consecrate' means to 'make holy', to set something or someone apart for God. It was used in the Old Testament as much of priests and prophets like the sons of Aaron or Jeremiah (Exod. 28:41; Jer. 1:5) as of animals for sacrifice (Deut. 15:19–21). To be made 'holy', to be set apart like this, is not for your own benefit, as some kind of reward or preferment. It is always for the sake of others. As the animals were sacrificed for the sake of the people, and as the priests and prophets were to serve the people, so Jesus sanctifies himself 'for their sakes' (17:19). The word 'for their sake' is *hyper* again, as when the good shepherd lays down his life 'for the sake of the sheep' and Jesus must die 'for the sake of the nation' (10:11; 11:51). It is the 'greater love' when someone dies 'for the sake of their friends' (see on 15:13). As Jesus 'consecrates' himself to die for our sakes, so we are made holy, 'sanctified in the truth' that, as God sent him into the world, so he can send us (17:18). Jesus could never have been accused of 'other-worldly' isolationism in his ministry to outcasts and sinners, but nor was he so identified with the world that his mission to save them was lost. This is what it means for his followers to be sent into the world, as he was, but not to be of it. It is indeed not easy to maintain that balance—but then, since it cost Jesus everything, even death on a cross, should we expect it to be any different?

PRAYER

Lord Jesus, take us not out of your world,
but protect us from the evil one;
sanctify us in your truth
that we may give our lives for the sake of others.

JESUS PRAYS *for the* CHURCH

Jesus has prayed to return to the glory he shared with God his Father before the creation (17:1–5). He has also prayed for his disciples whom he will leave behind in the world, although they are not of the world; the key to this balancing act is found in being 'consecrated for mission' (17:6–19). As Jesus reminded his disciples earlier, 'you did not choose me, but I chose you and I appointed you to go and bear fruit' (15:16). Now, Jesus looks beyond his immediate disciples to the result of that consecrated mission, to the fruit that they will bear. So he does not pray just on their behalf (*hyper* again), but for 'those who will believe through their word' (17:20). The good shepherd spoke of 'sheep of another fold' which he had to bring into 'one flock with one shepherd' (10:16); equally Caiaphas' ironic prophecy meant that Jesus was to die 'not just for the nation only, but to gather into one the dispersed children of God' (11:52). This desire for all to be brought into one is the concern of this final section of his prayer.

That they may all be one

So Jesus prays that all those who come to believe in him 'may be one'. Such unity is rooted in the life of God: 'as you, Father, are in me and I am in you, may they also be in us' (17:21). Jesus answered Philip's desire to see the Father with 'I am in the Father and the Father in me' (14:10). This unity between the Father and the Son is to be shared through the indwelling of the Spirit with all who love him (14:23; 15:9). Thus the command to 'love one another' is 'new', because it is no mere moral exhortation, but a sharing in the life of God, 'as I have loved you' (see on 13:34). Now Jesus brings together the unity he has with the Father and the love of the disciples for one another— but it is not just to generate warm feelings of togetherness. The purpose is for the continuing mission, 'that the world may believe that you have sent me'. The world does not naturally ponder the internal relationships of the Holy Trinity, but when it sees Christians living this self-sacrificial love, then it is challenged to think again.

Jesus shares the glory he has received from his Father with all his followers (17:22), and we obscure the world's view of that glory by the divisions and separations within the church. Not surprisingly, this phrase 'that they may all be one' has become the watchword of the ecumenical movement and the title of innumerable church reports, commissions and encyclicals. Unfortunately, there is little here about institutional or structural unity. The unity of the Father in the Son and the Son in the Father is a unity of relationship, a way of life lived in love. A disunited church is a scandal to the gospel and a stumbling block for the world, but the path to unity will be found more in loving and living and working together than in ecclesiastical reorganization. The world will know 'that you have sent me and have loved them even as you have loved me' only as Christians seek a unity arising out of 'I in them and you in me' (17:23).

That they may be with me

Finally, Jesus' prayer expresses his longing that all Christians might come to 'be with me where I am' (17:24). The prayer began with Jesus praying for himself to be glorified in the Father's presence with the glory he shared before the world was made (17:5). Now he wishes to share that glory with us as he draws this prayer—his last will and final wishes—to a climax, summing up his whole message and mission. He calls God 'righteous Father', the one in whom he has trusted throughout (17:25). It was because 'the world does not know you' that Jesus came into our world. As the one who does know the Father, he called disciples who came to know that he was sent by God. Because they accept that 'you have sent me', Jesus has made God's name known, revealing his very nature and character to them (17:26). What is more he continues to make it known, now and in the future, so that we may all share this unity of love, 'that the love with which you have loved me may be in them, and I in them'. In the End, therefore, we love each other not for our own sakes, nor even so that the world may believe, but because this is how we share the very life of God and come to be with him and in him for ever and ever, Amen.

PRAYER

Holy and righteous Father,
grant to your church such love and unity
that the world may believe and
all your children come to dwell
in your glory with your Son, Jesus Christ.

Betrayed *in a* Garden

Jesus has finally finished 'speaking these words' of the Farewell Discourses and his Prayer, and so now he takes his disciples out across the Kidron valley to a garden (18:1). We notice immediately that John's account of the passion is both similar to the others', and yet different. Here the garden is not named Gethsemane, neither is there sleep for the disciples nor agonized prayer for Jesus. Throughout the next chapters, John omits some bits well known from the Synoptics, but features other aspects. We must concentrate on his account and his particular emphases. Since he stresses how Jesus knows all things and is in control of everything, there is no place for agonized doubting now; it was hinted at earlier (see on 12:27), but now all is under control. Only John mentions the *wadi* of the Kidron, where a stream flowed alongside the temple, sometimes used to wash away the sacrificial blood. Also, only John says they 'enter' a 'garden', which reminds us of the struggle with evil in the Garden of Eden, and of the walled enclosure of the sheep-fold.

Judas and the forces of the world

The slopes across the Kidron from the temple still contain walled enclosures with olive trees; 'Jesus often met there with his disciples', so Judas 'also knew the place'. After the tolling of our funeral bell earlier, now the event it foreshadowed happens: Judas is identified twice as 'the one who betrayed him' (18:2, 5). While the other gospels say he brought a 'crowd', only John says it included a 'detachment of soldiers' and 'officers from the chief priests and Pharisees' (17:3). The first word, *speira*, denotes a Roman 'cohort', usually 600 or 1,000 men; sometimes it refers to a 'maniple', a unit of 200—either way a significant force. The 'officers' are the temple police which the Pharisees and priests—not known for working together—sent to seize Jesus at the Feast of Tabernacles (see on 7:32, 45–46). Thus John shows how all the forces 'of the world'—the political authorities, those in charge of the temple sacrifices and the interpreters of the law and scriptures—all united to arrest Jesus.

Furthermore they come with 'lanterns and torches', although the full Passover moon would make the night very bright in Jerusalem.

But they want to arrest the 'light of the world' and no amount of lanterns will illuminate the spiritual darkness foretold by Jesus into which Judas had gone (11:10, 12:35; 13:27, 30).

I am

Although Judas is 'standing with them' (18:5), no betrayer's kiss is needed in John. Jesus, who knows 'everything which is to happen' (cf. 13:1), steps forward to take the initiative (18:4). As the good shepherd, he sees Judas the 'thief' (12:6) and the armed bandits coming, and protects his sheep, behind him in the walled enclosure; force is not needed to take him—he offers his life of his own volition (see 10:18). When they say that they are seeking 'Jesus of Nazareth', Jesus replies 'I am'. Previously they have had difficulties arresting him (7:30, 44; 8:20; 10:39). Therefore they should have grabbed him after he identifies himself—but instead they are literally 'floored' and 'fell to the ground' (18:6). At the superficial level, this may be a result of their initial shock after the previous difficulties and the amount of force they have brought this time. Certainly they recover quickly enough to arrest him after he again asks them what they want and identifies himself (18:7–8). However, as so often in John the deeper level indicates that falling prostrate is the proper reaction to a divine appearance or the pronouncement of God's name (see Dan. 10:9; Rev. 1:17). After all the uses of 'I am' in this gospel to describe Jesus as something, 'bread of life', 'the true vine', and so forth, here it stands alone in the Greek, without even the 'he' supplied in most English translations (see also on 8:58 and 17:6). After asking God to protect the disciples 'in your name' (17:11), Jesus demonstrates the power of the name 'I am' here.

In serene control, Jesus tells them to let the others go. John says that this was 'to fulfil his word', making Jesus' words like scripture to be fulfilled (18:9; see also 18:32). In his prayer Jesus said that he had not lost any except Judas, fulfilling his earlier comment about 'the will of him who sent me that I should lose nothing he has given me (17:12; 6:39). Judas, the 'thief' cannot 'snatch sheep' out of the hands of the good shepherd (10:28). Jesus offers himself willingly, that his disciples might live.

PRAYER

Lord Jesus, when the world comes to extinguish your light,
may I stand safe with you, protected by the name of God.

89

From GARDEN *to* COURTYARD

When Jesus warned the disciples after washing their feet that they could not follow where he was going, Peter offered to lay down his life for Jesus (13:37). Despite Jesus' warning that he was more likely to deny him and everything in the Farewell Discourses about why and where Jesus is going, Peter still has not learned. All the gospels mention an attack on the high priest's slave, but only John says that it was Peter who drew his sword, and names the slave, Malchus, which comes from the Hebrew for 'king' (18:10).

Jesus tells Peter to put away his sword in words similar to Matthew's account (Matt. 26:52). The reason, however, recalls Jesus' prayer in the other gospels' accounts of Gethsemane: 'am I not to drink the cup that the Father has given me?' (18:11; see Mark 14:36). So John is familiar with the story of the agony, even if it does not fit into the way he is narrating things. Jesus' willingness to 'drink the cup the Father has given' reflects his serene control in John, while the metaphor of the 'cup' hints at the suffering and sacrifice of Jesus' death remembered in holy communion.

The disciples and the garden fade from view as the Romans soldiers and the Jewish police arrest Jesus; John uses the technical term *chiliarch* for the 'officer' in charge of a cohort of a thousand men (18:12). The use of so much superfluous force is also seen as only John says that they 'tied him up'; at the human level, the authorities think they are in control, but John is telling us all is really in the hands of God.

Annas and Caiaphas

They take Jesus to the house of Annas, who was high priest from AD6 to 15. Although the Romans then deposed him, he was followed as high priest by his four sons—and now by Caiaphas, his son-in-law! The wealth and power of this family, gained from their control of the temple animals and sacrifices, was notorious. Although he was officially 'retired', it is not surprising that Jesus is taken to Annas' house to 'assist the police with their enquiries'! After all, it was his son-in-law Caiaphas who advised that it was better for Jesus to die 'on behalf of the people' (18:14; see 11:52) and Jesus will be sent on to him next (18:24).

Peter by the fireside

John says that 'Simon Peter and another disciple followed Jesus' (18:15). Since the disciple was 'known to the high priest', some suggest that he must be one of the authorities who believed in Jesus like Nicodemus or Joseph of Arimathea; since these are both named elsewhere (e.g. 7:50; 19:38–39) anonymity here would be strange. Another possibility is Judas, who would have been allowed in, but is unlikely to have been accompanied by Peter. The obvious unnamed person, often linked with Peter, is the 'disciple Jesus loved' (see on 13:23). Whoever he is, he gains access into the courtyard, the *aule*, used only here and for the sheepfold (10:1, 6). Equally, Peter is left out at the 'door', mentioned for the first time since 'I am the door' (10:1–9). So the other disciple talks to the woman 'door-keeper', *thuroros*, which is used only here and for the 'gatekeeper' to the *aule* in 10:3. None of this is in the other gospels where Peter just wanders into the courtyard alone. These verbal echoes of the 'figure' of the door and the good shepherd are another example of John's multi-level writing; on the surface, it is just an ordinary courtyard, but at the spiritual level we see the good shepherd going to lay down his life for the sheep.

The door-keeper seems to know that the 'other disciple' is a follower of Jesus, since she asks Peter as he comes in, 'you are not one of this man's disciples as well, are you?' (18:17). The question expects the answer 'no', and, almost before he realizes it, that is Peter's reply. He is not yet under scrutiny or close questioning, but just wants to blend in quietly and get to the fire. But his reply, 'I am not' is the opposite of Jesus' ringing declaration in the garden, 'I am'. We wonder how Peter could move so quickly from protestations of being ready to die with Jesus one minute to denying him the next. In fact, it is a path we can all travel so easily, and it begins not with a great crisis but an off the cuff remark for a quiet life. Once denial has begun, however, the way back is all the more difficult when the pressure comes, as it soon will. No wonder Peter suddenly feels cold and warms himself alongside the very police officers whom he was attacking with his sword only a short time before (18:18).

PRAYER

Lord Jesus, you know how quickly my faith can move
from zeal to wanting the warmth of a quiet life,
have mercy and grant me your trust in God our Father.

JESUS BEFORE *the* HIGH PRIEST

Jesus was taken into the house of Annas, but before we could learn what happened, we were taken out into the courtyard to see how Peter was admitted and his first quiet denial of Jesus. We know from Jesus' warning to Peter that two more denials are to come (13:38). But before these, the scene shifts back into the house for Jesus to be questioned by the high priest. This oscillation between different scenes—what is going on inside and outside the same building—is common in films or drama to heighten the tension. John would win an Oscar for his narrative artistry as we switch between Peter out in the courtyard and Jesus inside the house—both being questioned, but reacting very differently. It is as though there are two trials going on and Peter's understandable panic and fear makes Jesus' serene composure all the more remarkable.

Jesus on trial before the Jews

Jesus is still in the house of Annas; he is sent on to Caiaphas in 18:24, but nothing is said about what happens there before he is passed on again from Caiaphas to Pilate (18:28). Thus this hearing in Annas' house is Jesus' only appearance before Jewish authorities—and even this is unofficial. Jesus has no trial before the Sanhedrin in John's final chapters. And yet, in many ways, much of the first half of this gospel was like a trial. After he healed the paralysed man on the Sabbath, Jesus was cross-examined by "the Jews" about his witnesses—John the Baptist, God the Father, the scriptures and Moses (5:30–47). His teaching was debated at the Feast of Tabernacles (7:16–24) and the attempt to make him judge the woman taken in adultery actually put him on trial, leading into an argument about whether he or his opponents came from God or the devil (8:1–11, 21–59). The healing of the blind man caused both the man and his parents to be investigated under the threat of excommunication (9:12–34), followed by an examination of Jesus' claim to be 'one with the Father' (10:22–39). Finally the Sanhedrin met after the raising of Lazarus and have already decided to put Jesus to death 'for the sake of the nation' (11:47–53).

This treatment of the trial reminds us of John's 'omission' of the institution of the holy communion; it is missing here, where we expect to find it in these last chapters, yet the whole of the gospel is shot through with sacramental things like bread, water and wine. Equally, the whole story of Jesus' ministry, of his words and works, the 'signs' pointing to his glory, has shown Jesus constantly on trial in his discussions and debates with "the Jews". An account of the formal hearing now is not needed. Far more interesting to John is the contrast between Jesus inside the house and Peter outside in the courtyard.

Annas' questions

John still calls Annas the 'high priest', even if his son-in-law Caiaphas is that officially. The close connection of the two is also seen in Luke (Lk. 3:2; Acts 4:6). The wily old arch schemer has not built his family empire up on the sacrifice trade to have it brought down by preacher boys from up north, especially one responsible for unfortunate demonstrations in his temple! So Annas has two areas of questioning—about Jesus' disciples and about his teaching (18:19). The authorities' anxiety about the growing numbers of disciples has already been mentioned (11:48; 12:19) and Annas is concerned that a threat to public order might be bad for business. Secondly, he wants to know if Jesus' teaching could make him a false prophet, for whom death was the penalty (Deut. 13:1–10).

John shows Jesus always in control, so now he appears to be in charge of his own interrogation. Jesus answers nothing about his disciples in order to protect them and he refuses to discuss his teaching. He points out that he has spoken in synagogues (6:59) and in the temple (2:19; 7:14, 28; 8:20; 10:23), places where 'all the Jews gather'. He has said 'nothing in secret', but 'openly'—*parresia* again—'to the world' (18:20; see 7:26; 10:24–30). Therefore there is no need to ask him; there are plenty of witnesses who heard what he said (18:21). It was against Jewish law to convict a person on their own testimony, as in the modern right to refuse to answer questions in court for fear of incriminating yourself. In the other gospels, Jesus is quiet and passive under examination, but John shows him rebutting the charges, serenely and confident.

PRAYER

Lord Jesus, thank you that your whole life bore witness to God;
grant that we too may speak openly to the world
and stand alongside us when we are on trial for faith in you.

REBUKES & DENIALS

The scene has moved from the garden to the house of Annas, the old high priest. We have seen that John is building the tension by oscillating between events out in the courtyard and the preliminary hearing taking place in the house. Annas wanted to question Jesus about his disciples and his teaching. Jesus, however, has refused to 'assist with enquiries'. He has said nothing about his disciples and has denied that any of his teaching was in secret. If the high priest wants to know about it, he should question the witnesses, not the defendant.

This reply is essentially a rebuke to the high priest for trying to get Jesus to incriminate himself, and it is taken as insolence by one of the police who hits him in the face (18:22). Cursing one of the leaders was forbidden by the Law (Exod. 22:28), and so Jesus should not answer a high priest like this. Jesus maintains his position: if he is wrong, then let them bring on the witnesses to testify to his crime. On the other hand, their immediate recourse to violence just suggests how right he is (18:23). Frustrated, Annas has no alternative but to send him off to Caiaphas, still all 'tied up' (18:24).

Peter's denial

The oscillation between Jesus and Peter continues: while Jesus is being taken to Caiaphas and questioned there, the director turns the cameras back into the courtyard to see how Simon Peter is getting on. Peter is where we left him, still feeling the chill and standing by the charcoal fire trying to get warm (18:25). Peter's denial of Jesus is often represented as a sad tale of cowardice or disloyalty, but actually it has been an act of courage and bravery so far. When Jesus, hurt by some of his followers giving up, asked if the disciples also wanted to leave him, it was Peter who blurted out his faith: 'Lord, where can we go? We believe you are the holy One of God' (6:66–69). Equally, at the last supper first he would not allow Jesus to wash his feet, but then he went to the other extreme of wanting to be washed all over (13:6–9)!

In his typically foolhardy manner, Peter put up the resistance in the garden and followed Jesus and the arresting party right into the lions' den. Gaining entry had been the problem, but with the help of the unnamed disciple he managed it—at the cost of a little white lie in agreeing with the doorkeeper's assumption that he was not a disciple. Now he is standing around with the police and the officials he was fighting not long ago. They also ask him the question inviting a negative answer: 'you're not also one of them, are you?' Having denied it once already, quietly to the doorkeeper, Peter cannot go back now and this more public denial takes him in deeper as again he replies 'I am not'.

Even worse, a relative of Malchus, the slave he wounded, thinks he recognizes him. For the first time, the construction of the question in Greek changes to expect a positive answer, yes: 'I saw you in the garden with him, didn't I?' (18:26). Suddenly there is no way out, and Peter is trapped where his rash devotion to Jesus has led him. He has no alternative but to deny it again, but, unlike the other gospels, John records no cursing or swearing of oaths here.

The breaking of the dawn

Then 'the cock crew' (18:27). Some intrepid commentators have conducted all night research on when cocks crow in Jerusalem, while others have noted that some texts forbid keeping cockerels within the holy city. This expression may even refer to the Roman early trumpet call at three in the morning, the *gallicinium*, to mark the start of the final watch of the night. Significantly, John omits any reminder here of Jesus' warning nor does Peter go out into the dark to weep. The cockcrow has signalled that the time of darkness—the night into which Judas disappeared to fetch troops with lanterns—is ending. It will soon be the start of the momentous day which will eventually bring forgiveness for all the insults and denials. Peter's love for Jesus took him into the courtyard where his courage failed him and he fell into denial. But Jesus' love for Peter will take him to the cross and beyond to another charcoal fire where it will all be put right (21:15–19). The enquiries will be answered, the insults forgiven, and the fallen restored, not only for Peter but for Annas and the whole world.

PRAYER

Lord Jesus, be with all those tempted to deny you
in the heat of the moment or the fire of persecution
and come again in your love to forgive and restore us.

ACCUSED BEFORE PILATE

It is 'now early in the morning', *proi*, the end of the last watch from 03.00 to 06.00 a.m. which has been spent at Caiaphas' house. We are not told what happened there. At daybreak Jesus is taken from Caiaphas' house to the Roman headquarters. After the oscillation between inside and outside Annas' house, John starts a new sequence of inside and outside the headquarters.

Entering the praetorium

John gives it the proper term, the 'praetorium' (18:28). Originally, in the field, this was the tent of the commanding officer, but by this time it is used for a Roman governor's residence. Usually, the governor of Judaea lived in the port of Caesarea, named after the emperor, on the Mediterranean coast. But at sensitive times like festivals, he would come with reinforcements to stay in Jerusalem in case of disturbances. The headquarters at this time would have been either the Antonia fortress on the East Hill overlooking the temple from the north or the Herodian fortress on the West Hill on the west side of the temple overlooking the whole city by what is now called the Jaffa Gate. They bring Jesus to whichever of these Pilate was currently using—but stayed outside.

'They themselves' would not enter such a Gentile building to avoid 'ritual defilement' which would prevent them participating in the Passover sacrifices and eating the lamb. Jewish law was cautious about impurities within a Gentile's house, not least that leaven may be there which was prohibited during the fast. There is an extraordinary irony here about religious leaders conducting barely legal hearings at night and plotting cynically to execute one man 'for the sake of the people', but drawing the line at dietary regulations. They want to eat the Passover lamb, but will kill the true Lamb of God who will take away the sins of all people (1:29; 11:50). It is easy for us to criticize, but how often are we so concerned for religious minutiae that we miss the more important matters of God?

Pilate

The governor has got used to these rituals, so 'Pilate went out to them' (18:29). He is so well known to both Christian and Jewish readers that the evangelist needs only to name him. Pontius Pilate was a Roman knight (the second rank, below senators) and governor of Judaea AD26–36; as a lesser imperial province, it merited only a prefect or procurator. Pilate is attacked in Jewish writings for his greed, murder and inhumanity. He tried to bring the Romans' standards, adorned with 'graven images' of the emperor, into Jerusalem on his first visit, and votive shields on another; he raided the temple treasury to pay for a new aqueduct and finally crushed a revolt in Samaria so severely that he was recalled.

Outside and inside

This powerful man is now reduced almost to a messenger boy, darting in and out of the headquarters. John has constructed the Roman trial in seven carefully balanced scenes oscillating between Pilate interrogating Jesus inside the praetorium and his conversation with the Jewish leaders outside:

1. Outside—18:28–32 The Jews demand death	7. Outside—19:12–16 The Jews obtain death
2. Inside—18:33–38 Pilate & Jesus discuss kingship	6. Inside—19:9–11 Pilate & Jesus discuss power
3. Outside—18:38–40 Pilate says Jesus is innocent	5. Outside—19:4–8 Pilate says Jesus is innocent

4. Inside—19:1–3
Soldiers mock Jesus as King

The balance of these scenes reveal that the trial is about power and kingship. In addition to Jesus' and Pilate's discussions, everything hinges around the middle scene where Jesus is scourged and mocked as king. There is also a contrast between the confusion outside and the calm debate with Jesus inside—and as Pilate runs between the two, he gradually moves from declaring Jesus' innocence to accepting the Jewish leaders' demand for his death.

PRAYER

Lord God, forgive us when we become so entangled
in our religious observances that we lose touch with your grace;
grant that we might honour Jesus as our true king.

ARE YOU KING *of the* JEWS?

The trial oscillates between Pilate's own interrogation of Jesus inside and those outside the headquarters. The first three scenes develop the theme of kingship, starting with Pilate's questions.

1—What is the charge?

Pilate begins outside with a reasonable request, to know the accusation; as governor, he should hold his own trial (18:29). The Jewish leaders are discomfited; the Sanhedrin decided that Jesus should die some time previously (11:53), a Roman cohort was involved in the arrest and they have done their own questioning. Petulantly they reply, 'if he were not an evildoer, we would not have handed him over to you' (18:30). In other words, 'we are working with you; trust us and do what we want'! The word 'handed him over' is the same as Judas' 'betrayed' (18:2, 5) which hints that all is not quite right. Slightly annoyed by their impertinence in using him as a rubber stamp, Pilate agrees that if they want to do it their way, they can use their own law and leave him out of it (18:31). But there is one difficulty: they do not have the power of the death penalty. Jewish sources say that they lost this right around AD30. The traditional Jewish execution was stoning, as the mob tried for the woman in adultery and for Jesus himself (8:5, 59; see Lev. 24:16; Deut. 17:7). But that is not what they need here. They want it done officially, by the Roman method of crucifixion. To the Jews, this would make Jesus accursed (Deut. 21:23); to the Romans it suggests a serious political offence—but to John, this is actually fulfilling Jesus' prophecy that when he was 'lifted up' he would draw everyone to himself (18:32; see 12:32–33; 3:14; 8:28).

2—Are you a king?

Mention of the death penalty sends Pilate back inside. That can only mean that they have brought him a revolutionary wanting to be a messianic king. He looks at Jesus, but the Greek word order expresses his surprise: 'you—*you* are king of the Jews?' (18:33). The emphasis is full of irony: at the real level Pilate is right, since Jesus is the King of the Jews—but he could not be more wrong at the ordinary human level. Jesus is not overawed by the governor's interrogation, but starts asking the questions himself, as though putting Pilate on trial. He does not admit or deny being King, but wonders whether Pilate worked it out himself, or did others ("the Jews" perhaps?) tell him (18:34).

Pilate responds with more questions: 'I'm not a Jew, am I?' (18:35). It is 'your own nation' (the word in Caiaphas' prophecy, 11:50) and chief priests who 'handed you over', again the word for Judas' betrayal: 'What have you done?' Finally, questions cease as Jesus replies, 'my kingdom is not of this world' (18:36). In fact, it is not a 'kingdom', or any place, at all; 'kingship' is a better translation. If Jesus wanted to be king in this world's terms, his disciples would be fighting on the streets for him, like many other groups at that time. Pilate does not really understand this, but he heard 'king': 'so you are a king then?' Jesus replies that these are Pilate's words and way of thinking, not his. Instead, he came into this world 'to witness to truth; everyone who belongs to the truth listens to my voice' (18:37). John's key themes like 'truth' and 'witness' here reveal his theological reflection on the meaning of this trial.

3—What is truth?

Unfortunately, like most politicians, Pilate does not have time for theology, asking, 'what is truth?' (18:38). Is he being cynical, sardonically dismissive—or perhaps wistfully wondering where truth can be found? Ironically the One who said 'I am the truth', the 'true bread' and the 'true vine', is standing before him, but he does not wait for an answer. He just turns around and goes outside again declaring that he finds 'no case' against Jesus. All the gospels mention a custom of releasing someone at Passover, which is not otherwise known. Pilate seizes upon this to be able to release 'the King of the Jews' (18:39). But those gathered outside are not so easily satisfied and refuse, calling for Barabbas instead (18:40). In yet more irony, *bar-abbas* means 'son of the father' and John says he was a 'bandit', like those who come to steal and destroy the sheep (10:1, 8). Perhaps he was a zealot freedom fighter, but John says no more about him. In later Christian imagination, he is portrayed as standing at the foot of the cross, a free man, realizing that the good shepherd dies as much for the thieves and the robbers, for Judas and Barabbas, as for the sheep.

PRAYER

Lord Jesus Christ, true King and Son of the Father
thank you that you died for me; help me to live for you.

HAIL, KING *of the* JEWS!

We have had three trial scenes so far: outside "the Jews" have demanded the death penalty, inside Pilate discussed kingship with Jesus, and then came outside again to declare his innocence in an attempt to release him. The rejection of this offer sends Pilate back inside the headquarters for the middle scene in which Jesus is mocked as king.

4—A crown of thorns and a purple robe

Pilate has Jesus 'flogged' (19:1). The Romans had several levels of corporal punishment, ranging from a beating to 'teach them a lesson' through to scourging with a whip of leather thongs and metal spikes which would rip the flesh from someone's back and might even kill them. Matthew and Mark suggest that Jesus received the full scourging in preparation for crucifixion (Matt. 27:26; Mark 15:15). Since Jesus has not yet been condemned, John seems to be thinking more a beating for 'wasting police time', to prove to the Jews that he is a pathetic king and no threat to Rome. So the soldiers plait a crown of thorns, like an emperor's wreath (19:2). The sun god was depicted with a crown radiating light, like that on the Statue of Liberty; the spikes of the date palm would provide a painful parody of this effect. Jesus is also clad in purple, the imperial colour, and greeted with a parody of the *Ave Caesar!*—'Hail, King of the Jews!'—except that their hands are offered not in salute, but a slap (19:3). At the human level, it is pathetic and ridiculous—but at the spiritual level, John hints at the irony that the true king is being crowned on his way to glory.

5—Behold the man

Pilate comes back outside for the fifth scene, which balances the third to stress Jesus' innocence again. The Jewish leaders outside still have not answered Pilate's original question about what the charges are (18:29). Pilate has investigated their request for the death penalty and can find 'no case against him' (19:4). To prove his point, he brings Jesus outside, still dressed as 'the king of the Jews'. A sorry sight he must have looked, and Pilate exclaims, *ecce homo*, 'what a man!' (19:5). At the human level, he is clearly just a poor chap, deluded perhaps, but certainly no threat to Rome, nor needing to be crucified. Nobody is going to follow someone in this state. And yet we can hear John's upper resonances echo, 'what a man indeed!' *The* man, 'wounded for our transgressions, beaten for our sins and by his stripes we are healed', the good shepherd suffering for 'the sheep who have gone astray' (Is. 53:5–6).

If Pilate thought that this pitiable spectacle would convince them to let him release Jesus, he was sadly mistaken. Infuriated by the parody of a 'king of the Jews' and outraged by the suggestion that Jesus might be '*the* man', the eschatological 'son of man' who would bring the kingdom of God, the chief priests and the temple police all shout out, 'Crucify him! Crucify him!' (19:6). In exasperation, Pilate gives vent to his frustration by suggesting that they should take him and do it themselves. They all know, of course, that it is not a serious proposal, since only the governor can do this—and Pilate repeats for the third time (like Peter's three fold denial perhaps?) that he can find 'no case against him'.

The Son of God

"The Jews" have no alternative but finally to admit that Jesus is not a revolutionary and reveal instead that the real charge is an offence against their law of blasphemy (19:7; see Lev. 24:16). They allege that Jesus has claimed to be 'Son of God'. Instead of Pilate referring it back to them as an internal matter, as he previously threatened (18:31), he is much more frightened by this (19:8). The beliefs of the Greeks and Romans were full of stories of 'sons of gods', semi-divine figures with miraculous powers appearing on earth—and he had just scourged this one! Perhaps he was superstitious and afraid of retribution. Alternatively, he may have been afraid that the Jewish authorities would report him to Rome yet again for not respecting the local laws and customs. Or perhaps his fear was simply the dawning realization that these people were not going to give up and let him get away with this, and so he has no choice but to go back inside for further investigations.

For REFLECTION & PRAYER

'What a man! The King of the Jews!'
Imagine the figure of Jesus, beaten and dressed up.
What is your reaction and what are you going to do with him?

No King *but* Caesar!

Pilate had thought it was all over; Jesus had been whipped and the idea that he was a king duly mocked, so everything was all set for his release, when those wretched religious leaders brought the gods and their offspring into it! Unsettled by this mention of semi-divine sons, he goes back inside for the sixth scene, which balances the second, when Pilate and Jesus discussed kingship.

6—Where are you from?

The kingship discussion arose from Pilate's question, 'What have you done?' (18:35). His argument with "the Jews" showed Pilate that the central issue is not what Jesus has *done*, but who he might *be*. So now he starts with a much better question: 'where are you from?' (19:9). The origins of Jesus have been debated throughout John. Nicodemus recognized he was 'from God' (3:2), although his colleagues denied this (9:29; see also 3:31–36; 8:21–59). Jesus has spent most of the gospel explaining where he is from, but now he is strangely silent. After all, Pilate did not wait for an answer to 'what is truth?' (18:38), so does he really want to know about cosmic origins?

Like most people in authority faced with a silence, Pilate starts to throw his weight around. He tells Jesus, 'I have power to release you and power to crucify you' (19:10). The word for 'power' is *exousia*, or authority, and we are straight into some heavy irony. Pilate can bluster about his authority, but the bedraggled prisoner before him is the one to whom God has given 'authority over all people', authority to 'give eternal life', to 'execute judgment', or make them 'children of God' (17:2; 5:27; 1:12). Pilate might think he has 'power' over Jesus, but the good shepherd knows that no one can take his life; only he has the 'power to lay it down and the power to take it up again' (10:18).

So Jesus breaks his silence to tell Pilate that the only power he has comes *anothen*, 'from above' (19:11). At the human level, he reminds Pilate that he depends upon the emperor's favour, but at the spiritual level, 'from above' answers Pilate's question about where Jesus comes from. He is 'the one from above' (see on 3:31 and 3:3). Pilate may appear in charge but 'the one who handed me over' is more responsible. The word 'hand over' is used for Judas the 'betrayer', who 'handed him over' (13:21; 18:3, 5)—yet more recently the priests 'handed him over' to Pilate (18:30, 35). This careful reply makes Pilate pause; someone with such a sense of his proper place and understanding of authority is not a hot-headed revolutionary.

7—Here is your king

Pilate goes out for the seventh and final scene, balancing the first requesting the death sentence. Despite his efforts to release him, the cries of "the Jews" are too much. They too realize that his power is from 'above', from the emperor. If Pilate releases Jesus, he is not 'Caesar's friend', a formal title (19:12; see on 15:14). Tiberius Caesar was emperor, a paranoid recluse on Capri, from where he considered everyone against him. In AD31, he even deposed his chief minister, Sejanus, a friend of Pilate. The early 30s, around the time of the crucifixion, was no time to have your loyalty to Caesar questioned.

Therefore, Pilate brings Jesus out to sit at his judgment seat and the irony continues. The Greek could mean that Pilate sits Jesus on the judge's bench—where he belongs since 'the father has given all judgment to the Son' (5:22). But at the human level, Jesus stands before his judge on the 'Stone Pavement' (19:13). A massive stone paved area has been excavated in the Antonia fortress with soldiers' dice games scratched on its surface. Since we are not sure which fortress was Pilate's headquarters, or when this pavement was built, its identification with the stones on which Jesus was sentenced is not as clear as tour guides assume—but to stand there today is a moving experience.

At noon on the Friday of Preparation, when the Passover lambs were slaughtered, the Lamb of God is sentenced (19:14; see 1:29). Pilate makes one last attempt, offering Jesus' broken figure to the Jews, 'Here is *your* king', accepting their charge for execution. But they do not want him, repeating, 'Crucify him!'. Pilate replies, 'crucify your king?' Their cry 'we have no king but Caesar' passes their own sentence. Their only king was supposed to be God (Jdg. 8:23; 1 Sam. 8:7) or his 'anointed' (Ps. 2:2). In accepting the pagan emperor, they were not just refusing Jesus, but any messiah and ultimately God himself, renouncing his rule and breaking his covenant. Judgment has been given.

PRAYER

Lord Jesus, Lamb of God and true Judge
may I have no King but you.

The KING IS CRUCIFIED

Through these seven balanced trial scenes, Pilate moved from mocking Jesus to a grudging respect for his kingship while "the Jews" rejected the rule of God, preferring Caesar. Now Pilate 'hands him over to them', using the word for 'betray', after the actions of Judas and the priests (19:16; see on 19:11). 'To them' means "the Jews" who have finally got their way and so the soldiers take him for crucifixion.

The Cross on Calvary

Jesus 'carried the cross by himself' (19:17). There is no mention here of Simon of Cyrene who helps in the other gospels, since John stresses that Jesus is in control throughout the Passion. He is taken to the 'place of the skull', probably a skull shaped rocky outcrop on the edge of the old city, called Golgotha in Hebrew, or 'Calvary' in Latin. The traditional site is now enclosed within the Church of the Holy Sepulchre, with two altars built over the rock which pilgrims can touch underneath. 'There they crucified him' (19:18). It is easy today to miss the horror which John's terse comment would have communicated to the ancients. Being roped or nailed in an upright position with your arms outstretched makes the body fluids collect in the chest. Death is caused eventually through 'drowning', or suffocating as breathing becomes difficult. It could take days, unless the person died earlier of the wounds from flogging, heat exhaustion or heart failure from the traumatic stress. Temporary relief for breathing could be obtained by sitting on a small 'saddle' half way up the cross, but this only prolonged the agony. The physical horror and the public humiliation was such that it was expressly forbidden for Roman citizens to be crucified; it was only used for slaves or local criminals. Jesus is crucified 'with two others'; John does not tell us if they were thieves or zealot fighters, nor of Luke's account of one repenting (Lk. 23:39–43). His focus is totally on Jesus in the centre.

Jesus of Nazareth, King of the Jews

The title INRI on depictions of the crucifixion comes from the Latin for 'J(I)esus of Nazareth, King of the Jews' (Rex Iudaeorum), the inscription which Pilate had written in all three ancient tongues

(19:19–20). Hebrew was the language of the Jewish faith, Greek was the language of culture, spoken by everyone and containing the beauties of literature and philosophy, and Latin was the official political language of the state. Proclaiming Jesus as king in the religious, intellectual and social realms fulfilled Jesus' prophecy that he would draw everyone to himself when he was 'lifted up from the earth' (12:32). Flushed by their success in the trial, the chief priests are horrified that Jesus should be officially proclaimed like this. After resisting all Jesus' 'I am' statements earlier in this gospel, now they want to insert 'I am' into the charge to undercut its absolute claim, 'this man said, "I am King of the Jews".' (19:21). But this time Pilate is obdurate, refusing with the pithy 'what I have written, I have written' (19:22). They brought the prisoner on a capital charge and rejected him even when he was crowned in purple, stating their loyalty to 'no king but Caesar'. It is too late for word games now; Jesus' kingship stands and the cross declares it for all Jews and Gentiles to read. Jesus reigns, even from the wood of the cross, as in crucifixes of him in regal robes as *Christus Rex*. Such is John's account of Jesus still in control.

Parting his garments

Part of the humiliation was being executed naked in public view. The soldiers would keep the person's clothes as a 'perk' for the messy job. John shows that the crucifixion party was a *quaternion*, a four-man unit, who divided Jesus' clothes between them. His tunic, however, was 'seamless' (19:23). Josephus says that the priest's tunic (see Lev. 16:4; Exod. 39:27) was seamless, made from a single thread because of the law's prohibition against mixing different sorts of cloth. Some commentators have suggested that Jesus' robe was 'priestly' therefore; an old legend says that Jesus' mother Mary made 'the Robe' herself, while Cyprian said that his clothes' four shares represent the four corners of the earth and the seamless robe is the undivided church! John has none of these, preferring his theme of fulfilment, as the soldiers cast lots for it (19:24; Ps. 22:18). The world gambles over castoffs while 'God reigns from the tree', offering life in every language.

PRAYER

Jesus our King, crucified for all nations,
pour out love from your cross
over all the corners of the earth.

The KING'S LAST WORDS

The soldiers have finished crucifying Jesus and shared out his clothes; there is nothing left now, but to wait for death to come. John's focus moves to the foot of the cross, where there are four women: the mother of Jesus; his mother's sister; Mary wife of Clopas, and Mary Magdalene (19:25). Jesus' mother is not named, nor is her sister; comparison with the other gospels suggests that she might be Salome, the wife of Zebedee, mother of James and John (Mk. 15:40; Matt. 27:56). A condemned man's family and friends could witness an execution, and people had to be near to read the charge written over the cross. The soldiers would ensure no one attempted to rescue anyone from the cross! Hearing a dying person's last words can be difficult no matter how close you are, and each gospel represents Jesus' end differently, reflecting their interpretations. Mark has one dark cry of desolation (Mk. 15:34), which is answered by a supernatural earthquake in Matt. 27:52; Luke, however, has three profound sayings of forgiveness and trust (Lk. 23:34, 43, 46). John also has three sayings, continuing his theme that Jesus is still in control.

Woman, behold your son

First, Jesus sees his mother and the unnamed 'disciple whom he loved'. As the eldest, Jesus would have provided for his mother, brothers and sisters since Joseph's death; but his brothers do not believe in him (7:5). If the 'Beloved Disciple' is John son of Zebedee and if Mary's sister is his mother Salome, then John would be Mary's nephew and Jesus' cousin, which may be why Jesus entrusts his mother to John (19:26-27). Neither is named: Jesus calls her 'woman', as he did at the wedding in Cana when his 'hour' had not yet come (2:4). Now the 'hour' has arrived (13:1; 17:1); from 'that hour', the disciple takes her 'to his own', as Jesus came 'to his own' and made the disciples 'his own' (1:11; 13:1). At the surface level, John shows Jesus still in control, ensuring that his mother and friends were cared for after he was gone. At the deeper level, some Catholics interpret Mary as the mother of the church, symbolized by the disciple. On the other hand, since the mother is given into the disciple's care, she may represent Judaism being entrusted to the church. Yet others see them as a new

Adam and Eve, beneath another Tree and being obedient this time.

I thirst

Once more, John stresses Jesus' knowledge. Having known that all was under control and loved 'his own' disciples 'to the end' (13:1–3), now Jesus knows that everything has 'ended', 'all was now finished' (19:28). The same word is used for 'end' as he 'finishes' scripture: 'knowing all was fulfilled, said to fulfil scripture'. Hanging on a cross in the Mediterranean heat would make anyone thirsty. But Jesus says 'I thirst' more to fulfil scriptures like Ps. 69:21 and his own desire to 'drink the cup that the father gave me' (18:11). The soldiers had a jug of 'sour wine' to help them with their thirsty work, and so they put a sponge full on hyssop and hold it up to him (19:29). Because hyssop is not a very strong plant, some scholars prefer the reading 'javelin', *hyssos*, found in some late manuscripts. It is more likely that John was thinking of how hyssop was used to put the lamb's blood on the door frame so that God would 'pass over' his people (Exod. 12:22–23), thus making another link with Jesus as the true Passover lamb.

It is finished

Jesus has received the wine and knows that 'all was now finished' (19:28). So when he cries out 'It is finished' (19:30), it is another of John's typical two level statements. On the surface, it looks like it is all over, Jesus is finished and everything has been a failure. Yet John's theme of Jesus being in control invites a further look: 'it is accomplished', 'fulfilled', all brought successfully to the proper conclusion. The word is also used to settle a bill; the price has been 'paid on the nail'. Then 'Jesus bowed his head', like someone going to sleep, and 'gave up his spirit'. He is still in control, with these active verbs; there is nothing passive about John's passion; no one takes the life of the good shepherd, but he gives it up (10:17–18). When Jesus died, he 'handed over' his spirit, breathing his last over the beloved disciple, Mary and the others at the foot of the cross. As he promised, it is 'to your advantage that I go away' so that he could pour his parting gift of his Spirit upon them (see on 14:16, 26; 16:7).

PRAYER

Lord Jesus, thank you for all you accomplished on the cross;
make me your beloved child and pour your Spirit upon me.

The DEATH of the KING

The Romans would usually leave a crucified body hanging on the cross to be picked clean by animals and birds, as a warning to others, like the old gibbets for hanged highwaymen at cross-roads. According to John, it is the Day of Preparation for the Passover, when the lambs were sacrificed (19:14). The priests would not even enter Pilate's headquarters in case they became ritually impure (18:28). It was even more important, as both the Sabbath and Passover approached at sunset, not to defile such a special day with bodies hanging around (19:31). Jewish law considered that 'anyone hung on a tree is under God's curse' and therefore 'the corpse must not remain all night upon the tree; you shall bury him that same day; you must not defile the land' (Deut. 21:22–23; see Josh. 8:29). A crucified man died from suffocation as the body fluids collected in the chest, and he could get temporary relief by hauling himself up to breathe. Therefore, death could be hastened by breaking the legs, so that he would sag down and die more quickly. The priests ask Pilate to do this, not out of compassion for the dying, but so that their religious festival would not be spoiled by messy corpses! Once more, how easy it is for us to be so concerned with our rituals that we miss both human compassion and what God is doing.

Blood and water

The Roman soldiers smashed the legs of the other two to stop them prolonging the agony and to hasten their deaths (19:32). But when they come to Jesus, it is unnecessary, since he is already dead (19:33). To make sure, a soldier thrusts his spear into Jesus' side and 'at once blood and water came out' (19:34). This simple statement has provoked enormous comment from the early Fathers to modern medical investigations. Since John stresses its importance (19:35), we might expect to find his usual levels of interpretation here. At the surface level of human physiology, both the flogging and crucifixion would cause the body fluids to collect in his chest. Some doctors say that the blood would separate out from the more colourless fluids, which would look like water when the spear opened the bottom of the chest cavity. Others suggest that the blood came from his heart being ruptured, suggesting that Jesus died of a broken heart—literally! John stresses at the physical level that Jesus was really human and died a real human death. Because of the ancient Greek 'dualism' between the physical world and the divine realm, the idea that God could become human was ridiculous—and that he might die even more outrageous! The 'Docetics' (from the Greek *docein*, to seem or appear) argued that Jesus only 'seemed' to be human and just 'appeared' to die, while actually he was rescued by God. Muslims also believe that Jesus did not die, but only a 'likeness' was crucified (*The Qur'an*, sura 4:156–9). But John is clear: Jesus died, and blood and water came out of his side.

New life from death

As often, there are many interpretations of John's deeper meaning for the blood and water. Since Jesus dies as the true Passover lamb, blood recalls how the lamb's blood was sprinkled by the priests (2 Chron. 35:11). On the other hand, water recalls Jesus' promise that out of his *koilia*, heart or chest, will flow 'streams of living water', which John interpreted as the giving of the Spirit after he had been glorified in death (7:38–39). Some early Fathers saw here the two-fold baptism of water and baptism of blood, or martyrdom, faced by their people in the persecutions. Others interpret it as the Lord's gift of the two sacraments: water for baptism, and blood for the wine of communion. We have noted the connection of water with baptism and the Spirit before (e.g. 3:5; 7:38–39), while blood comes only in the discourse about eating his flesh and drinking his blood (6:53–56). After the hints of bread and wine, vines and cups through John's account of Jesus' last night and day, another reference to the sacraments here is very possible.

The mystery of Jesus' death on the cross for us is so deep that none of these interpretations will ever fully exhaust it. We can only stand at the foot of the cross, like the disciple who witnessed it (19:35)—and marvel. From that messy, all too human death pours a flood of spiritual benefits of forgiveness and new life in the Spirit, freely given to us and to all God's people.

For REFLECTION & PRAYER

Rock of ages cleft for me, Let me hide myself in thee;
Let the water and the blood, From thy riven side which flowed
Be of sin the double cure, Cleanse me from its guilt and power.
A.M. Toplady (1740–78)

The KING IS BURIED

After describing Jesus' three last sayings and the flow of blood and water from his side, suddenly John inserts a narrative comment with two of his key words both used twice, 'witness' and 'truth' (19:35). John the Baptist was a 'witness' to Jesus at the very start (1:7, 19, 32) and many of the informal trials between Jesus and "the Jews" were about which witnesses were 'true' (e.g. 5:30–38); Jesus has also claimed to be 'the truth' and 'the true vine' (14:6; 15:1). Both words are linked to the 'Spirit of truth' who will 'bear witness' with the witness of the disciples (15:26). The use of these words here suggests that we were right to see hints of the Spirit in Jesus' 'handing over his spirit' and in the flow of water and blood (19:30, 34). The witness' testimony to the truth is repeated at the end of the gospel, where the witness is clearly the 'disciple Jesus loved' (21:24). Here he is present at the foot of the cross with Jesus' mother and now reports what he saw (19:26). At the end of the gospel, John stresses that he is writing 'that you may believe' and he states the same purpose here (19:35; 20:31). At this crucial moment of the crucifixion, the writer wants us to understand both the truth and the significance of what he is saying.

Scripture is fulfilled

Further corroboration comes from the fulfilment of scripture. John has not used this idea much until the cross, when both the dividing of the garments and Jesus' thirst were to 'fulfil scripture' (19:24, 28). Now the fact that he died before the soldiers could break his legs fulfils the requirement that the Passover lamb should not have any bones broken (19:36; see Exod. 12:46; Num. 9:12). So John's deeper level continues the irony that the priests have sacrificed Jesus as the true Passover lamb. He may also recall the Psalmist's belief that God protects his righteous people, ensuring that their bones are not broken (Ps. 34:20).

The final scripture quoted comes from Zechariah, whose themes have recurred so often recently. His prophecy that 'your king comes to you, humble riding on a donkey' was fulfilled in Jesus' entry into Jerusalem (12:15; Zech. 9:9). His 'worthless shepherd' who did not care for God's people was behind Jesus the good shepherd's criticism of the religious leaders' lack of care for people like the blind man (10:12–14; Zech. 11:16). The scattering of the disciples after they lost the good shepherd also picked up his prophecy (16:32; Zech. 13:7–8). Yet Zechariah looks forward to a 'fountain which will cleanse Jerusalem' (Zech. 13:1) reminding us of the flow of water and blood from Jesus' side. Now John quotes Zechariah's lament of Jerusalem mourning for a first-born son as 'they look on the one whom they have pierced' (19:37; Zech. 12:10). The king who came riding humbly in peace laid down his life like a good shepherd, pouring out the fountain of life from his side. As Jesus prophesied, when he is 'lifted up' on the cross, he draws everyone to him; some look at the 'one pierced' and oppose him even in death—but for all who 'look on him' and believe, his death brings eternal life.

Burial in another garden

Jesus' death brings two of the Jewish authorities more fully into the light. Joseph of Arimathea has been a disciple 'in secret … out of fear of the Jews' (19:38; see 12:42). Now he requests Jesus' body from Pilate; if Jesus really was guilty as a king against Caesar, his body should be left exposed as an example, while the Jews only buried criminals in a common grave. By granting Joseph's request, Pilate again implies that Jesus is innocent. Equally, Nicodemus, 'who had come to Jesus by night', finally comes out into the open, bearing lavish gifts fit for a king (19:39). Josephus describes the vast amount of spices used at the burial of King Herod the Great. Now the 'King of the Jews' is buried with a 'hundred pounds' of spices and linen—all in accordance with Jewish burial customs (19:40). He was betrayed in a garden, and is now buried in a garden nearby (19:41; see 18:1). No communal criminals' grave is used, but 'a new tomb in which no one had ever been laid'. Jesus receives a right royal treatment. Because time was short on the Day of Preparation, 'they laid Jesus there' (19:42). In fact, what was being prepared for them would be beyond their wildest imaginings…

PRAYER

Lord Jesus, you were laid in the tomb
and sanctified the grave to be a bed of hope to your people;
grant that our dying may be so done
that we live in you for ever.

100 JOHN 20:1–10

THEY HAVE TAKEN AWAY *the* LORD

The arrival of the Sabbath caused Jesus to be brought down from the cross and buried in a nearby tomb (19:42). Now it is early on Sunday, *proi* again, just before dawn, the time when they took Jesus from Caiaphas to Pilate on Friday morning (18:28). Mary Magdalene comes to the tomb 'while it was still dark' (20:1). Like Nicodemus coming to Jesus by night, or Judas going out into the night (3:2; 13:30), Mary is still in darkness, the black despair of grief and desolation. We saw with another Mary the custom of visiting a tomb for three days to lament, waiting for the person's spirit to depart as the body decomposed (see on 11:17, 31). Today was Mary's first opportunity, so she is up early. As she arrives, she sees that the covering stone has gone. We who know the story must remember that she would not deduce that Jesus had risen. Rather, she would assume that either the authorities had been unable to leave Jesus' body alone and had taken him off, perhaps to a communal grave, or, even worse that tomb robbers had been lured by the rich spices and cloths.

A race to the tomb

So she ran to get help from Simon Peter who is still seen as the leader, despite his denial of Jesus. As so often, he is with the 'other disciple', who got him into the high priest's courtyard (18:15). He is now identified as 'the disciple Jesus loved', who was present at the last supper and the crucifixion (13:23; 19:26). To these two, she pours out her story: 'they have taken the Lord out of the tomb, and we do not know where they have laid him' (20:2). Like many in grief, she wants to tell the story of her loss, a story which will be repeated like a cracked record to anyone who will listen. Both disciples dash to the tomb, but the beloved disciple 'outran Peter, and reached the tomb first' (20:3–4). If he is the witness behind this gospel, he would have been younger than Peter. In the early light of dawn, he can see 'the linen grave cloths lying there', probably on a shelf cut into the rock, but he does not enter, as he waits respectfully for the elder disciple (20:5).

The grave cloths

Simon Peter arrives out of breath, all huffing and puffing—and goes straight in (20:6). This is the impetuous Peter who hit Malchus the high priest's slave in the garden and followed his master with the other disciple even into the courtyard where his rash actions led to denying Jesus only a couple of days ago (18:10; 15–27). So now, he does not stop, but enters immediately to find the linen grave cloths still lying there (20:6). Obviously, the authorities are not responsible, for they would not have undressed the body; tomb robbers might— but only to take the spices and cloths, and leave the corpse. The cloth or napkin for the head was 'rolled up by itself' (20:7). When Lazarus came out of his tomb, he still had this cloth around his face, with his body so wrapped up that he could only shuffle out (11:44). Yet Jesus' body has gone and left these cloths. What could have happened?

The beloved disciple believes

The other disciple finally enters—and goes beyond Peter, in three terse verbs: he 'entered', he 'saw', he 'believed' (20:8). Somehow the cloths suggested that the body had passed through them. His insight invites comment about this disciple and Peter. After all, he always goes one better: he leans against Jesus at the last supper and Peter asks a question through him, just as he gained access for Peter to the high priest's courtyard (13:23–25; 18:16). Now he 'outran Peter', arrived first and was the first to believe (20:4, 8). Some suggest that he represents a 'superior' church, perhaps Gentile Christians against Peter's Jewish Christians, or the evangelist's community against the mainstream church under Peter (see Introduction, pp. 20–21). Yet this gospel consistently shows Peter as the leader of the disciples; if the beloved disciple is an 'ideal figure' going beyond even Peter, that is the calling John issues to all his readers. Despite his belief, both disciples still did not understand the scriptures which suggested resurrection (20:9; see e.g. Ps. 16:10; Hos. 6:2). Therefore something very strange happens: they see all this and then—'they went home'! (20:10). If only they had waited with Mary at the tomb, their questions would have been answered by Jesus himself, but 'they went home'. It is not enough to see like Mary, to enter like Peter or believe like the beloved disciple, if all we do is go home afterwards and carry on regardless.

PRAYER

Christ is risen! He is risen indeed!
Lord give us the eyes of faith to see, and believe, that you are alive.

I HAVE SEEN *the* LORD!

After Peter and other disciple have gone home, Mary stays outside the tomb, frozen in her grief (20:11). She has been through the desolation of watching Jesus die on the cross; at least she was there, unlike Peter (19:25). But now she suffers a second grief with the loss of his body. She wanted to weep for him, to have something to hold on to in her pain—but even that has gone.

Messengers in white

Bent double in her agony, she peers into the tomb and sees two figures in white, keeping watch at the head and foot of where Jesus had lain (20:12). John says they are 'angels', which means 'messengers'. Mary is so locked into her tears that she does not realize who they are, since she does not react as people in the Bible usually do when they see angels. She is too wrapped up in her own concerns to be frightened or awe-struck. She just wants to be left alone in her grief. Instead, they question her: 'woman, why are you weeping?' (20:13). On the surface this is a silly thing to ask someone at a grave; the answer is obvious and the question intrusive. Yet at a deeper level, they are right to ask—for if Mary only knew what we know about Jesus, she would be weeping tears of joy. But she replies with almost the same words she told Peter and the beloved disciple (see 20:2). It is the cracked record of a bereaved person, telling the same story over and over and over again, becoming ever more personal; Jesus is now '*my* Lord' and '*I* do not know where they have laid him', not 'we'. Engrossed in her grief, she does not wait for a reply, but turns away.

The gardener?

As she turns around, she becomes aware of someone else standing behind her, whom she was too occupied to notice before; even now she does not recognize that it is the very person she is looking for (20:14). So great is her desire to mourn alone, she looks away again, since she does not face him until he calls her name (20:16). Jesus, too, will not leave her alone, but repeats the angels' question, 'woman, why are you weeping?' For the moment he calls her 'woman', as he did his mother long ago in Cana and from the cross

(2:4; 19:26). In another 'echo', he adds the first words he spoke in this gospel, which he repeated to those who came to arrest him in the garden: 'whom are you looking for?' (20:15; see 1:38 and 18:4, 7). Mary misses these allusions and mistakes him for 'the gardener'. Impervious in her grief, she repeats her story; if he has moved the body, 'tell me where you have laid him and I will take him away'. She just wants to find Jesus' body, to hold on to it and grieve in peace. So the cracked record goes round and round and only a miracle will change it. And that is exactly what happens, as Jesus moves from 'woman' to gently whispering her name, 'Mary'. The sheep know their shepherd's voice when 'he calls them by name and leads them out' (10:3). Recognizing the good shepherd's voice, she turns again to face him, 'Rabbouni', my master! (20:16). The heart of this personal encounter with the risen Jesus is encapsulated in those two names, 'Mary', 'Master'. 'They' have not taken him anywhere; there was nothing passive in the passion, and he is still in control now: he has risen from the dead!

A new relationship for a new message

But Mary is still the same, she wants to cling on to him, to possess him as before. Jesus explains that in their new relationship she cannot 'hold on' to the risen Christ. Instead, she has a task, to be the apostle of the resurrection; Jesus sends her to go and tell the news to the disciples who would have met him themselves if only they had not 'gone home'. In this gospel, everyone gets a new task after meeting Jesus, as he brings a new covenant relationship: we are brothers and sisters with Jesus, children of 'my Father and your Father, my God and your God' (20:17; see Lev. 26:12; Jer. 31:33; Ruth 1:16). Having seen God's messenger angels, Mary becomes one herself: she goes *angellousa*, 'announcing' to the disciples how Jesus has replaced her cracked record with a new song: 'I have seen the Lord'—and declaring all the wonders he had told her (20:18).

This is the heart of every Christian's story, that the risen Jesus meets us and calls us out of our selfish concerns to become an angel, announcing to everyone, 'I have seen the Lord'.

PRAYER

Lord Jesus, speak through my tears,
call me by my name and give me a new song to sing
—that you are risen and alive for evermore!

102

SENT OUT *in the* SPIRIT

Mary saw some angel-messengers at the tomb, but through meeting the risen Jesus she became a 'messenger' herself. The same happens now to the disciples in a climactic scene which draws threads together from throughout the gospel. In the Farewell Discourses, Jesus explained that it was to the disciples' 'advantage' that he went away, so that he and the Father could send the Holy Spirit as 'another Paraclete', an advocate or comforter (16:7). While the Spirit's role includes some 'comfort' in Jesus' leaving gift of peace in a hostile world, he comes not primarily for our benefit but to teach us and to witness to the truth for the sake of the continuing mission (14:26–27; 15:26). Through the resurrection of Jesus and the gift of the Spirit, the mission of God the Holy Trinity is passed on to us.

Peace be with you

On that Sunday evening, the disciples are all gathered together, perhaps where they had the last supper, behind locked doors out of 'fear of the Jews' (20:19). But no locked doors can prevent Jesus keeping his promise, 'I will not leave you desolate; I will come to you' (14:18). So he comes and stands among them, and says 'peace be with you'. At the last supper he left them his parting gift of 'shalom', a peace 'not like the world gives' so that their hearts need not be 'troubled' (14:27; 16:33). Like all bequests, the disciples receive this gift after the giver has died— but unusually, he brings it in person! He had also promised that although they would feel pain as sharp as childbirth, they would rejoice when they saw him again (16:22). Now he shows them his hands and side and 'the disciples rejoiced when they saw the Lord' (20:20).

As the Father sent me, so I send you

Jesus has repeatedly stressed that he had been sent into the world by God his Father, 'the one who sent me'. In the Farewell Discourses he was preparing the disciples for their mission of being 'sent'. Apostles, 'those sent', are not greater than the one who sent them, and they should expect to be treated as the master was (13:16; 15:20). But the converse is also true that 'whoever receives one whom I send receives me; and whoever receives me receives him who sent me' (13:20). Jesus prayed for those he would send into the world 'as you have sent me into the world' (17:18). Now that moment has arrived. First, he gives them his gift of peace and then follows it with his mission charge: 'Peace be with you. As the Father has sent me, so I send you' (20:21). The apostles, the 'ones sent', are not given a new task to do; they are to carry on Jesus' mission. The Father 'sent' Jesus in the past, but Jesus 'sends' them on a continuing mission in the present and the future. An old Jewish proverb says 'a man's representative is as the man himself'. We are the 'body of Christ' here on earth; if the world receives us, then it receives Jesus who sent us, and in receiving him, it receives God the Father, the source of all mission.

Receive the Holy Spirit

To carry out someone's commission you need the power to act, and the authority to speak, on their behalf. First these frightened disciples, huddled in a locked room, need power to go anywhere, so Jesus 'breathed on them' (20:22). It is like God breathing 'the breath of life' into Adam or breathing upon the valley of dry bones (Gen. 2:7; Ezek. 37:1–14). C.S. Lewis depicts it well as Aslan breathes upon the children in Narnia whenever they need strength for the tasks he gives them. So now Jesus fulfils his promise of sending them the Holy Spirit (16:7)—except he makes a delivery in person as he breathes upon them and says 'Receive the Holy Spirit'.

Having fulfilled his promises to be with them and bring peace and joy, Jesus now gives them not just the power to go into the world, but also his authority. As the Father sent Jesus, so he sends his disciples. As the Father 'gave authority to execute judgment to the Son' (see 5:19–29), so Jesus gives them the task of forgiving and retaining sins (20:23). The work of liberation involves forgiving, letting go and releasing—the same word is used to 'unbind' Lazarus' bandages (11:44). The other word, 'retain', 'hold on' appears only here in John—but throughout Jesus has warned that the coming of light into darkness produces shadows, the 'critical moment' when some prefer to remain in their sin and blindness. To be sent into the world as Jesus was sent inevitably brings the possibility of acceptance or rejection.

PRAYER

*Risen Lord Jesus, breathe your peace upon us
and send us out in the power of your Spirit.*

THOMAS: *from* DISBELIEF *to* FAITH

Thomas is immortalized as 'Doubting Thomas', an unfortunate nickname which does not do him justice either in this story or earlier in John. He is first mentioned when Jesus is returning to Judaea to raise Lazarus—and Thomas says 'let's go and die with him' (11:16). He is not really a doubter, more of a depressed donkey, the loyal pessimist, like Eeyore, who looks at ground level and sees the thistles. At the last supper, he did not understand what Jesus was saying and wanted to know the way physically (14:5). Yet this is the apostle who, according to tradition, went all the way to found the church in India. Something must have happened to get him to look up from the physical level!

I will not believe

Thomas was absent when the risen Jesus first came to the disciples behind the locked doors (20:19, 24). As the pessimist down at the physical level, perhaps he withdrew into his pain and grief. It is totally understandable, something many of us do. The problem is that we keep away from church when we need it most—and then we miss the fun when Jesus turns up! Being told what a good time everybody else had when you were absent only compounds the problem. Now the disciples all repeat Mary's message: '*we* have seen the Lord' (20:25). Thomas again wants the physical level—literally: 'unless' he can physically touch Jesus' wounded body, 'I will not believe'. At least he is honest. He is not an agonized doubter, wrestling in an effort to believe. He is an honest sceptic who just wants some physical evidence.

Be not faithless, but believe

On the next Sunday evening, the community are gathered together again perhaps to break bread in communion. Thomas is with them this time: he may be a pessimist, but he is a loyal one who was ready to go with Jesus to die. Despite his scepticism, he is still here. The doors are locked as before, but Jesus again comes and stands among them greeting them with the same gift: 'Peace be with you' (20:26; cf. v. 19).

Jesus knows about our questions. So he gives Thomas his answer, inviting him to touch him at the physical level (20:27). Jesus told Mary not to touch him because she was clinging on to the old way of life. For Thomas, the chance to touch Jesus is the way to a new life. People progress differently spiritually; what will help one might hinder another. Everyone comes to faith differently in this chapter: the beloved disciple believes from empty grave cloths, Mary when Jesus calls her name, the disciples from seeing him come and stand among them, and now Thomas from touching him. Except that we are not told that Thomas actually touches Jesus; perhaps the appearance and the invitation are enough for him. So Jesus tells him 'Do not be faithless, be faithful.' Nothing is said about doubt. It is about getting faith where there was none—and Jesus' word is enough. Thomas replies with a full confession: 'my Lord and my God' (20:28). This echoes the claim of the emperor Domitian to be called 'Dominus et Deus noster'. Thomas moves from the surface to the summit of Christian faith. 'My God' recalls the prologue (1:1) while Jesus echoes Thomas' 'believing' and 'seeing'. The blind man came to see and believe, while the religious leaders became blind by not believing (9:38–41). As in his high priestly prayer, Jesus lifts his eyes beyond the disciples to the wider church and blesses 'those who have not seen yet believe' which includes you and I who read the gospel today (20:29).

That you may believe

Now John addresses us directly with his purpose in what sounds like the original ending of the gospel. The first half ended with a summary about Jesus' signs echoing the beginning with John the Baptist (10:41–42). Thomas' declaration has taken us back to the prologue, while the writer reminds us of the 'signs' (see 2:11). But 'Jesus did many other signs' of which these are a selection; John had so much material that he had to choose which fitted his purpose, 'that you may believe that Jesus is the Christ, the Son of God' (20:30–31). Those titles take us from John the Baptist denying that he was the Christ through all the other expressions of faith like Martha's (1:19–20; 11:27). But faith is not an end in itself; through faith John wants us to 'have life in his name', like Thomas and all who met the risen Jesus.

For REFLECTION & PRAYER

My Lord and my God!
Imagine you are in the room when Jesus appears.
What do you want to see, hear, touch, or ask? What is your reaction?
Are you like Peter, Mary, Thomas, or are you the unnamed disciple?

GONE FISHING

After the climax of Jesus' resurrection and appearances to Mary, the disciples and to Thomas, the last verses handed the baton on to the reader in what seemed like the end of the gospel. Most scholars consider this chapter to be a later addition, perhaps written in a slightly different style. Also, it is difficult to fit the story into the sequence of chapter 20 and the early church in Jerusalem. On the other hand, the story recalls many key themes from the gospel and no manuscript is without it. It deals with some 'loose ends' from the gospel, especially about Peter and the beloved disciple and their relationship. So it may be better to see it as an epilogue, balancing the prologue at the start.

Jesus is always in control in John, even through his trial and death. The same is true at the resurrection as he called Mary by name in her grief and gave peace to the disciples locked in by fear and brought faith to Thomas. The one person not sorted out is Simon, brought by his brother Andrew and called Peter, 'the rock', by Jesus (1:42). He is impetuous, the one who is quick to state his faith, and then at the last supper, moves from not letting Jesus wash his feet to wanting to be washed all over (6:68; 13:6–10). Yet Peter has been decidedly 'rocky' and wobbly lately: in the garden he lashed out at Malchus, and in the courtyard his rashness led to his denial (18:10, 15–27). His impetuosity made him rush to the tomb, behind the younger beloved disciple, and he was first to enter it (20:6–7). Then he 'went home'; presumably he was with the disciples when Jesus appeared, but he was not mentioned.

Old ways

Now he really has 'gone home', back to 'the old place', the Sea of Tiberias or Galilee (21:1; 6:1). He is also with old friends, Thomas the loyal pessimist and Nathanael of Cana who does not think anything good can come from Nazareth (1:45–51). In addition to this gloomy pair are the sons of Zebedee and two others. The beloved disciple must be one of them, hence his traditional identification with John, son of Zebedee (21:2, 7).

In the old places with old friends, Peter returns to his old way of life: 'I'm off fishing' (21:3). He is still the leader; going fishing is his idea, but the others follow him—and it is 'night'. This may be a good time to go fishing on the Sea of Galilee, but night has been used symbolically for the hour of darkness in John, what Nicodemus came out of and Judas went into (3:2; 13:30). So it is not surprising that they return to their old ways at night. But, of course, we cannot go back: it is fruitless, and they catch nothing all night. When we have done something bad, or something has gone wrong in our lives, the temptation is to retreat back to old friends, old places, old habits to try to forget, yet it does not work.

The stranger on the shore

Now Jesus arrives, in control as always, taking the divine initiative at just the low point, when everything is fruitless. Every morning, the new light of God comes into the darkest hour. Once again it is daybreak, *proi*, the time when Peter had committed his threefold denial and Mary found the tomb empty (18:27–28; 20:1). Jesus comes and stands on the sea-shore, but they are so sunk in the old ways that they do not even recognize him (21:4).

So Jesus takes the initiative, with a friendly shout, 'Hi, guys!' or 'Lads!' It is a pleasant enquiry, but he already expects a negative answer: 'you have caught no fish, have you?' and they sadly agree (21:5). Then he gives them a simple instruction to try the right hand side, where they catch too large a shoal to haul the net into the boat (21:6). Commentators debate whether this is meant to be a miracle and further evidence of Jesus' divine knowledge, or just reflects a trick of the light whereby people on the shore can see below the surface more easily than those on top of it in the boat. Certainly, John's gospel is all about learning to look below the surface for the deeper meaning—and, not surprisingly, the 'disciple Jesus loved' did just that. The vast number of fish is typical of Jesus, the super-abundance like turning 150 gallons of water into wine, or feeding the five thousand. So, as at the tomb, this disciple has a flash of insight: 'It is the Lord!' (21:7). Peter's response is equally typical: his first impulse is to gird his clothes around him to cover his nakedness, jump straight in and swim to greet Jesus.

PRAYER

Lord Jesus, when we are tempted to go back to the old ways,
call out to us to look more deeply, that we might see you.

237

BREAKFAST *with* JESUS

Fishing was Peter's idea but he has abandoned ship, leaving the others lurched over the side dragging the net in (21:8). When they come ashore, they find 'a charcoal fire'. The use of *anthrakia* for the fire immediately recalls the high priest's courtyard, where Peter warmed himself at the *anthrakia* there (18:18)—the only two places the word is used in the New Testament. Peter does not need reminding: the evocative smell of charcoal would provoke all too strong a memory of that night and a hint of the conversation to come. The fire already has bread and fish on it, another verbal echo (21:9). While the fish in the net are the common *ichthys*, the fish on the fire is *opsarion*, dried fish, which appears in the New Testament only here and in the little boy's lunch at the feeding of the five thousand (6:9–11). Since that miraculous feeding is the only other event in John to take place near the sea of Tiberias (6:1; 21:1), the link is unmistakable. So the writer very cleverly pulls the threads together in this final scene.

153 fish

Before Jesus can deal with Peter's denial, he has to warm him by the fire, and feed him breakfast. So he tells them to 'bring some of the fish you have just caught' (21:10). Peter springs into action—impetuous as ever, or perhaps trying to be helpful to make up for his lapse—and hauls the net ashore single-handedly with 153 fish (21:11). 153 is a very precise figure. It is not impossible that one of them, amazed at the catch, sat down and counted them to be able to tell fishermen's tales! But after all the deeper meanings in John, this number has given commentators a field day. Since the letters of the alphabet were also used as numerals in Hebrew and Greek, some have tried to use *gematria*, adding up the numerical values of the letters, just as 666 makes the 'number of the beast' in Rev. 13:18. Thus some have reckoned that the Greek for 'Simon' equals 76, plus 'fish' *ichthys* equals 77, giving a total of 153.

The Fathers had many symbolic interpretations. Cyril of Alexandria took it as 100 (for the Gentiles) plus 50 (the Jews) plus 3 (for the Trinity). Augustine noted that 153 is the sum of all the numbers from 1+2+3+ up to 17; 17 can be made up from a full 10 for the commandments plus a perfect 7 for the gifts of the Spirit. 153 dots can be arranged into an equilateral triangle with 17 along each side; the ancients believed that such 'triangular numbers' stood for completion. Finally, Jerome thought there were 153 types of fish species in the world. So this catch represents the universal haul of all people brought to Jesus, in a net which is 'not torn'; since 'torn' is the verb from *schism*, the 'division' we saw among "the Jews" (7:43; 9:16; 10:19), the unbroken net signifies the undivided church, hauled in by Peter, representing the clergy, or even the Pope! The variety and ingenuity of these solutions, each reflecting the commentators' interests rather than the original readers', should make us pause this time in the search for John's deeper meaning. Perhaps all we can say is that 153 is a very large number, which may represent universality or completeness.

Come and eat

Meanwhile, back at the fireside, Jesus is serving breakfast (21:12). John stresses the reality of the resurrection—hallucinations or ghosts do not cook fish! The disciples 'knew it was Jesus', yet they must have been full of questions. All the resurrection appearances suggest that Jesus was recognizable, eventually, yet somehow different. His old ways and habits are still there—yet transformed. So Jesus answers their questions with a familiar action: 'he took bread and gave it to them, and did the same with the fish' (21:13) These words recall how he fed five thousand by this same lake (6:11). We saw then that 'taking' and 'giving' are eucharistic and the reflection of the communion is below the surface here. Pictures in the catacombs and early churches use images of fish and bread for the communion as often as the cup of wine. So this 'third appearance to the disciples' (21:14) is a lovely picture of the risen Jesus coming to find Peter and the others when they have gone back to their old ways. He makes a meal for them, as he did in the good old days. But the smell of the charcoal fire and the bursting net hint that it is all different since the denial in the courtyard and the empty cross and tomb. They should be out fishing for people, bringing the whole universe to be completed in Jesus who feeds them with his risen life through loaves and fishes, bread and wine.

FOR REFLECTION AND PRAYER

*Go and have an 'early breakfast' with Jesus
at a church service near you.*

DO YOU LOVE ME MORE THAN THESE?

Breakfast is finished, but the lingering smell of the charcoal fire is a potent reminder that something is still hanging around. Peter showed willing by jumping into the sea to greet Jesus and leaping to get more fish. But Jesus has to take the initiative after he has cared for Peter physically, warming him at the fire and feeding him. So the two of them go for a stroll after breakfast, as we see when the other disciple turns up later (21:20). Along the water's edge, Jesus starts his gentle, but firm questioning. He addresses him formally, 'Simon, son of John'—as he did when they first met (1:42). Then he nicknamed him 'Peter', but recently he has been more 'rocky' than 'solid-rock'! Now is his chance to put it right. Interpreters are divided about 'do you love me more than these?' Perhaps Jesus waves his hand at the boat and the net and the fish; Peter has gone back to the old ways, to his old business—but does he love Jesus more than that? Or maybe Jesus indicates the other disciples; at the last supper, Peter wanted to follow him even to death (13:36–38); he got further than everyone else except the 'other disciple'—but then denied him three times.

Lord, you know everything

So Jesus asks him three times if Peter loves him, once for each denial. Jesus uses *agapao* for 'love' in the first two, while Peter replies consistently with *philo*, which Jesus adopts the third time. Some suggest that Jesus is asking for a higher love, *agape*, but Peter can only offer friendship, *phile*, which Jesus settles for. However, most ancient and modern commentators argue that there is little difference in these words elsewhere in John and so not too much should be made of it here.

It is the threefold questioning which causes Peter to be 'hurt', literally 'grieved' (21:17). He has not yet dealt with his feelings about his loss of nerve in the courtyard, the loss of Jesus on the cross and losing his position among the disciples—and now Jesus asks three times. Yet it is the healer's knife, cutting out the old wound, to let Peter to affirm his love three times. He can only fling himself on Jesus' knowledge: 'you know everything'. When our pain and shame is so near the surface, we have to rely on the Lord's full understanding which looks deeper at our love beneath. Under Peter's denial was a love which followed Jesus almost to the end.

Feed my sheep

Having dealt with the painful stuff about the past, Jesus helps Peter move to his present ministry and his future destiny. When the 'good shepherd' was betrayed by Judas 'the thief', Peter may have ran away like 'the hireling' (10:10–12), but now he is to be a shepherd too. His threefold profession of love receives three commissions: 'feed my lambs', 'tend my sheep', 'feed my sheep' (21:15–17). The Good Shepherd gives us the task of caring for the sheep, but they remain his, '*my* sheep'. He sends us as Father sent him (20:21). So Jesus reinstates Peter not for his own sake, to make him feel better, but for his task of caring for the church. So often we talk about 'my ministry', 'my job', 'my decision for Christ'—but it is never mine at all. It is always *his* calling for *their* sake; it is Jesus who calls us and others who are to benefit.

The cost of being a shepherd

Finally, Jesus warns Peter of the cost of this love (21:18). The 'hireling' may run away but the 'good shepherd lays down his life for the sheep' (10:11–12). Peter has gone back to the old ways of his youth, girding up his belt and going fishing when he feels like it. Later he would write that pastoral care does not mean 'lording it about over those in your charge' (1 Pet. 5:1–6); it involves 'humility', sacrificing yourself and letting others make demands. Eventually it will crucify him. When he is older, 'you will stretch out your hands and someone else' will help him dress; but the deeper meaning is that he will stretch out his hands as someone ties him to a cross beam. Jesus used similar hints 'to indicate the kind of death' he would die (12:33; 18:32); now he suggests the same fate for Peter, whose death will also 'glorify God' (21:19). Again, we think of the *Quo vadis?* legend of Peter fleeing Rome but returning to be crucified upside down after meeting Jesus carrying a cross. Like Peter, we all want to be restored when we let Jesus down and we are all called to care for others, whether our vocation is to be Pope or unnoticed in a back pew—but are we prepared to follow all the way?

PRAYER

Lord, you know everything; you know that I love you.
Grant that I may feed your sheep and follow you to the end.

FOLLOW ME

Jesus warmed and dried Peter by the fire, fed him with fish and bread; then he restored him to his pastoral care of God's people and hinted at his glorious martyrdom to come. Only one thing remains to be said, 'Follow me' (21:19). It is Jesus' last word, yet also his first. After Andrew brought his brother Simon to Jesus at the start and he renamed him Peter, Jesus' first words were 'follow me' (1:42–43). At the last supper, Peter asked Jesus, *quo vadis?*, 'where are you going?' When Jesus said that Peter could not follow then, Peter declared that he was ready to follow to death (13:36–37). So now Jesus reminds him of all that with the same two simple words, 'follow me'. It is the call at the very start of our Christian journey, but the call is also to lifelong discipleship, repeated every day until we die.

Yet, how easily we are distracted! As they are walking along, Peter makes the typical mistake of looking back over his shoulder. He sees the 'disciple Jesus loved' also 'following' him and Jesus (21:20). Just to be clear who this is, the evangelist reminds us of his first appearance, reclining in the special place next to Jesus at the last supper and asking Jesus Peter's question about the betrayer (13:23–25). Ever since, he always seems to be with Peter, yet usually going that little bit further (see 18:15–17; 19:26–27; 20:2–8; 21:7).

Lord, what about him?

'When Peter saw him', he could not resist it. It is all very well for Jesus to put Peter through such painful questioning, giving him instructions for leading the church and his future martyrdom—but what about the next chap? So one final time Peter opens his mouth and puts his foot straight in it: 'Lord, what about him?' (21:21). The lifelong journey of following Jesus is one every individual must make—but we do so in community with others. Therefore there is always the temptation to compete, to want to know what they are doing or even to try to control them. But that is how the bad shepherds treated the blind man (9:24–34). Christian pastoral care is not about dictatorship or even interference. We are more like sheep dogs than shepherds, bringing people to Jesus the Good Shepherd, and their destiny is with him, not us. Thus Jesus' reply to Peter is rather brusque, essentially 'mind your own business'! The other disciple's future is 'between him and me; your job is to follow me' (21:22).

The problem is that the Christian community are also interested in what Jesus says to the others, and so 'the rumour spread that this disciple would not die' (21:23). The writer points out carefully that Jesus did not say this; he simply told Peter it was not his business 'if it is my will that he remain', using the word for 'abide', *meno*, so beloved of the Farewell Discourses (see 14:2, 10, 17; 15:4–10). The obvious inference is that people were expecting Jesus to return before this disciple's death; if he had recently died, this would explain their anxiety and why the writer wants to put the record straight.

Bearing witness

The call to follow for Peter involved bearing witness even to death. The Greek for 'witness' is *martur-*, which gives us the English 'martyr'. In the end, Peter and the other disciple are always together in their witness. Peter witnesses by his martyrdom, but 'this disciple is the one who bears witness to these events and has written them down and we know his witness is true' (21:24). These last two verses appear to be an authentication by some early church leaders (after his death?) that the unnamed disciple has been the eye-witness, the authority behind the story. Furthermore, by using his key words like 'witness' and 'true' they show how much they have made his witness their own (see on 19:35 above). And so this epilogue ends as the last chapter of the gospel did, reminding us of the vast number of things Jesus did of which these are only a selection (21:25).

FOR REFLECTION AND PRAYER

Think of a time when you were impetuous and regretted it,
spoke or acted first and thought later;
have you slipped into denying your faith,
or worked all night with nothing to show for it
and envied another Christian who seems better?
The risen Christ comes in the new light,
tells us where to catch new resources, invites us to breakfast,
gently questions and restores us and wants us to care for others.
Hear Jesus calling 'Follow me'.
What is your response?

GLOSSARY

In accordance with the purpose of the series, technical terms have been kept to a minimum and we have tried to explain them where they have been used in the studies. Several important terms are collected together here for ease of reference.

Apocrypha   Literally the 'hidden' books; other 'scriptures' written mostly in intertestamental times and placed in some Bibles between the Old and New Testaments; Catholic and Orthodox tradition accept them as more authoritative than do Protestants.

Christology   The study of the person of Jesus, especially in relation to God; thus a 'low' Christology may treat him as a prophet, while a 'high' Christology sees him as divine and explores his place within the Trinity.

Eschatology   The study of the End (*eschaton*) of everything—death, judgment, end of the world, heaven and hell, eternal life.

Intertestamental   The period between Old Testament and the New Testament times, usually taken from Alexander the Great's conquest in 331BC to the early first century AD.

Maccabees   The family of a priest Mattathias who led the resistance to Seleucid emperors who controlled Judaea in the second century. Three of his five sons became important leaders—Judas Maccabeus, Jonathan and Simon. Simon's son, John Hyrcanus, secured the future for the Hasmonean dynasty in the new independent Jewish state.

Mashal   A 'riddle' or figurative saying, often given by rabbis in answer to a question to provoke the listener to further thought.

Mishnah   Jewish oral traditions about the Law, collected together and written down during the second century AD; usually forms the first part of the Talmud.

Synoptics   The first three gospels, Matthew, Mark and Luke, so called from the custom of 'looking at them together' (*syn-opt-* in Greek) to look at how they compare in the use of their material.

Talmud   The collection of Jewish laws and traditions.

FOR FURTHER READING

*'I suppose the world itself could not contain the books
that could be written.'*

The evangelist's despairing comment (21:25) about the possible books on Jesus has been borne out in the number of books about John. I have learned so much from so many scholars and commentators. This annotated list is only a selection, but I hope it will be helpful if you have enjoyed this commentary.

General Introductions

John Ashton (ed.) *The Interpretation of John*. Philadelphia: Fortress, 1986.
A collection of significant essays on John from 1923 to 1972.

Richard A. Burridge. *Four Gospels, One Jesus?* 2nd ed. Grand Rapids: Eerdmans, 2005.
A general introduction to studying the gospels, including John.

Barnabas Lindars, SSF. *John*. JSNT Study Guide. Sheffield Academic Press, 1990.
A brief and easy to read introduction to all the main issues.

D. Moody Smith. *The Theology of the Gospel of John*. Cambridge University Press, 1995.
A more detailed coverage of the gospel's setting and theology and the issues raised.

Mark W.G. Stibbe. *John's Gospel*. New York: Routledge, 1994.
An introduction to a literary reading looking at hero, plot, genre, style and polemic.

Shorter Commentaries

These are all a few hundred pages in length and take the gospel in sections, including application for preaching and devotional use.

William Barclay. *The Gospel of John*. Daily Study Bible. Edinburgh: St Andrew Press, 1955.
The classic daily commentary packed with spiritual insights and undergirded with good scholarship; still essential reading today, although some of the illustrations are now rather dated.

Diarmuid McGann. *Journeying Within Transcendence*. New York: Paulist, 1988.
A fascinating reading which mixes Catholic spirituality with a Jungian psychological perspective.

Lesslie Newbigin. *The Light Has Come*. Grand Rapids: Eerdmans, 1982.
A marvellous exposition which draws on Newbigin's experience in India and applies it all to modern Western culture.

William Temple. *Readings in St John's Gospel*. New York: St Martin's, 1955.
A classic spiritual reader written in the late 1930s when Temple was Archbishop of York.

Stephen Verney. *Water into Wine*. London: Collins Fount, 1985.
An interesting set of studies drawing on nearly fifty years of study first as a soldier in the Second World War and subsequently as a priest and bishop.

Detailed Commentaries

These are more extended treatments of the gospel verse by verse dealing with all the academic and critical issues. Many are volumes within larger series dealing with the whole Bible.

George R. Beasley-Murray. *John*. Word Biblical Commentary Vol. 36. Dallas, Texas: Word, 1987.
A good steady treatment following a traditional approach with useful general comments.

Raymond E. Brown. *The Gospel According to John*. Anchor Bible Commentary Vols. 29 and 29A. New York: Doubleday, Vol. 1. 1966; Vol. 2 1970.
Still the classic extended commentary, over 1200 pages of articles, notes and comments on every verse and issue, yet packed with helpful observations for preachers and teachers.

D.A. Carson. *The Gospel According to John*. Grand Rapids: Eerdmans, 1991.
A careful scholarly treatment from an evangelical perspective.

Barnabas Lindars. *The Gospel of John*. The New Century Bible Commentary. London: Marshall, Morgan & Scott, 1972.
Helpful analysis drawing on years of teaching and scholarship.

John Marsh. *Saint John*. Philadelphia: Westminster, 1978.
A lot bigger and fuller than it looks (700 pages) and still very useful.

Mark W.G. Stibbe. *John*. Sheffield Readings. JSOT Press, 1993.
An interesting new approach; shorter (224 pages), taking the gospel section by section in the light of modern literary analysis.

Ben Witherington III. *John's Wisdom*. Louisville, Ky.: Westminster John Knox, 1995.
A good up to date commentary with insightful sections on how to preach and teach the gospel in church life today.

Commentaries on the Greek text

E. Haenchen, Hermeneia, 2 vols, Philadelphia: Fortress Press, 1984.
C.K. Barrett, New York: Macmillan, 1955; 2nd ed. Philadelphia: Westminster, 1978.
J.H. Bernard, ICC, New York: Scribner, 1929.
B.F. Westcott, Grand Rapids: Eerdmans, 1954.